Faith, Love, and Mercy

Faith, Love, and Mercy

Homilies for Catholic Life

Richard R. Roach, SJ

Edited by Peter Weigel

with a Preface and editorial consultation by
Anthony Annett
and a Foreword by
Peter Ely, SJ

WIPF & STOCK · Eugene, Oregon

FAITH, LOVE, AND MERCY
Homilies for Catholic Life

Copyright © 2015 Richard R. Roach. All rights reserved. Except for brief quotations in critical publications or reviews, no part of this book may be reproduced in any manner without prior written permission from the publisher. Write: Permissions, Wipf and Stock Publishers, 199 W. 8th Ave., Suite 3, Eugene, OR 97401.

Scripture quotations unless noted are from *The New Jerusalem Bible*, copyright © 1985 by Darton, Longman & Todd, Ltd. and Doubleday, a division of Random House, Inc. Used by permission. All rights reserved.

The majority of the other Scriptural quotations are from the New Revised Standard Version Bible: Catholic Edition, copyright © 1989, 1993 the Division of Christian Education of the National Council of the Churches of Christ in the United States of America. Used by permission. All rights reserved.

Wipf & Stock
An Imprint of Wipf and Stock Publishers
199 W. 8th Ave., Suite 3
Eugene, OR 97401

www.wipfandstock.com

ISBN 13: 978-1-61097-186-7

Manufactured in the U.S.A.

Contents

Foreword by Peter Ely | vii
Preface | ix
Acknowledgments | xiii

Part I: Select Solemnities, Feasts, and Special Days

1. First Sunday of Advent | 3
2. Solemnity of the Immaculate Conception of the Blessed Virgin Mary | 10
3. Solemnity of the Nativity of the Lord (Mass of Christ) | 15
4. The Blessed Virgin Mary, the Mother of God; The Giving of the Name Jesus | 21
5. The Epiphany of the Lord Father | 32
6. Baptism of the Lord | 41
7. Annunciation of the Lord | 50
8. Ash Wednesday | 56
9. Palm Sunday of Our Lord's Passion | 63
10. The Lord's Supper (Holy Thursday) | 71
11. Good Friday | 77
12. Easter | 82
13. Second Sunday of Easter: Divine Mercy Sunday | 87
14. Solemnity of the Ascension | 94
15. Pentecost | 100
16. Holy Trinity Sunday | 111
17. Solemnity of the Transfiguration | 122
18. The Solemnity of the Assumption | 127

| 19 | All Saints Day and All Souls Day | 133
| 20 | All Saints Day | 137
| 21 | All Souls Day | 140
| 22 | The Solemnity of Christ the King | 146

Part II: Select Thematic Homilies

| 23 | Catholic Ecclesiology and Authority | 155
| 24 | Eucharist and the Lamb of God | 163
| 25 | Faith and Reason | 172
| 26 | On Anti-Catholicism and Some Modern Ideologies | 180
| 27 | Vanity, Humility, and Contemporary Gnosticism | 192
| 28 | The Humility of the Cross | 202
| 29 | Loving One Another | 207
| 30 | Perseverance | 214
| 31 | Christ as the Way, the Truth, and the Life | 224
| 32 | We Are All in God's Hands | 231

Bibliography | 233

Foreword

I FIRST MET RICHARD ROACH when we were Jesuit philosophy students at Mount Saint Michael's in Spokane, Washington. I was his senior in religious life, already in my third and final year at the Mount when Richard began his studies there, but he was junior in age and life experience. Usually the more advanced students helped show the way for the newcomers. But with Richard, it was different. He brought with him even then a certain authority that came from the depth of his convictions, and made him a person to respect even when one did not agree.

Our shared enthusiasm about philosophy and love of intellectual pursuits, along with the faith that had brought us to enter the Society of Jesus, formed the basis of a friendship that lasted until Richard's death on November 7, 2008. I was privileged to be with him at his last breath. We taught together before ordination as "regents" at Jesuit High School in Portland Oregon, studied theology at Regis College in Toronto, shared a memorable car ride from Toronto to Seattle, and were ordained in Seattle on June 14, 1969.

Up until the end of his life, I continued to be amazed at the vigor of Richard's intellect. Once I brought Richard to the home of my brother, John, in Spokane. John asked Richard how he defined IQ. The answer was succinct, "intellectual energy." Richard certainly had it to a high degree. He thought deeply about things, read widely, experienced significant transformations of his own views, and challenged others, sometimes at their discomfort. IQ surely must also include the capacity for insight, understanding, and grasp of complex issues and Richard had that too.

Richard's restless intellect was coupled with an abiding faith. In his dying days, I realized how deep it was. Occasionally I would begin a prayer at his bedside without making the sign of the cross. He would make me start over. It wasn't a liturgical scruple but a desire that his dying always be under the sign of Jesus's cross.

Richard deeply loved the people of Saint John Vianney Parish. His time there was the fullest and happiest of his years of priestly ministry.

Those of us who knew Fr. Richard Roach and all who will read these pages owe a debt of gratitude to Peter Weigel, Tony Annett, and the others who put together this selection of homilies. Richard loved teaching. In his days at Saint John Vianney on Vashon Island, he taught mainly through his carefully prepared homilies. We are blessed to have some of them collected together here. I can imagine Richard smiling as he sees his words, so lovingly crafted, now available in this new form for meditation and reflection.

Fr. Peter B. Ely, S.J.

Preface

THE AUTHOR OF THIS collection of homilies, Richard R. Roach, S.J., was a man of extraordinary talents and intellect, with a deep love of God and the Church. He had a profound effect on the lives of those who knew him.

Fr. Roach was born in Seattle in 1934, and converted to the Catholic faith from Congregationalism while still an undergraduate at the University of Washington. Following a stint as a jet pilot in the United States Air Force, he entered the Oregon Province of the Society of Jesus in 1958, and was ordained a priest in 1969. Along the way, he studied philosophy as a young scholastic at Mount Saint Michael's in Spokane, taught at Jesuit High School in Portland, and studied theology at Regis College, the Jesuit School of Theology in Toronto.

Following his ordination, he received a doctorate in religious studies from Yale University, where he studied under noted moral theologian James Gustafson. He also considered a major influence the great historian of Christianity, Jaroslav Pelikan.

Recognized as among the best minds of his generation, Fr. Roach began teaching theology at Toronto, and then at Marquette University in Milwaukee, where he stayed for almost twenty years. During this period, he developed close friendships with leading Catholic intellectuals of the time, including G.E.M. Anscombe and her husband, Peter Geach.

While at Marquette, he also had a profound influence on many students over the years, with a reputation as an excellent pastoral priest and a strong advocate of Catholic identity. He frequently said Mass in the Milwaukee area, where some local Catholics still recall the exceptional quality of his homilies.

After taking early retirement, Fr. Roach moved to New York and became a scholar in residence at Columbia University's Catholic campus ministry.

At that point, his life took a different turn. Already in his sixties, and following an impressive career in academia, Fr. Roach was asked by his order to enter parish life and become a pastor. He moved back to Seattle, his hometown, and beginning in 1998, served as pastor of Saint John Vianney Church on bucolic Vashon Island. Despite his primarily academic background, Fr. Roach grew into the role expertly. He became a much-beloved pastor, with a reputation for excellence throughout the Archdiocese of Seattle. He remained there for a decade.

Fr. Roach died on November 7, 2008, following a battle with pancreatic cancer. He faced a painful death with courage, dignity, and absolute acceptance of God's will.

The homilies in this book grew out of his time at Saint John Vianney.

As a pastor, Fr. Roach deployed his scholarly background to great effect in his weekly homilies. He retained his professor's knack for conveying key theological truths with accessibility and vigor. Each week, he would diligently prepare his printed homily, an exercise in which he took a great deal of pride. He would deliver an abbreviated version from the pulpit, with his trademark eloquence and charisma, and he would then send the printed version by email to all who expressed interest–not only in his parish, but throughout the country, and indeed, across the world.

Over the years, he developed a dedicated following of people who delighted in their weekly email from Vashon Island. And despite his busy schedule, he would always find time to answer emails from far and wide, exploring the issues raised in his homilies.

This collection of homilies presents a mere snapshot of Fr. Roach's prodigious output spanning a decade of writing. The selection has been carefully chosen to reflect the major way-stations of the liturgical year and the major themes of his preaching–faith and reason, mercy and justice, humility and obedience.

Accordingly, this collection has a two-part structure. The first part hews closely to the liturgical year, while the second part presents a selection of themed homilies that deepen the discussion of the issues introduced in the first part. To aid the reader, the main editor, Peter Weigel, has included short summaries preceding each homily. These summaries simply orient the reader to key themes, and are not meant to anticipate every topic. In places, the Editor shortened the original homilies for easier reading, while normally trying to leave the body intact. Sometimes it made sense to remove content more germane or comprehensible to the parish audience and the time it was written. Fr. Roach's particular views are often his own, and not always those of others involved with this book.

We selected this collection to give a true sense of the man and his teaching of authentic Catholic faith. We also wanted to situate these homilies in their proper context, tied intimately to parish life and the liturgical seasons.

What makes this collection of homilies stand out? Fr. Roach believed that too many modern homilies tended to trivialize the truths of faith and condescend to the congregation. Steeped in the rich and deep Catholic intellectual tradition, he felt strongly that glossing over this great legacy was tantamount to cheating people.

As Fr. Roach was fond of saying, "I like my faith *neat*, not watered down." As a result, his homilies could be long, frequently complex, and always challenging—and this was precisely what people loved about them. He was meeting a real unmet need in Catholic catechetics. He was teaching, guiding, and nurturing people in the faith, week-by-week, homily-by-homily. He strove to emulate the Ignatian charism of evangelizing through careful moral and religious instruction, centering devotional life on the Gospel message.

But these homilies were far more than just theoretical expositions. They were deeply practical, showing the person-centered and experiential approach of Jesuit education. In each homily, Fr. Roach was keen to tie the readings of the day not only to the underlying teachings of the Church, but also to what was going on in the wider world at that particular moment. Accordingly, you will find references in this collection to the sex abuse scandal, the terrorist attacks of September 11th, American electoral politics, and Dan Brown's *Da Vinci Code*. You will see scholarly rigor tinged with a personal touch and a deep affection for the people of Vashon. Above all, you will see a priest who was tirelessly committed to the Church and the truths of the faith.

Fr. Roach recognized the importance of understanding the culture to be able to intelligently critique it. He frequently makes subtle but important points that often escaped the attention of others, whether on the meaning of doctrine, culture, belief systems, or habits of contemporary Catholics. Over and over again, he would warn against the illusory appeal of cultural Catholicism, the prevalence of Gnosticism in the culture, the lingering influence of Jansenism, the dangers of fundamentalism, and misguided ways of understanding Christ's sacrifice for our sins.

Unlike some modern Catholic apologists, Fr. Roach stood above politics and partisanship, preferring the deeper theological insight over the cacophony of competing ideologies. He cared only about the integrity and internal consistency of the Catholic faith, which sometimes brought him criticism both from left and right—on issues like abortion and contraception on one hand, and war and social justice on the other. For Fr. Roach, his Catholicism always came first, and he refused to squeeze it into the narrow categories too often demanded by society. (In seeking the *Nihil Obstat* and *Imprimatur* for this book, as Fr. Roach would have wanted, the Archdiocese of Portland responded that current policy is to put only catechetical works through the process.)

Those of us lucky enough to know Fr. Roach as a friend loved him deeply and learned so much from him. He made a deep impression on so many different people, especially those closest to him. We miss him dearly, and we cherish his memory.

We will always remember him at his happiest—reclining in a comfortable chair, a glass of wine in his hand, his beloved dog on his lap, expounding upon the issues of the day with a furrow in his brow, a glint in his eye, and a joyous laugh that was never far away.

It is our hope that readers of the book can also share some of Fr. Roach's insight. More than that, we hope these homilies continue his lifelong mission in the Society of Jesus, bringing souls to the love of Christ and his saving truth. We believe that readers will derive great spiritual benefit from the writings of someone who was one-of-a-kind, a true man of God.

Anthony Annett

Acknowledgments

To Fr. Richard R. Roach, S.J., (d. 2008) as a longtime friend and the author of these homilies, I owe deep gratitude. When this project was still just an idea, he only modestly encouraged it. Remembering his life of service and intellectual vigor strengthened my resolve to see the book into print after his death. Fr. Patrick Lee, S.J., Provincial of the Oregon Province of the Society of Jesus from 2008–2014, graciously granted permission for publication of Fr. Roach's homilies. I am grateful to Fr. Peter Ely, S.J., a close friend of Fr. Roach in the Society of Jesus, for writing the Foreword. Invaluable editorial advice and encouragement came from Tram Nguyen, Darlyn Sullivan, Matthew Sullivan, and Anthony Annett, who contributes the Preface. Tony Annett's significant consultations with me made him effectively co-editor as the book took final shape. Fr. Rees Doughty and Mark Hamilton also offered ideas and encouragement, as did others appreciative of the homilies. Teresa Abney copyedited and formatted the manuscript. Washington College in Maryland generously granted me a sabbatical allowing for the book's timely completion. Thank you all.

Peter Weigel, Editor

Part I

Select Solemnities, Feasts,
and Special Days

Chapter 1

First Sunday of Advent

(December 3, 2000)

Scripture Readings

First Reading—Jer 33:14–16; *Responsorial Psalm*—Ps 25; *Second Reading*—1 Thess 3:12–4:2; *Gospel Reading*—Luke 21: 25–28, 34–36.

Summary

Fr. Roach explains the Catholic meaning of Advent and its penitential significance. He contrasts this traditional account with the historical secularization of Christmas in the United States. First, Christ's birth points to his Passion, Death, Resurrection, and return in judgment. Christ's return (*Parousia*) reminds us of how we receive God's grace to follow Christ in "seeking justice all of our lives." It calls us to seek the truth about God and ourselves, which should prompt our repentance. Advent is thus a time of soul-searching and penance. The real joy of Christmas becomes a solemn one where we consider our finality as persons.

Homily

WHEN CELEBRATING OUR LITURGY for this Sunday, we will have a brief homily that refers to these Scriptures. But, instead of a written homily based principally on the sacred Scriptures, I want to take this time to address the problem we as Catholics face in observing Advent in the midst of a culture that has already started to observe its secularized version of Christmas, the American Christmas.

We first need to know what is Advent, and why we observe it. Advent is the time set aside in the liturgy for us to prepare not only for Christmas, which commemorates the birth of Our Lord Jesus the Christ, but also for the coming of Christ as our judge on the last day. It is a solemn season. We used to observe it in much the same way we observe Lent, but less strictly. In the Eastern rites of the Church, the season is longer and still is observed like Lent. It is supposed to be a time of thoughtfulness and some soul-searching. During Advent, we should renew and deepen our understanding of why we need to be redeemed (saved), and why we anticipate our Savior's return on the last day of this era as our judge. And, we should know what to expect when this event occurs. With these reflections, we prepare ourselves to rejoice at Christmas because they enable us to understand better what the birth of Jesus the Christ means for us.

We need to think about Our Lord's Second Coming—more properly referred to as the *Parousia* (Greek for "presence" or "arrival")—because this event will give finality to our lives as the human family. Our personal judgment at the moment of death gives us finality, individually. The general judgment gives us finality as the human race. We will then see our lives in the context that defines us. Until then, some of our questions will not as yet have had an answer. In the *Parousia*, we will understand how mercy and justice come together, and see all matters of justice resolved. The general judgment will confirm our personal judgment, and resolve any questions we may have about it. God gives justice as the finality of our human race. If we appreciate this truth, we will seek justice all of our lives. Need I add that justice requires truth as a prior condition?

In what I would judge is one of the most brilliant moments in the history of thought, Saint Thomas Aquinas taught the basics of what we call the Natural Law. The great saint said that in addition to the basic inclinations we have as substantive animals, as rational beings we are inclined to know the truth about God and to live in society.[1] This two-fold inclination gives rise to the obligation to seek the truth wherever it may be found, and to pursue justice. We pursue justice so that we may live in society as he created us to live. For this living, we must be just. Otherwise, society is the place where we harm and kill each other, where we debase each other and end up dying

---

1. *Summae Theologiae* Ia q.94 2c. Aquinas's "Summary of Theology" has a widely used English translation by the Fathers of the English Dominican Province (1947), which is readily found online.

degraded. We have these natural inclinations that give rise to our obligations because of the way in which God created us. Because we are unable to fulfill these obligations unaided, and because sin has made it even harder for us, God has provided a remedy. His remedy takes us beyond what he originally created for us into his own life. We call everything that comes to us directly from God, grace, because the word "grace" implies that what God gives us God gives freely and not as something God owes us. In gracing us, God confirms what he has created and goes beyond it (i.e., crowns nature with what is beyond nature, which we then call supernatural). Jesus, as God's Word, is the truth about God, so he satisfies our inclination to seek the truth about God. Further, Jesus inspires us to seek all other truth, because he reveals that all of creation has meaning. And, Jesus, again as God's Word, is God's very justice in person. He inspires us to create a just society. Jesus, thereby, confirms what the Creator wrought, and enables us to fulfill the creation. Contemplating the Second Coming (the *Parousia*) helps us appreciate all that I've tried to say here, and understand our living here and now.

The birth of Jesus—Our Lord's First Coming—is the "advent" of God's way of preparing us for our finality. Advent means "to come to." God first came to us in person when Jesus was born. God comes again to us in person when Jesus returns in glory. We will realize our finality in that Second Coming. We need to ponder everything about Jesus from the first advent through to his resurrection in order to prepare us for our finality. Before the birth of Jesus, we as humans could sense only a dark and/or frightening finality to our lives. Therefore, in his birth, Jesus brings us light. Jesus is like the light we speak of when we say that there is light at the end of the tunnel. Jesus also is the light that enlightens our minds so that we may understand why we are living and what we are living for. If we cooperate with him, Jesus slowly makes us wise. Therefore, the birth of Jesus is something to celebrate with joy. We do this when we celebrate those Masses dedicated to the memory of his first advent, which Masses we call, simply, Christmas.

By the way, we used to refer a number of special days with the suffix, "mas": Michaelmas, Candlemas, and Lammas, to name three. Michaelmas (now the Feast of the Archangels Michael, Gabriel, and Raphael) on September 29th begins the fall term at British Universities; Candlemas (the Feast of the Presentation of the Lord in the Temple) on the February 2nd initiates the spring term. Lammas reaches back to King Alfred in the eighth century. It takes place on the 1st of August, and what it celebrates is disputed. Although perhaps the most important, Christmas is just one of these "mas" days.

Our challenge is to relate the truth about Advent and Christmas (including the Christmas season that this year lasts through the 8th of January) to the celebration in this country of what are called the holidays that began at least by Thanksgiving. This secular celebration has a tangential relation to Catholic faith and practice. Those who have secularized this season have been unable to replace the term "Christmas" and remove all reference to the birth of Jesus. The secular celebration also often includes some bowdlerized version of his gospel. Still, they have succeeded in burying these residual elements of Catholic faith under a mountain of magic and consumerism. I used to be of the mind that we should try to reclaim the holidays. I now think it is impossible. So, especially for the sake of the children, I think we should find a way to enjoy the secularized holiday while observing what authentic faith calls us to celebrate through the liturgy of the Church. It is a little schizophrenic. One has to walk on two, often diverging, paths at once. And, one has to be able to explain the tangential relationship between the secular party and the Church celebration, especially to children.

I think the key to keeping the holiday party and the Catholic faith distinct lies in the history of the party. First, it is essentially an American party that has taken over the world. In its pseudo-messianic spread, the holidays are not unlike the religions invented in the U.S. in the nineteenth-century. The many religions invented here, including fundamentalism, have spread around the globe, just as Santa Claus and his holidays have. (American culture is perhaps the most powerful culture the human race has ever witnessed.) Secondly, as I've just said, one can date the creation of Santa Claus, as we know him. Creating him was the beginning of the holidays.

Before we turn to the poem that really created our Santa Claus, we may profitably spend a bit of time on his pre-history. American Protestantism originally rejected Christmas, vigorously. It was a wicked, "popish" Catholic, Roman, bad thing! For example, in the Commonwealth of Massachusetts, until 1681, it was a crime to bake Christmas cookies. Yet, not all of the original settlers were as stringent in rejecting all things Catholic as the Puritans. A number of Dutch immigrants had settled in New York. Although virtually all Protestant, they were reluctant to part with their beloved *Sinterklaas* (Saint Nicholas). Either on the eve of his feast day or Christmas eve or New Year's eve, Santaclaw, as he had become in the colonies, came and filled the stockings or wooden shoes of good little boys and girls with oranges, Dutch crullers, juicy sweetmeats, cookies and nuts. Bad little boys and girls found birchen rods in their stockings or wooden shoes. A powerful lesson! Moving the lesson from the eve of the saint's feast in the Catholic calendar helped de-Catholicize the event. At this point, the event was still Dutch and not yet our American Christmas.

Despite the fact that it was more or less simply a way to train children, the whole thing was too Catholic for most Protestant ministers. They railed against this observance. Two anti-Catholic stories used to counteract the observance will help one appreciate how strongly they railed against the event. One attack changed the legend about the sainted bishop of Myra, Saint Nicholas, providing dowries for poor girls. Instead, he was described as a lecher who had de-flowered the girls, and the gold he gave was pay-off. In another less virulent attack, Catholic mothers were excoriated. It was said that they sent their children to bed hungry so that when they found food in their socks the next day they would thank Saint Nicholas, thereby becoming practitioners of the "wicked" practice of venerating saints. Earlier in the history of this country, anti-Catholicism was really something!

Against this background, an anonymous author on December 23rd in 1823 published a poem in the *Troy Sentinel* (Dutchess County, New York State). The poem was entitled "Account of a Visit of Saint Nicholas." Most of us know the poem by its opening line: "'Twas the Night Before Christmas." I think this anonymous author was a sweet guy, and I don't think he had any anti-Catholic intent. Nevertheless, although he refers repeatedly to Saint Nicholas (or Saint Nick), he so describes him that in the popular imagination he ceases to be a Catholic saint and becomes exactly what the poem says he is: "He was chubby and plump, a right jolly old *elf*, / And I laughed when I saw him in spite of myself; . . . " (Emphasis added.) Even if the Dutch had transformed him into a child's disciplinarian, they had left him a saint. I think they had distorted him as a saint; nevertheless, he was still a man, not an elf! The poem transforms him from a man into an elf. He no longer is someone to venerate, which the Protestants despised. He now is magic, not reality. He is now free to be known by his American Dutch name—Santa Claus. And, the American Christmas is born!

The American Christmas was born secular, too. Go back and re-read "'Twas the Night Before Christmas." There is not a reference to Christianity in the poem, except calling Nicholas, Saint Nicholas; and, the use of the term "Christmas." But, we must remember that the meaning of the suffix, "mas", had been totally forgotten, and we pronounce "Christmas" in such a way that one does not hear "Christ." Say "Christmas" and then say "Christ Mass." The poem, which I think is wonderful, is nevertheless secular.

American Christmas is a magic time. Elves and flying reindeer belong to magic land. I obviously do not think there is anything necessarily wrong with the fantasy of magic. For example, I've endorsed Harry Potter in these writings. Still, even children learn to tell the difference between magic and reality. The secular, American Christmas is magic. Here in the Church, we celebrate reality.

To substantiate factual claims about American Christmas that I've made in this essay, consult "Yes, Virginia, There WAS a Santa Claus," the sixth chapter in *Author Unknown: On the Trail of Anonymous* by Don Foster. Foster demonstrates that Major Henry Livingston, Jr. wrote "'Twas the Night Before Christmas," not Clement Clarke Moore who, after Livingston's death, accepted credit for the poem. Livingston seems to have been a delightful and cheerful family man, whereas Moore seems not to have been so. Moore was a Protestant seminary professor, who initially had been opposed to celebrating Christmas.

Before I close this essay, we should attend briefly to the sacred Scriptures read and proclaimed at this Mass. The first reading from Jeremiah virtually repeats Jeremiah 23:4–6. I said virtually because there is a slight variation. The key verse in both passages of the New Revised Standard Version Catholic Edition [NRSV-CE] translates traditionally as "'The LORD is our righteousness.'"[2] The New Jerusalem Bible translates: "'Yahweh-is-our-Saving-Justice'"[3] (Jer 33:16d; the hyphens in the NJB rightly indicate that the sentence actually is a name). Historically, Jeremiah is contrasting the name that the Messiah (i.e., the Christ) will give to us as a people with the name of a reforming king, Zedekiah, which means "Yahweh is my (not 'our') Saving Justice." (Zedekiah reigned in Jerusalem nearly six-hundred-years before the birth of Jesus.) With hindsight, the Church came to see that the prophecy applied to Jesus, who is "*our* saving justice" or "*our* righteousness" (Emphasis added). The contrast with the name, Zedekiah, teaches what I tried to explain at our celebration of the Solemnity of Christ the King. What we have directly from God that saves us, God gives us as a people, not merely as individuals. The only individual to whom "righteousness" or "saving justice" belongs by right is Jesus, because he is God as well as human. Whatever righteousness or saving justice that you or I have within us comes through our participation in the living Body of Christ, which is visible as his Church. Jesus shares with those who will share with him.

The second reading needs little or no explanation, if you don't read on past the last verse read out at Mass. When Paul starts to enumerate some of the instructions he "gave through the Lord Jesus,"[4] the text has an ambiguity

---

2. National Council of Churches, 1989 and 1993.

3. *New Jerusalem Bible*, Wansbrough, 1985. Fr. Roach normally quotes from this translation unless otherwise noted.

4. Readings for the liturgies for these homilies (1999–2008) are from the *Lectionary for Mass for Use in the Dioceses of the United States*. (2nd Edition, 1998–2002). The single first volume for Sundays, Solemnities, Feasts of the Lord and the Saints began to be used for Masses starting in 1998. The *Lectionary* uses its own translation based on the *New American Bible* translation from 1970 with New Testament revisions (1986), with certain modifications to the *Lectionary* translation reflecting linguistic controversies. Fr. Roach only very occasionally quotes from the *Lectionary* and is otherwise quoting other translations, as will be indicated.

that misleads people into worrying about sexual feelings (attractions). The key verses (4–5) in my judgment should read: " ... each one of you knows how to take a wife for himself in holiness and honour, not with lustful passion, like the Gentiles who do not know God; ... " [1 Thess 4:4–5]. Paul is inveighing against reducing a wife to the status of chattel used for a husband's sexual pleasure. He is not attacking sex and the pleasures associated with it. He is following in the tradition found in the great Book of Tobit in our Old Testament (excluded from the Protestant Bible). A moral of that book is that husbands should love their wives as persons, not merely as sexual objects. I'm stating the moral with language that developed centuries after the book was written. The ancient language, which Paul also used, distinguished between honorable sex and mere lust. All sexual energy and attraction should be channeled to support love and respect for other persons. Otherwise, it degenerates into lust.

Finally, when hearing the gospel proclaimed, we need to bear in mind that, just as with the beginning (Genesis), so with the end of this universe, all biblical descriptions are poetic, neither scientific nor literal. In the New Testament, the poetic images usually are taken from the Old Testament. In this gospel, our Lord teaches us to live with our finality in mind. We will be individually and generally judged. We don't know when; we know only that, as the Son of Man, Jesus will so judge us.

Chapter 2

Solemnity of the Immaculate Conception of the Blessed Virgin Mary

(December 8, 2006)

Scripture Readings

Gen 3:9–15, 20; Ps 98; Eph 1:3–6, 11–12; Luke 1:26–38.

Summary

The homily explains what the Immaculate Conception means for us. By a "prevenient grace" anticipating Christ's many merits, God "intervened in the conception of the Blessed Virgin Mary to block the transmission of the effects of the sin at the origin of the human race." Its significance, however, is not limited to Mary. The Immaculate Conception celebrates Christ born fully human yet sinless, as incarnate in "a sinless Mary by the power of the Holy Spirit." Finally, our share in that grace marks us as adopted sons and daughters of the Living God. The Immaculate Conception thus properly illuminates the fullness of, referred to in the angelic salutation, "Hail, full of grace."

Homily

*T*HE FULL TITLE OF this solemnity reminds us that we are celebrating as immaculate the conception of the Blessed Virgin Mary. Her conception resulted from the virtuous marital intercourse of her parents, whose names we believe were Anna and Joachim. (Joachim we know especially by his name in Spanish as the patron of a major central valley in California, *San Joaquin*.) The conception was immaculate not because no sexual intercourse took place, because sexual intercourse did take place; the conception was immaculate because by a special grace (referred to in theology as a *prevenient grace*) granted in anticipation of her son's merits. This grace freed Mary from inheriting the effects of the sin at the origin of the human race (usually referred to as original sin).

We should face and answer these two questions concerning the truth about Mary's Immaculate Conception: Why do we not find this truth stated explicitly in the sacred Scriptures? And, why did it take some time for the Church to become fully aware of this truth? Actually, the two questions have one answer. This answer can be summed up as follows. God's revelation is not a text or a code of law, but a person like you and me. All inspired texts (i.e., the Bible) as well as sound morality are subordinate to the person, Jesus, and God has revealed them only insofar as through the texts and by obeying the "laws" that we come to Jesus.

Jesus the Christ is God's final revelation, because if one knows who Jesus actually is, one knows there can be no revelation in addition to who Jesus is. Revelation consists of what we cannot know about God except God reveals whatever it is. Then, remembering that God is rational, we know that God cannot reveal more about himself than reveal himself in person. It's like this: A pen pal (or, using more contemporary language, someone you communicate with by instant messaging or some other use of the Internet) can write you and tell you about him/herself (think of God communicating with human beings as recorded in the Old Testament), and then the pen pal can board a flight and come in person to see you (think of God becoming one of us—i.e., Incarnate—as Jesus the Christ, as reported in the New Testament). Jesus is true God as well as true man (i.e., he is both fully human and God). He is God Incarnate and in person. Anything more we could possibly come to know about God is extracted, as it were, from Jesus, who is God's Word, also known as God-with-us; and since Jesus is the second person of the Trinity, he is God in person. The pen pal (or instant messenger) has arrived.

The New Testament records our Lord's arrival and gives us a great deal of important information about him, but not all. Saint John closed his gospel with these words (chapter 21 was added by a disciple after John's death):

"There were many other signs that Jesus worked in the sight of the disciples, but they are not recorded in this book. These are recorded so that you may believe that Jesus is the Christ, the Son of God, and that believing this you may have life through his name" (John 20:30–31 NJB). The memory of Jesus preserved by God the Holy Spirit in the Church that Jesus founded (i.e., the Catholic Church) retains, even when not recalled clearly, the significance of all these signs. As the faith is challenged, what we didn't fully appreciate or realize then comes to the fore, and the Church becomes able to state the truth in a clear way, not as new revelation, but as an improved understanding of Jesus and what he means for us. This is a schematic presentation of how the truth about our Lady's conception came to the fore.

After we came to believe and appreciate who Jesus is, especially as Savior, and to better understand why his teaching began with a call to repentance—"Repent, and believe the gospel (i.e., the good news)"—we had to ask ourselves, "Did he mean that in some sense everyone is sinful?" (A person needs to repent only if there is something sinful about the person.) Saint Paul began to answer this question, and in doing so added some confusion. "Well then; it was through one man that sin *came into the world*, and through sin death, and thus death spread through the whole human race *because everyone has sinned*" (Rom 5:12, second emphasis added; I urge all to read Rom 5:12–21). Did Saint Paul mean that innocent babies had sinned? It was painfully clear during Saint Paul's time that some innocent babies, even many innocent babies, died. Was this the sure sign they'd sinned even before they knew right from wrong or were able to choose freely? Today we say quite simply, "Of course not!" But, we recognize innocent babies still die, and in the poorer parts of our globe they die at the same rate, or even at a faster rate, than when Saint Paul lived. But, with Saint Paul, we know that these horrors derive ultimately from sin at the origin of the human race. This original sin has been frighteningly amplified by the actual sins of so many who have come along since the first sin. Since the beginning, a vast multitude has sinned freely and deliberately and in dreadful ways, including those who presently are sinning. A key point to remember always is that this mess (referred to as the sin of the world) had a start, and God did not start it.

Regrettably, we all inherit the effects of that original sin, with two exceptions. From the beginning, we saw clearly that Jesus is sinless. Among other reasons we saw this clearly came from the truth, as the old saying has it, that a blind person cannot lead another blind person, or they both fall into a ditch. Instead of being blinded by sin, Jesus as he walked among us had the sight of the sinless so that he could lead us sinners out of the darkness, which our sinfulness, both inherited and actual, causes. As the author of the Letter to the Hebrews made clear, Jesus is like us in all things except sin (cf. Heb 2:14–18, and then especially 4:14–16). The question then came up, "How was Jesus born sinless when he was conceived and born a member of our sinful human race, and born sinless in a stronger sense than even an innocent baby is sinless?" In other words, "How did Jesus become Incarnate—that is, human exactly as we are—without inheriting the sad effects of the sin at the origin of the human race?" We figured out the answer. By a special and unique prevenient grace, his mother, the Blessed Virgin Mary (who was without doubt a member of our sinful race because she was the daughter by natural procreation of a man and woman who had inherited original sin) when conceived did not inherit the effects of the sin at the origin of the human race. We state this truth by saying that she was immaculately conceived.

A "prevenient grace" is a grace that anticipates the merit whereby the grace is won. Jesus wins all grace through his meritorious life, especially his suffering and death, in order to bring God's merciful love to each of us. In anticipation of our Lord's merits as one of us through his expiatory sacrifice, God intervened in the conception of the Blessed Virgin Mary to block the transmission of the effects of the sin at the origin of the human race. This was her Immaculate Conception! We celebrate because this wonder resulted in our Savior being born a sinless human, in the fullest sense both of human and sinless because he became incarnate in and was born of a sinless mother by the power of God the Holy Spirit. Jesus, therefore, was completely human, one of us, although internally free from what happened at the origin of our human race. Then, Jesus suffered fully unto death from the external effects (especially the sins of others) of that original sin. His mother suffered, although differently, from the sins of others as well as her son did. Although she suffered less physically than her son, she suffered more painfully than the rest of us who suffer from sin because she too was sinless. (Sinfulness reduces our capacity for suffering.)

I hope we'll all say an extra "Hail Mary" today and rejoice in the wonders of the truth that this solemnity celebrates!

The first reading for this solemnity inspired the statue known as the Immaculate Conception. This traditional statue depicts our Lady standing on the globe with a snake under her feet. Older members of the parish will remember these statues. The depiction comes from the choice Saint Jerome made when translating the pronominal adjectives in verse 15 of today's first reading; he had to choose between his, her, and its. He chose "her," so in his translation the verse reads as follows: "I (God speaking to the snake) will put enmities between thee and the woman, and thy seed and her seed ("seed" means "offspring"): she shall crush thy head, and thou shalt lie in wait for her heel" (Douai/Rheims translation of Saint Jerome's Vulgate).[1] No contemporary translator follows Saint Jerome's choice. Our iconography, until quite recently, did. [The imagery means that the snake (Satan) tries to kill the Mother of God; instead through her son she kills him.]

Our response came from Psalm 98.

The key verse in our second reading is the following: "Thus he (i.e., God) chose us (you and me) in Christ before the world was made / to be holy and faultless before him in love, / marking us out for himself beforehand, to be adopted sons (and daughters), / through Jesus Christ" (Eph 1: 4–5a). The phrase "chose us in Christ" refers in part to the prevenient grace whereby the Blessed Virgin Mary was immaculately conceived. Our share in this grace did not bring it about that we were immaculately conceived; instead, we were marked out to be *adopted* sons and daughters of the living God. But the similarity remains in other ways. Just as our Lady had to freely accept the grace for its full effects (i.e., for the Incarnation to take place), so we must freely accept what God has marked out for each of us—i.e., to be his adopted son or daughter. Our Lady's words of acceptance are in today's gospel (Luke 1:26–38). She replied to the angel Gabriel: "You see before you the Lord's servant, let it happen to me as you have said" (Luke 1:38 NJB). We, too, should accept God's offer.

Today's gospel is well-known. This passage recounts the Annunciation. For this solemnity, in addition to the verse quoted in the preceding paragraph, the key verse is the one we use in our wonderful prayer, the Hail Mary. The verse records the words with which the angel Gabriel greeted the Blessed Virgin Mary: "Hail, full of grace." The NJB translates these words as follows: "Rejoice, you who enjoy God's favour!" (Luke 1:28). Having come to recognize the truth that our Lady was immaculately conceived, we better understand that the fullness of grace or God's favor that the angel Gabriel referred to meant Mary was immaculately conceived.

---

1. The *Douay-Rheims Bible* saw its New Testament finished in 1582 and the Old Testament in 1610, with major revisions by Bishop Richard Challoner from 1749 to 1752. Douay-Rheims served as the standard Bible for English-speaking Catholics well into the twentieth century.

Chapter 3

Solemnity of the Nativity of the Lord (Mass of Christ)
Life that is the Light (December 25, 2003)

Scripture Readings

The Vigil of Christmas: Isa 62:1–5; Ps 89; Acts 13:16–17, 22–25; Matt 1:1–25.

The three Masses commemorating the Nativity of the Lord on the 25th of December:

Midnight Mass: Isa 9:1–6; Ps 96; Titus 2:11–14; Luke 2:1–14.

Mass at Dawn: Isa 62:11–12; Ps 97; Titus 3:4–7; Luke 2:15–20.

Mass during the Day: Isa 52:7–10; Ps 98; Heb 1:1–6; John 1:1–18.

Summary

The homily explains how John's Prologue unveils the true meaning of Christmas and Christ's new direction for our lives. God sends his Word that we may have truth and life if we submit. Christ is authoritatively present in the Church and particularly in the Eucharistic Sacrifice (the Mass). Followers of Christ are saved by incorporation into Christ's life, his new humanity. This happens through his Church and initially through Baptism. Mary's lifelong virginity importantly signifies that this new humanity is not handed on through procreation but as Fr. Roach explains, "So, the Church he founded incorporates people into his life, the life of the new humanity, initially through Baptism." Fr. Roach notes the central message of Christmas is that the Word came to dwell among us, offering truth and grace; In Christ, we receive "the grace to forgive and the truth about God" and share in Christ's life as members of his Body.

Homily

THE SACRED SCRIPTURES TELL us about the birth of Jesus the Christ in two ways. Somewhat fanciful narratives are the first and most popular way. These two narratives, called the Infancy Narratives or Infancy Gospels (Matt 1–2; Luke 1:5–2), are bare-boned facts fleshed out with legendary material first handed on by word of mouth. As legendary material always does, this material may record some dates incorrectly, and might have been imaginatively expanded. Nevertheless, the narratives rest on bedrock fact. Jesus was born of a virgin named Mary who had conceived by the power of the Holy Spirit. Her legal husband named Joseph cared for her and the child. The birth took place in Bethlehem of Judea. The child was raised in Nazareth of Galilee. Joseph, a carpenter who [according to an early tradition] was probably a widower when he agreed to serve as the boy's foster father, seems to have died before the boy became an adult and a public figure.[1]

The narratives make clear to those who know how to read them that Mary's virginity was a life-long sacrifice that she, with her husband, made in order that she may serve as the mother of the new humanity. In the words of Saint Paul, Jesus is the new Adam. Mary knew that the new humanity born as her son would not be handed on to future generations in the ordinary way, i.e., by what we call reproduction or procreation. Instead, a person born into this world through ordinary conception and gestation would become incorporated into the new humanity of her son by some work of the faith he would inculcate. So, the Church he founded incorporates people into his life, the life of the new humanity, beginning with the Sacrament of Baptism. The continuing birth of the new humanity, whose first appearance we are celebrating, comes by sacrament. In the words of Saint John's gospel used on this day, the new humanity, i.e., the children of God, are those "who were born, not of blood or the will of the flesh or of the will of man, but of

---

1. Brackets around a single word or brief phrase are editorial modifications (often Scripture references) added to Fr. Roach's original text. Bracketed passages containing full sentences and paragraphs are Fr. Roach's own asides.

God" (John 1:13; NRSV-CE).[2] Being born again of God takes place in the Sacrament of Baptism. And, just as the life that began when our mothers conceived us, the life of our new humanity can be lost through sin—i.e., by sins of omission or commission or, in other words, by what we do or what we fail to do.

The Infancy Narratives appeal to us because we all like stories. But, stories are limited as ways of telling the truth. Stories as conveyers of truth can be neutralized by people wrapping the stories in sentimentality, or by treating the figurative as literal. So, aware of these limitations to telling the truth of our Lord's birth by story, Saint John the Evangelist told the story of our Lord's nativity in strong, philosophical sounding language. He thereby made the Christmas story unequivocal. We call his account of the Nativity of the Lord, the Prologue to the Gospel according to John.

This is how it begins: "In the beginning was the Word, and the Word was with God, and the Word was God" (John 1:1). In a way we cannot understand while on this side of the grave, the one and only God who always is thinking, can distinguish himself from what he thinks, which is his Word and as such also is the one and only God. "He (the Word) was in the beginning with God" (John 1:2). In other words, God's Word has been with God from the beginning, which means from all eternity. The original creation, as the Bible tells us about it, began "In the beginning" (Gen 1:1). All that existed at the "beginning" was eternity. So, the Word was with God in eternity, since only God is eternal. The Word is God as expressed or thought to himself. "All things came into being through him, and without him not one thing came into being" (John 1:3). In other words, God thought about creating before he created. And, God thought about everything.

"What has come into being in him was life, and the life was the light of all people" (John 1:3-4). Although the manuscripts may have preserved this sentence imperfectly, the meaning is clear. God's thoughts about life are realized in his Word. If we share this life as the Word (i.e., the Christ) lives, and not just as God created life, we become enlightened about the meaning God gives all life, even our own individual lives. The created life we received from God through our parents is incomplete and lacks direction and meaning. The uncreated life that God's Word lives is the direction and meaning we all yearn for and desperately need. Jesus, who is God's Word become human, lives this direction and meaning we all yearn for and desperately need. If we share in his uncreated, eternal life, we find our meaning. This meaning has been offered to all people. It is Catholic (i.e., universal) faith. "The light shines in the darkness and the darkness did not overcome it" (John 1:5).

---

2. Throughout this homily, Fr. Roach uses the NRSV-CE translation.

At this point in his prologue, Saint John the Evangelist tells us about the other John, Saint John the Baptist, "There was a man sent from God, whose name was John. He came as a witness to testify to the light, so that all might believe through him. He himself was not the light, but he came to testify to the light. The true light, which enlightens everyone, was coming into the world" (John 1:6–9). The Baptist's testimony led people to repent, as we all need to do before receiving our Lord. The change of heart that we call "repentance" (the original Greek word literally means change of heart or mind) requires us to recognize how we are implicated in this world's evils through what we have done or failed to do, or both. Then, we are required to show our sorrow, especially by making what reparation we can and by changing for the better. Then, and only then can we believe with a faith that receives Jesus the Christ.

"Believing" has come to mean something quite different from what Saint John had in mind when he wrote his prologue nearly two thousand years ago. We use the word for something equivalent to "in my opinion," "it seems to me," or "I think that." This use of the word "believe" has nothing to do with what John meant when he wrote that the Baptist was testifying to the light, "so that all might believe through him" (John 1:7). The Baptist intended his testimony to enable us to recognize God's authority in Jesus [see John 1:10–13]. Believing Jesus means submitting one's heart and mind to God!

In the second paragraph of this homily, we saw that the persons "who were born, not of blood or of the will of the flesh or of the will of man, but of God" (John: 1:13) are those who have been incorporated into the new humanity, which is the eternal life of the person, Jesus, whose nativity we celebrate today. Birth into his life is assured through the Sacrament of Baptism, assuredly lost through deadly sin, and assuredly regained through the Sacrament of Penance. Saint John made clear that God assured "all who received him (i.e., Jesus the Christ), who believed in his name" (John 1:12), that they would be made God's children, which means sharers in the eternal life that God's Word brought into the world when born as one of us and named Jesus. We might have forgotten what "believe in his name" means.

To believe in Jesus's name means to submit with all our hearts and minds to God's authority residing in Jesus. "Name" is a Semitic way of saying "presence." Where Jesus is present, there we submit to him. There is no mistaking that our Lord's real presence is within the Church he founded. His presence is focused in the Church's assembly and in her principal act of worship, which is the Eucharistic Sacrifice, popularly referred to as the Mass. There, the bread really becomes Jesus—who is the Bread of Life—and there the wine really becomes his blood poured out for our salvation. In the

Church, God the Holy Spirit preserves the memory of Jesus until he comes again, so that we can fulfill his command to "Do this in memory of me!" Believing in Jesus means submitting to God's authority. Submitting to God's authority in the person of Jesus the Christ, as remembered in the Church he founded, is what we call faith.

Once Saint John had made clear these truths about faith, he wrote that Jesus was born as one of us: "And the Word became flesh, and lived among us, and we have seen his glory, the glory as of a father's only son, full of grace and truth" (John 1:14). This is the truth of Christmas in one sentence!

My dear friends, in good biblical language you and I are flesh. This means we die. But, eternal life, life that cannot die, has become enfleshed. (Incarnation means enfleshed.) So, flesh has been offered a second life. Let us meet the conditions God has set down and graciously accept his gift.

The rest of the sentence uses a metaphor lost to us. Ancient biology, not overturned until modern times, thought that the father's seed (we still use the Latin term for seed, *semen*) contained the whole new human being. The mother provided only nurture. We were thought to be like the oak tree. The acorn contained the new tree. It needed the ground only as a place to grow. (Some soil was better than other soil.) When the Bible or ancient creeds speak of the "father's only son," the words mean that the son fully replicates his father. So, God the Father and God the Son are equally one and the same God, differing only as they are related one to the other. The Son has all the grace and truth found in the Father.

"John testified to him and cried out, 'This was he of whom I said, He who comes after me ranks ahead of me because he was before me'" (John 1:15). Saint John the Evangelist wrote this repetitive verse because he wanted to emphasize that Saint John the Baptist knew that Jesus was from eternity. Everyone knew that John the Baptist was the elder in terms of who was born into this world first. Saint Elizabeth was advanced in her pregnancy when Mary, our Lord's mother, visited her. Mary had just begun her pregnancy. (Cf. Luke 1:39–45; note that the Visitation follows immediately upon the Annunciation, at which time Mary became pregnant with Jesus; and Elizabeth was already great with child.) The Baptist was older than the Christ, yet he said that the Christ "was before" him, since he knew that the Christ was from eternity. Before the beginning, there is only eternity.

"From His (God's Word's) fullness we have all received, grace upon grace" (John 1:16). "Grace" names freely given gifts of love, especially a merciful and transforming love. We were created in love; we are redeemed in an even greater love. "The law indeed was given through Moses; grace and truth came through Jesus Christ" (John 1:17). It is indeed good (i.e., a grace) to know the difference between right and wrong. And, Moses did more than any other human being to help us with this distinction. Nevertheless, we all know that this distinction can be used. I've wanted badly to write a book entitled, *The Immoral Uses of Morality*. Morality can be used immorally to judge, to hurt, and to stop up forgiveness and mercy in order to put people down and make them miserable. It can also be used to cultivate self-righteousness. Yet, we cannot possibly get along without morality, while morality leaves us needing, desperately needing, something more. What we desperately need came through Jesus the Christ. It is "grace and truth": the grace to forgive and the truth about God, as well as the truth about ourselves, and what we do or fail to do, and what our lives mean—truths no mere morality or value system can give us. Only the life and light of God's Word gives these truths!

"No one has ever seen God. It is God the only Son, who is close to the Father's heart, who has made him known" (John 1:18). Merry Christmas!

Chapter 4

The Blessed Virgin Mary, the Mother of God; The Giving of the Name Jesus
Dark Chocolate (New Year's Day, 2006)

Scripture Readings

Num 6:22–27; Ps 67; Gal 4:4–7; Luke 2:16–21.

Summary

The title invokes the bittersweet joy of the hope seen in Christ and Mary's examples. Fr. Roach explains this by joining Jesus's name ("Yahweh saves") and Mary as "God bearer" (*Theotokos*). Jesus's circumcision sees his first shedding of blood for us. The New Testament replaces circumcision with baptism into the new People of God. Christ's joy was bittersweet, knowing all that would happen to him, including dying for our sins. Mary's trials, too, see hope mixed with sorrow. She is our exemplar for living our faith. Calling Mary "Mother of God" protects belief in the Incarnation. The Incarnation also means that God's primary revelation is Christ as a person. The Church authoritatively preserves the memory of Christ. Christian revelation thus cannot be reduced to inspired writings or a set of laws. It cannot be dismissed as merely poetic or mythological truth, as Fr. Roach observes a contemporary noted author doing. The sermon on Jesus receiving his name appropriately closes discussing biblical titles for God.

Homily

*T*HE CHRISTMAS SEASON IS a difficult time for the priests who serve you. We all experience the tension between the season as commercialized and celebrated differently from the spirit established in the Mass of Christ from which the holiday takes its name. As mentioned [recently before], some of the celebration that varies from the Church's original intent is quite good. Some families use the occasion to strengthen familial bonds of love and support and to celebrate their blessings, which they find in each other and in their friends. This is very good. Unfortunately, for many other [families], this is an expensive time of forced and organized joy that occasions forms of depression known from popular music as "Blue Christmas." The commercial American Christmas gone bad is very sad, but not our concern in this homily. Here, we want to discern clearly the difference between the joy of the good American Christmas, and the spirit of this season as it emanates from the history of our liturgy and the life of the Lord whose birth and infancy we celebrate.

The good American Christmas, which remains good even when commercialized, began in the nineteenth century in New York.[1] I liken this good American Christmas to rich milk chocolate fudge loaded with butter and sugar and nuts, and very sweet. On the other hand, the spirit of the Christmas season in the liturgy of the Church as it remembers the birth and infancy of Jesus, concluding with his entrance onto history's stage as a young man, I liken to bittersweet dark, dark chocolate.

This metaphor leads to our distinguishing between two kinds of joy. The enjoyment of the sweet and buttery milk chocolate is light, carefree, and happy; whereas the joy of the bittersweet is a strange and quite different joy. This joy is more like hope. Saint Paul referred to this joy as "hoping against hope." When Saint Paul wrote this strange phrase, he was referring to Abraham, our father in faith as our liturgy refers to him. Abraham was an old man and his wife was decades beyond menopause when God's messenger told him they would have a son. (cf. Gen 17.) Saint Paul wrote the following about how Abraham received God's promise: "Hoping against hope, he (Abraham) believed that he would become 'the father of many nations,' according to what was said (by God's messenger), 'So numerous shall your descendants be'" (Rom 4:18; NRSV-CE).[2] The joy of dark chocolate is "hoping against hope." It is the joy that only God the Holy Spirit can provide.

---

1. See the first homily in this volume, *First Sunday of Advent*.

2. Fr. Roach is again quoting from the NVSV-CE this entire homily. The next sees his return to his customary use of the NJB.

This joy accompanies us even when we are dying, even when our losses seem unsupportable, even when we suffer horribly; it is the only joy that can enter into life's darkest moments. This is the joy of dark chocolate. This is the spirit of Christmas.

If you grasp the distinction I've tried awkwardly to make with this chocolate metaphor, then you see why priests dread Christmas. Many people come to the Masses of Christ surfeited on buttery milk chocolate expecting the Mass to serve as the climatic piece of fudge; instead, the liturgy serves up the bittersweet and dark.

There is a great American slave spiritual honoring the birth of Christ with a line in the lyrics that says of the Baby Jesus, he was born for to die. It took the Africans held in chattel slavery in the United States to understand the true meaning of Christmas. Then, came the American Civil War. It was the bloodiest war of the nineteenth century, yet the original American Santa Claus visited the troops and brought them joy, the bittersweet, authentic joy of Christmas. I strongly prefer the Santa Claus of Thomas Nast's illustrations for the *Harper's Weekly* drawn during the Civil War to what appears came to the fore in the advertisements of the Coca-Cola company and in the shopping malls of today. For me Nast's illustrations capture perfectly the bittersweet joy of Christmas.

The great solemnity which this year we celebrate on the first day of the new calendar year reminds us of the bittersweet, because we remember during this solemnity the first day Jesus shed his blood for our salvation. Jesus received his name on the eighth day following his birth, immediately following his circumcision, according to Jewish custom and law. When he was circumcised, Jesus bled. (The Jewish community refers to circumcision as *Bris* or *Brit Milah*, which means the circumcision of the covenant.) These were the first drops of the blood that saves us from our sins.

Father John Endres, S.J., a Scripture scholar of the Oregon province, hosted me when I was in Rome to preside at the wedding of friends from Ireland. He led me back to the principal Jesuit church of Rome, the Gesú. I had not visited this wonderful edifice since I'd been in Rome fifty years ago as a young pilot in the United States Air Force. It was there that I tried to decide if I was truly called to join the Society, which I obviously did. In the urgency of my prayers at that time, I did not pay attention to the magnificent painting over the main altar. Instead, I concentrated on the shrine of Saint Ignatius of Loyola, which is a side altar. When Father Endres took me back, he focused my attention on the great painting from which the church receives its name (Gesú is Italian for Jesus). The painting shows our Lord's circumcision immediately following which he received his name, which means "Yahweh saves." This painting rises above the main altar of our flagship church because Saint Ignatius of Loyola wanted the new order he founded in the sixteenth century named the Society (or Companions) of Jesus. Today's solemnity commemorates the naming of Jesus, and we Jesuits consider this solemnity our name day.

"After eight days had passed, it was time to circumcise the child; and he was called Jesus, the name given by the angel before he was conceived in the womb" (Luke 2:21; the concluding verse of today's gospel).

Father Endres told me how he had served as a guide for a group of his fellow Scripture scholars from Israel on their first visit to Rome. They, of course, were Jewish. When, at the conclusion of the tour, he brought them before the high altar of the Gesú and pointed up to the great painting of the circumcision of our Lord, they were all amazed and one of the scholars broke into tears. The young scholar who wept explained her tears by saying that this was the only place in Rome where she had seen that Jesus is a Jew.

If one reads chapter 17 of Genesis, particularly verses 12–14, one hears God command circumcision as the sign of his covenant with Abraham and his descendants according to the flesh. We learn from this that God expects those with whom he relates, those with whom God is bound in covenant, those whom God saves, to belong to a people and live as members of God's people. In Jesus, the new covenant (also called the New Testament) has the same requirement of active membership in God's people, but with different signs. The sign that replaces circumcision is baptism followed by confirmation. The sign that repeatedly affirms living membership in God's people is the Holy Eucharist. Living with hope in Jesus the Christ requires these signs!

Replacing circumcision with baptism is a principal subject in the New Testament. I used the concordance of the Authorized Version to estimate the number of times this change of the sign of covenant with God comes up in the New Testament.[3] I simply counted the number of references to circumcision in that translation. I counted fifty-five references. Not an obscure issue in the New Testament! We should learn from this how illusory is the idea that one can count on God's saving and merciful love while repudiating active membership in the new People of God Jesus established, and which we enter through baptism into the Church he founded.

The first pope, Saint Peter, addressing principally non-Jews who had received baptism, although Peter, a Jew, included his own people who were baptized in the new people, wrote about our Lord's new People of God as follows: "But you are a chosen race, a royal priesthood, a holy nation, God's own people, in order that you may proclaim the mighty acts of him who

---

3. Authorized Version refers to the *King James Bible*, or King James Version, first printed in 1611.

called you out of darkness into his marvelous light. Once you were not a people, but now you are God's people; once you had not received mercy, but now you have received mercy" (1 Pet 2:9–10). The reason we know that the audience for these words consisted principally of non-Jews comes from what Saint Peter, a Jew, wrote when referring to his audience as once a non-people, whereas Saint Peter's own people had been a chosen people for many centuries. The Second Vatican Council built its description of the Church Jesus founded in the Council's *Dogmatic Constitution on the Church* [*Lumen Gentium*] principally upon these two verses. Understand these verses, and one has begun to understand the Church.

In conclusion, we may say that Jesus belonged to the chosen people from the moment the event we commemorate today took place. He then bore the name "Yahweh saves." And when it came his turn to found a new people, his Church, he insisted without hesitation that those who follow him join his new People of God and live as active members. He began the founding of this new People of God by shedding blood as he, although still an infant, had shed his blood when he was signed by circumcision as a member of the older chosen people. Jesus, then, made the People he newly organized into his own Body by shedding his blood on the Cross and then rising from the dead. While walking this earth with us, our Lord's joy was dark and bittersweet. His joy in this life was the darkest chocolate. May the blessings of the real Christmas be yours now and throughout the new calendar year.

We turn now to the other part of this solemnity—the Solemnity of the Blessed Virgin Mary, the Mother of God.

First, all Catholics must clearly understand what the appellation "Mother of God" means. The third ecumenical council of the Catholic Church (the Council of Ephesus held in 431) made this title into a central piece of our system of belief so that heretics would not succeed in undermining and even denying the Incarnation.

From early on in the life of the Church and widespread today, there have been many who want to undermine or deny that Jesus is God's Word, and is God in the same sense that the Father and the Holy Spirit are God, i.e., one and only one God. The Council of Ephesus adopted the Greek word *Theotokos* to describe our Lady. *Theotokos* means literally God-bearer, bearer as in a mother bearing a child. Thus, the Latin translation of the council's documents rendered *Theotokos* as *Mater Dei*, literally Mother of God. In context, the meaning is quite clear. Mary gave birth to a whole person who, while fully human, was also God. Jesus is the Incarnate Word of God, and son of the Blessed Virgin Mary. He is the new humanity of which Mary is the Mother *par excellence!* Mary is the new Eve. Jesus does not gain his divinity from his mother (a preposterous idea); he does receive his humanity from her; but Mary gave birth to no abstract humanity; she gave birth to a man who received the name of Jesus, and who also is God. By the way, this third ecumenical council was held in the town where Saint John the Evangelist took care of our Lady until she fell asleep (Dormition) and joined her son Jesus (Assumption). Centuries later, Muslims conquered the town, which now is part of modern Turkey. Still, heroic Catholics maintained the shrines, some of which remain to this day.

There are many among us with Protestant friends who undermine the faith by refusing to refer to Mary as the Mother of God; instead, they refer to her only as the Mother of Jesus. Some are unaware how this undercuts historical Christianity. Among us are many who have friends who deny explicitly or implicitly that God has revealed himself by becoming one of us. Insofar as they accept God's existence and any revelation, they reduce this to inspired writings and laws. We cannot hear often enough how this regression to mere writings eventually destroys faith.

In this country among people who are nominally Christian, some even nominally Catholic, we find the same phenomenon: many who forget the significance of Jesus as God's Word, and instead elevate the text of the Protestant Bible into an exclusive status as God's Word. This phenomenon follows directly upon the Protestant dogma of *sola scriptura* (only Scripture). One of the supreme advantages of earning a doctorate in religious studies has been to comprehend firsthand how nothing remains of the historical Christian system of belief (i.e., the full and true faith) if one has only a text and uses the techniques of contemporary scholars to unpack the meaning of the text. Only the sacred Tradition of the Church saves the facts on which faith rests. In my doctoral studies, I learned that the choice was between being Catholic or at best a pious agnostic. It is essential that young people in college understand the conclusions contemporary scholarship draws concerning matters of faith. Otherwise, they will lose their faith.

Colleges and universities of any quality today are blanketed by one view of religion. These intellectuals hold as definitive the claim that what people call faith cannot in principle have anything to do with ascertainable fact. Religion is not a matter of truth that includes facts; religion deals only with the kind of transformative truths we rightly associate with great poetry, with ancient mythology, with psychotherapy, and so forth. In other words, for these intellectuals, the resurrection of Jesus cannot include the fact of a tomb that was empty because a dead man came back to life, an event we can date approximately. Instead, the resurrection is a kind of poetry that inspires hope in the face of adversity and death. Neither more nor less! That this hope is, as our liturgy says, "sure and certain" contemporary intellectuals, except for the few Catholics among them, deny. Instead they regard such belief as preposterous.

It is very important to know why contemporary intellectuals, except for a few Catholics, hold this view. They are all quite bright enough, and quite well educated enough to know that no writings could guarantee such a fact as the resurrection. They know that such a fact could be guaranteed in only one way: namely, an authoritative witness. And the only way the truth from an authoritative witness could last through the centuries would require an institution to preserve the truth of what was witnessed. Given human sinfulness, such an institution would require divine protection. In other words, if the claim that the tomb was empty because Jesus rose from the dead is factual, only the Church Jesus founded and God the Holy Spirit protects could verify the claim.

Contemporary intellectuals choke on the idea that there is a teaching authority that knows something they can't know for themselves. Hence, some conclude that at best religion is poetry containing some values while providing some transformative psychology. Others prefer to regard religion as a disease.

If you have children in college, even nominally Catholic colleges, or if your children went to prestigious preparatory schools, you may be sure they've been exposed to this anti-Catholic prejudice in at least one of its many forms. If anyone wishes to see this view of religion presented in a smart, short form, read Karen Armstrong's new book, *A Short History of Myth*.[4] Remember that Armstrong is an ex-nun, ex-Catholic. I find her fascinating and quite off-putting. From my point of view, she's catalogued more religious leaves than I would ever even want to catalogue while never having found the tree on which they grow. By the mercy of God, I found the tree and see no point in trying to count all the leaves.

The conclusion of her book is weirdly elitist. She seems to think the role formerly played by mythology, which for her includes the vital element in all religions, now is played by novels. Among the novels she lists, she adds one famous painting and one famous poem. I laughed out loud because only a small number of educated people would know the works on this list, whereas living mythology has always been a cultural phenomenon for the masses. Mythology is pop culture when and wherever the mythology is alive.

From early on in our day, mythology has been exported around the world beginning from southern California. Movies, popular music from country to rock and roll, to rap and everything in-between, as well as most

---

4.. Armstrong, *A Short History*.

everything on radio, TV, and now on the Internet—all this is today's mythology; not for the love of God. T.S. Eliot's *The Waste Land*, which is the famous poem that Armstrong cites as modern mythology. Eliot's *The Waste Land*, for those who are not familiar with the poem, is a deliberately obscure Modernist poem that requires footnotes and is a challenge for even the well-educated to read. It's brilliant, but not accessible as was Homer's poetry (*The Iliad* and *The Odyssey*), which contained living mythology. The least educated could hear the blind poet Homer tell his tales. His tales contained mythology that lived. Only a few can comprehend a reading of *The Waste Land*.

For her book, Karen Armstrong counted an impressive number of leaves on the great tree of mythology and again missed the tree itself. She missed the roots of the tree sunk deep into the soil of the masses. She failed to realize that this tree was never a small potted plant in the conservatory of the elite. And, she missed the trunk of the tree as well: the trunk which consisted of the belief of the masses that their mythologies contained facts, even some historical facts. Regarding this last, perhaps she thought Agamemnon, Achilles, and Helen of Troy were not mythological. I still say she counted leaves and missed the tree.

There always are flaws and errors of this magnitude in the thinking of today's anti-faith, anti-Catholic claimants. Please don't let this thinking with its errors deceive the young people whose education you are paying for. Because there are instances of ancient mythology interwoven within our sacred Scriptures and used to teach truths that do not require facts, the young will be taught that all is non-factual myth. They will not be taught that there also are facts, especially historical facts, upon which our faith rests in the same Scriptures. For instance, Jesus actually rose from the dead, and as Saint Paul stated clearly, "If Christ has not been raised, your faith is futile and you are still in your sins" (1 Cor 15:17). I wouldn't waste my time with "religion" if those who witnessed the empty tomb and saw the risen Lord had not told the truth, and if their witness had not been truthfully preserved in the Church he founded. I then also would be an old man who expected nothingness soon.

Those who read this homily and also hear it proclaimed will know how little of it I preach. I've put the rest in the written form for a variety of reasons, principally for those who are in college. Still, this part of the homily needs proclamation because it is the core of the solemnity that honors the Mother of God.

The shepherds told our Lady what they heard from the angels the night she gave birth to Jesus. What they heard was the subject of our homily for the Masses of Christ. This Mass coming eight days later overlaps what we heard on Christmas, but focuses us on this key statement about our Lady after she heard what the shepherds had to say: "But Mary treasured all these words and pondered them in her heart" (Luke 2:19). Do we also treasure what the angels told Mary, and do we ponder what they said in our hearts? If we do, we're still wondering what it means that a savior has been born for us and why he is called son of David and Messiah (or Christ) and Lord. We also are wondering why this is good news (gospel) of great joy for all the people, and what is the peace promised for those on whom God's favor rests. As we ponder what the angels said, we come to see the baby more clearly. Today, we see the first blood he shed.

Mary pondered all her life. Many have wondered why the sacred Scriptures tell us so little about her. I see no great mystery in this silence. She was given no knowledge infused by God into her mind telling her all about her mysterious son. No, she had to live by faith and learn just as you and I do. It seems to me the reason for the nearly complete silence about her in the New Testament is obvious: she is the epitome of obscure men and women about whom no one will write a great book and who must learn by prayer and pondering upon Jesus, as you and I must do, what the dickens life is all about. She is our hope and joy that in this learning we may succeed. We can be like her. She so pondered the wonder of her very unusual son that she was able to follow him to the foot of the Cross on which he was executed.

I think only Saint John, because he too was there, understood how her life of pondering the mystery of her son led her to the foot of his Cross. There, before dying, Jesus gave her to John and through him to us (John 19:25–27).

If we but ponder as she did, God's grace will lead us through life to that strange joy whereby it becomes possible to endure great suffering with sure and certain hope. The strange joy like very dark, bittersweet chocolate wherein we find the meaning of our lives is the same bittersweet joy that gave Mary the courage to stand at the foot of her son's Cross while he died. She had seen his first blood when he was circumcised; immediately following his death she witnessed blood and water flow from his side, the side the centurion pierced with a spear (John 19:34). Only the bittersweet joy of someone who has pondered the mysteries of faith can understand how Mary survived her suffering and loss. You and I, dear friends, need this kind of joy many times in our lives. It is the true joy of Christmas. Therefore, let us follow her example and ponder what we've heard in our hearts, so we too will be prepared.

Our first reading came from the Book of Numbers (6:22–27). The liturgists chose this reading to emphasize the importance that the ancients in general and our Lord's people in particular placed on the meaning of a name. The last verse of the reading says this: "So they shall put my name on the Israelites, and I will bless them" (Num 6:27). The name put on the Israelites was the Tetragrammaton now transliterated into English as Yahweh (cf. Exod 3:13–15; use NJB with notes). And, as I've said above, the name Jesus means "Yahweh saves."

Our Lord's name lost two syllables as it went from Hebrew to Aramaic, to Greek, to Latin, and finally into English. Traditionally, translators substituted Lord for Yahweh (all but those who translated the sacred Scriptures following the scholarship that produced the first edition of the Jerusalem Bible in French). The translators substituted Lord for Yahweh in part because observing Jews did not use the Tetragrammaton for fear of violating the second commandment. Also for reasons I won't go into here, the translators until recently commonly transliterated the Tetragrammaton incorrectly. Their error is how we acquired the word "Jehovah." Furthermore, the New Testament never uses Yahweh; the writings that make up the New Testament use only Lord or what Yahweh means—particularly the first part of the Tetragrammaton, the Yah, which means I AM. Finally, this reading contains a translation of this blessing, which Protestant ministers most commonly use; but the ministers use the blessing with Lord, not Yahweh. Therefore, for this homily I used the NRSV-CE, which in regard to transliterating or translating the Tetragrammaton is more traditional than the NJB. Unfortunately, with this choice, the last verse of today's reading becomes unintelligible. I'll explain, but first here is the blessing: "The Lord bless you and keep you; / the Lord make his face to shine upon / you, and be gracious to you; / the Lord lift up his countenance / upon you, and give you peace" (Num 6:24-26 NRSV-CE; each instance of "Lord" replaces Yahweh).

The last verse, which I've quoted above, states that with this blessing the priests of Aaron will place the name of Yahweh on the people and thereby bless them. Name is very special and means among other things presence. The name Yahweh makes God present to the people and thereby blesses the people. In this sense, the name Yahweh foreshadows the Real Presence in the Eucharist. The conventional or traditional translations neuter this blessing by removing the name, which by the way means I AM WHO I AM. Nevertheless, the blessing remains a beautiful prayer. We invoke the name of Jesus because we believe that in Jesus the Lord saves us.

We respond to this reading with verses from Psalm 67. This psalm opens with a verse that almost repeats the blessing from the Book of Numbers: "May God be gracious to us and bless us / and make his face to shine upon us" (Ps 67:1). I love using the metaphor of God's face because we've seen God's face in Jesus. I pray Jesus will smile on us, which is what I take shining to mean.

The second reading comes from Saint Paul's Letter to the Galatians (4:4–7). The liturgists chose this reading to honor our Lord's circumcision: "But when the fullness of time had come, God sent his Son, born of a woman, born under the law, . . . " (Gal 4:4). Eight days after he was born from the womb of Mary, the Mother of God, he was as it were born under the law as God first gave that law to Abraham, thereby making him the father of a people God chose for his own (cf. Gen 17:12–15).

In the rest of this reading we meet again the term of address, *Abba*, Aramaic for Father. We must never sentimentalize this term. Essentially, it is what we say when we pray as our Lord taught us—"Our Father." The use does mean we recognize that we are called in Jesus to be children of God. But, as such, we remember how Jesus used this term to address his Father when he was struggling in prayer while in the garden of Gethsemane seeking the strength to do his Father's will, his *Abba's* will. Again, we come upon dark, bittersweet chocolate. God the Father gave Jesus the strength, and Jesus died, a victim of our sins in order to bring us the merciful love his Father had embodied in him. Dare I say it, he died joyfully, strengthened by that dark joy which enables the human spirit to endure the evils of this world in the sure and certain hope of the resurrection.

Jesus signaled this dark joy in various ways by directing the attention of all who witnessed his dying to the twenty-second Psalm. This psalm that begins in misery and a deathly feeling of abandonment ends with an affirmation of joy. The beginning: "My God, my God, why have you forsaken me?" [Also please note the] ending: Ps 22: 27–31. Only the strange joy born on Christmas makes it possible to sing this song in the face of adversity and even death, death on a Cross. Let us ponder! Perhaps, we need to cultivate a taste for dark chocolate and not just sweet, buttery fudge.

Chapter 5

The Epiphany of the Lord Father
(January 8, 2006)

Scripture Readings
Isa 60:1–6; Ps 72; Eph 3:2a–3, 5–6; Matt 2:1–12.

Summary

The Epiphany celebrates God's manifestation "as human and resident with us in the world God created." The Maji signal Jesus is the awaited Messiah for all peoples. The second reading discusses calling God "Father," a metaphor signifying him to be the transcending source of authority and merciful love. The metaphorical intent behind the title is easily misjudged. The Catholic view of seeing God behind all legitimate authority limits all merely human authority. A postscript further explains translating biblical terms.

Homily

EPIPHANY MEANS APPEARANCE OR manifestation. Thus, this solemnity celebrates the appearance or manifestation of the Lord God as human and resident with us in the world that God created. This solemnity is older than the celebration of Christmas and in its original form included reference to our Lord's birth, but always focused on the public appearances of our Lord. The first and most important public appearance took place when our Lord asked Saint John the Baptist to baptize him in the River Jordan. After setting the scene by introducing the Baptist, Saint Mark began his gospel with this appearance, i.e., the baptism of our Lord (cf. Mark 1:1–11). Matthew and Luke, as we know, placed a theological narrative about our Lord's birth before beginning his public history (the first two chapters of both gospels). Then, both Evangelists report our Lord's baptism. Saint John the Evangelist wrote a prologue that proclaimed what the Incarnation means and wove in reference to the other Saint John who was the baptizer (John 1:1–18). The Evangelist then reported about the Baptist and Jesus, but did not report it as the major appearance inaugurating our Lord's public life. To announce our Lord's appearance in public, John chose to report the way in which our Lord manifested himself at a wedding feast in Cana of Galilee (John 2:1–12) as the beginning of his public life of teaching. In this way, Saint John emphasized the role of the Blessed Virgin Mary both at the beginning and at the end of our Lord's public life. It was Mary who requested the wondrous conversion of water into wine at Cana, and it was she who stood at the foot of the cross as her son died (cf. John 19:25–27). In its original form, this great Solemnity of the Epiphany celebrated all these initial appearances among us of our Incarnate Lord.

Of course, epiphany also means manifestation, so the solemnity could not pass over the manifestation Saint Matthew reported in his theological narrative celebrating our Lord's birth: namely, the star whose appearance fulfilled ancient prophecy and led wise men from Persia to honor the baby Jesus. [*Magus* is Latin, or *magos* in Greek, for a learned man among the Persians; *magi* (Greek, *magoi*) is plural, i.e., learned men. These learned men also administered the government. Their wisdom included a sophisticated astrology. Thus, these men "read the stars."] We find the prophecy the Star of Bethlehem fulfilled in the Book of Numbers (24:17). The verse is part of the prophecy of Balaam son of Beor, an amusingly reluctant prophet. He was engaged to prophesy against the Israelites. Instead, the Lord God, who used an ass in the process, forced Balaam to prophesy truthfully against the enemies of the Israelites. As he was prophesying truthfully, Balaam said: "a star is emerging from Jacob, / a scepter is rising from Israel, / to strike the brow of Moab, / the skulls of all the children of Seth" (Num 24:17bc [NJB]). The star presaged the birth of a king who would conquer the enemies of the Israelites represented in this verse by Moab and the children of Seth. [One finds the history of Balaam in the Book of Numbers from 22:2 to the end of chapter 24.]

Rabbis in our Lord's day understood the star mentioned in this verse as shining on the birth of *the* Messiah (i.e., *the* Christ). This rabbinic understanding later played a major role in the history of the Jewish rebellion against the Roman Empire, the rebellion Jesus refused to lead. A man named Simeon Ben Kosiba led the final, futile Jewish rebellion against the Roman Empire (AD 131–135). Rabbi Akiba, who is one of the founders of what today we refer to as normative Judaism, dubbed this leader of the rebellion Bar Kocheba, which means Son of the Star. With this naming, Rabbi Akiba declared the rebel leader the messiah. "Son of the Star" meant that in the Rabbi's mind the rebel leader fulfilled the prophecy in Numbers 24:17. Saint Matthew in his theological narrative had already told us that Jesus fulfilled this prophecy. Saint Matthew's narrative tells us that Jesus is the Messiah (the Christ). The story of the *Magi* states that Jesus fulfills the prophecy from Balaam in the Book of Numbers. Thus, Saint Matthew's theological narrative is primarily about the star that announces the appearance of God–with–us; then, the narrative embellishes the appearance of the Incarnate One with the account of wise men who traveled from Persia to Bethlehem. In other words, why they traveled is most important: they followed the star Balaam had predicted. Then, the narrative affirms two more important truths.

First, the *Magi* are not Jewish. Therefore, the fulfillment of the prophecy about a star, which would herald the birth of the Messiah, is not just for the chosen people. The fulfillment is Catholic. In other words, the Messiah or Christ, is for all peoples. The second truth has two aspects. The first aspect consists in the *Magi* recognizing that the baby has been born a god/king. It was not unusual in ancient times, even among the chosen people, to think that in some sense a real king was godlike. To use contemporary idiom, a king channeled divinity. This is what the *Magi* thought they were honoring with their gifts of gold, frankincense, and myrrh. These were gifts worthy of a god/king, but tradition (small "t") has assigned to each a specific significance: gold for his royal status, frankincense for his divinity (we burn incense to honor God because incense rises with sweet aroma as do our prayers and because it was an expensive sacrifice), and myrrh, a pungent resin with a bitter taste, to foreshadow his bitter death.

Mention of the gifts in Matthew's gospel also is a literary allusion to Isaiah 60:6. This verse appeared in our first reading for this solemnity. The prophecy was written late in the sixth century before the birth of our Lord, around two centuries after the great prophet's death in the eighth century BC. Isaiah inspired a school of prophets who used his name. This prophet wanted to console Jewish exiles and persuade them to take advantage of the largesse of the Persian king who had conquered their Babylonian oppressors and return to Judea from which the Babylonians had exiled them. Returning us from exile in sin to God's grace is the work of our Lord whom the *Magi* honored with gifts mentioned in Isaiah, gifts which were fit for a king.

The other aspect of the *Magi* recognizing our Lord's royal status, even as a baby, leads to today's second reading. The reading consists of a snippet from a section of Saint Paul's Letter that leads up to a prayer. Before we turn to the prayer, which links this New Testament passage to the *Magi*, we should note how Saint Paul used the word "mystery." The term refers to something one cannot know except the person with the knowledge reveals what he/she knows. In this case, God alone knew for sure that he intended the same inheritance for the gentiles God had promised the chosen people. God revealed this catholicity in Jesus. In other words, Saint Paul's use of the term "mystery" means something we now are able to know because God has revealed it. The term does not mean a puzzle, as it does when referring to a mystery story in our day.

The prayer this passage prepares us to listen to begins as follows: "This, then, is what I pray, kneeling before the Father, from whom every fatherhood, in heaven or on earth, takes its name" (Eph 3:14–15). When the *Magi* knelt before the baby Jesus and did him homage (Matt 2:11), they were in effect addressing Jesus as "Father" in the sense that the ancients understood this appellation. Their primary meaning for "Father" was not Dad, as we use "Dad." "Father" first and foremost designated the being who had authority over one.

In the writings that make up our Old Testament, "father" refers almost exclusively to the patriarch of the family. The patriarch embodied authority and although he does beget children, his children did not look upon him in quite the way we look upon our dads. In the New Testament, as Saint Paul made clear in the verse quoted above, God is the Father in the patriarchal sense of the authority figure who begets children and loves them. This shift from using the term primarily, if not exclusively, for one's earthly father to referring to God as Father was adumbrated in the writings accepted into the Hebrew Bible, which is the sole Bible for the synagogue, and also is used by Protestants as their Old Testament. Although adumbrated in the Hebrew Bible, the use is not common; whereas calling God, Father, is ubiquitous in the New Testament.

The shift from earthly father to heavenly father took place as an essential element in the prophecies that prepared people for the coming of the Messiah. I believe the three verses of Second Samuel 7:14–16 report the shift. In these verses, speaking through the prophet Nathan, Yahweh said the following to David about his descendants (i.e., his dynasty), referring first to David's son, Solomon: "I (Yahweh) shall be a father to him and he a son to me; if he does wrong, I shall punish him with a rod such as men use, with blows such as mankind gives. But my faithful love will never be withdrawn from him as I withdrew it from Saul, whom I removed from before you. Your dynasty and your sovereignty will ever stand firm before me and your throne be forever secure." Jesus is the final son and heir of the Davidic dynasty. Jesus fulfills this promise in his person. This promise is referred to elsewhere in the Old Testament, most famously in verse 7 of Psalm 2.

Later, Isaiah the prophet (the Isaiah himself whose name his followers would use) in a prophecy that comes from him in the eighth century before the birth of Jesus referred to a son he predicted would be born as "Wonder-Counsellor, Mighty-God, / Eternal Father, Prince-of-Peace" (Isa 9:6). In context, it is clear that this son will be a heir of the Davidic dynasty. The Church has seen these titles as referring to God–with–us, namely, Jesus the Christ. [This verse closes the first reading for this Mass—Isa 60:1–6.]

Fortunately, we have a longer Old Testament preserving our memory of the period that immediately prepared for our Lord's birth. In our complete Old Testament, we learn how the righteous person who is not a direct descendant of King David can call God his Father. In a famous passage about a righteous person whom the wicked were intending to kill, the wicked said of the righteous one: "In his opinion we are counterfeit; / he avoids our ways as he would filth; / he proclaims the final end of the upright as blessed / and boasts of having God for his father" (Wis 2:16). This verse from a book the Protestants excluded from their Canon of inspired writings not only prepared people for Jesus who is the righteous one, but also says that God is his Father not just because he is heir to David's throne. God is the Father of the righteous even if they have no claim on David's throne. Therefore, both as the righteous one without equal and as heir to the throne of King David, Jesus could teach us to pray "Our Father," because he knew what calling God "Father" really means. Unfortunately, referring to God with a masculine term causes many [people] great difficulty in our day.

The "Father" of the prayer that Jesus taught us is neither Dad nor Mom. Father is a principal term for authority in the world of patriarchy, and the entire world was patriarchal until quite recently. Most of the world still is. Unlike words, such as king or god, "father" also suggests that authority cares for those whom the authority lords it over, as one hopes that biological fathers care for their children. Jesus taught us that his Father is God, the one and only, and not only completely benign in our regard, but also mercifully loving. Nonetheless, by using the term "father" as he did, Jesus also taught us that God is the ultimate and only authority from which all other legitimate authority derives. If the lesser authority is not from God, which means that the authority is at least compatible with God, we as Catholics are not obliged to submit to the authority; we may even be obliged to resist the authority.

Jesus, as one of us before his death and resurrection, would never have thought with his human mind that addressing God as Father implied males are superior to females. Even a secularist trying to discredit the faith has to note that Jesus alone as a major religious leader truly saw women as equal to men. He made this most clear when he abrogated (i.e., wiped out) the provision in the law of his people that provided for the male divorcing the female, but granted the woman no rights (cf. Deut 24:1–4). Multiple passages in the Gospels record how Jesus abrogated this sexist divorce law (Matt 5:31–32; 19:1–9; Mark 10:1–12; Luke 16:18). Jesus would be appalled at those who would re-write the prayer he taught us as "Our Father/Mother who art in heaven," because he would know they had misunderstood what he intended when he used the term "Father." To reinforce what our Lord intended, I shall risk paraphrasing the prayer he taught us: Our Authority which art in heaven, hallowed be thy designation; may thy counsel and rules prevail on earth as they do in heaven. Give us this day our daily bread and forgive us our sins as we forgive those who have sinned against us. Lead us not into temptation, but deliver us from the Evil One. Amen!

I do not recommend using my paraphrase of the Our Father in prayer. I've written it only to make a point. The point I've tried to make is exactly the same point Saint Paul made before the prayer our second reading prefaces. Here again is the sentence that leads into the prayer: "This, then, is what I pray, kneeling before the Father, from whom every fatherhood, in heaven or on earth, takes its name" (Eph 3:14–15). Playing with the word "father" and making it into an issue in the feminist struggle for equality distracts from, or obliterates completely the significance of the term in the Catholic system of belief, which is the only system of belief faithful to the whole of the Bible. "Father" is the metaphorical use of a term to refer to God, which term literally refers to the most basic form of human authority throughout history, but which also can be a term of endearment. The radical Catholic ideal whereby all legitimate authority comes from God and remains legitimate only when in harmony with God's counsel and purposes limits all human authority, including the authority of the Church God's Word founded.

The Church does hold some of God's authority, but in a clearly limited or constitutional fashion. Jesus signaled giving divine authority to the Church he founded when our Lord empowered his Church to forgive sins, which only God can do (cf. John 20:22–23; Matt 16:19 and 18:18). But, even this empowerment is constitutionally limited. God retains all ultimate authority, thereby limiting all human authority.

We state this radical Catholic ideal by calling God our Father and saying with Saint Paul that "every fatherhood, in heaven or on earth, takes its name" from God the Father. Thus, God requires that all human authority be constitutionally limited. The limitations derive from the dignity God has assigned each human being. Then, God's own authority is "limited" by God's own love, intelligence, justice, and wisdom.

There are numerous other references to the truth that God alone is the final authority in our lives, all other authorities deriving their legitimacy from God and subordinating themselves to God. My favorite statement of this truth is one our Lord made when excoriating hypocrites. Jesus said: "You must call no one on earth your father, since you have only one father, and he is in heaven" (Matt 23:9). When I was a young Protestant boy, I often heard our Lord's hyperbole recorded in this verse used to attack Catholic practice, particularly the custom of addressing a priest as "Father."[1] Such a misuse of our Lord's hyperbole obliterates what he meant. Instead of what the misuse implies, Jesus actually used hyperbole to denounce an unconstitutional usurpation of God's authority by those who at best exaggerated their claim to share in this authority.

The radical character of this Catholic belief about authority is the reason why overreaching human authorities always persecute the Church. China, Islamic governments, and Cuba are but three outstanding instances of this persecution in our day, but not the only instances. Other forms of the persecution tend to be subtler.

Appreciating this truth breaks down the wall many would like to create between religion and politics. As citizens able to vote, we are responsible for how elected officials use their authority we give them. How we handle our responsibility is as significant an expression of our faith as are other aspects of our living. We either exercise our responsibility as God wants us to, or not. There are numerous examples in the political life of this country at the moment. To name one: where do you stand on the presidential use of authority to wiretap? To name another: have the officials you voted for adequately held the agencies that regulate and evaluate the safety of coal mines to account? God calls us to account for these positions as much as God calls us to account for prayer and receiving Holy Communion.

The *Magi* knew that legitimate authority came from God, and they recognized this authority resident in a baby born in Bethlehem two thousand years ago. The *Magi* recognized God's epiphany as one of us.

Before leaving the subject of this Epiphany, we should note that our response to the first reading came from the Psalm 72. The opening verse of this psalm is a worthy prayer asking God to insure that our governing officials follow God's rules (Ps 72:1–2).

---

1. Fr. Roach was raised as a Congregationalist.

Postscript

Translations are treacherous. People who follow these homilies know that I most frequently use the New Jerusalem Bible. I do so because I trust the translation, in part because of the excellent notes. Nevertheless, I often check the translation against other scholarly work. While preparing this homily, I was cross-checking the NJB translation with the NRSV-CE, and I came across a horrible mistranslation in this most highly touted English translation.

The NRSV-CE mistranslated the verses from Saint Paul's Letter to the Ephesians (3:14–15) that I used in the body of this homily to make the point about what "Father" in the Bible really means. I quoted the NJB in the homily. The verses are quoted in the homily printed above. The mistranslation of the two verses as found in the NRSV-CE follows: "For this reason I bow my knees before the Father, from whom every family in heaven and on earth takes its name." The *Magi* did not kneel before a family; they knelt before a god/king. Saint Paul did not say that every family took its name from God; he said "every fatherhood" derived from God the Father. There is a great difference. Even before it became customary to address all priests as Father, Catholic faith recognized a fatherhood that does not beget children through sexual intercourse. The faithful always have recognized spiritual fathers. Celibacy from Saint Paul, who was a celibate, to the present is worthy only when in the service of spiritual fatherhood.

Of course, I should add in a partial defense of the NRSV translation that our use of brother and sister for fellow members of the parish does indicate how God's family is not biological. But, the begetter of the family is God the Father who employs spiritual fathers to assist in accomplishing his purposes. The mother of the family is the Blessed Virgin Mary, assisted by her spiritual heirs. The Blessed Virgin Mary is the spiritual mother of us all and as such the Mother of the Church. Unfortunately, these facts do not justify the mistranslation.

Obviously, the translators for the NRSV were avoiding the term "father" because they thought it sexist. In doing so, they lost the meaning of what Saint Paul wrote. I find this ideologically motivated tampering with language a bit frightening, not because I believe translations are more faithful if they are "dictionary" literal. I know better. The "dictionary literal" often falsifies the meaning. Nor do I find this frightening because I oppose using language that supports our vision of the equality of men and women, because with the Church I believe this vision comes from God the Holy Spirit. Regularly, I make small adjustments in liturgical texts to provide language I think better supports equality. Therefore, I hope all see that what frightens me in this mistranslation is not an effort to find language that supports equality, but the failure to understand what the older language meant.

This failure reveals how little many who allegedly are religious scholars actually understand about the religions they study. I urge those in college or prep schools and their parents to be on the alert for the influence upon religious studies of the latest prejudices. The verses mistranslated in the NRSV show how deadly to true understanding well cultivated prejudices can be.

Chapter 6

Baptism of the Lord
Sin (singular) and Sins (plural)
(January 11, 2004)

Scripture Readings

Isa 40:1–5, 9–11; Ps 104; Titus 2:11–14, 3:4–7; Luke 3:15–16, 21–22.

Summary

The homily considers what sin involves, and that Jesus's baptism shows us a way out. Sin can mean individual wrong acts, the inherited weakness of original sin. It can also refer to the general disorder of the world. Baptism gives us life in Christ, and aids us in overcoming weakness. In gratitude for this, we should love God and others while seeking justice. Christ's baptism sees him identify himself with us as caught in sin, and also with those harmed by our sins. Failure to see this identification with those who suffer can lead to false piety. Christ's baptism and ours shows us that the exercise of merciful love in Jesus is "the one encompassing solution to the problem of evil," which characterizes Catholic faith. Finally, we should remember that full justice and recompense will come only with God's judgment.

Homily

MANY KEY CONCEPTS USED in the New Testament to express our faith are complex. One of these is the concept of "sin." We tend to think that this word denotes only what a person does when he/she does something wrong; whereas many times, both in the New Testament and in our liturgy, when the word is used, it denotes not individual wrongdoing, but a complex condition that has resulted from a lot of wrongdoing. It is helpful to sort out this complexity, and there is a simple way to begin.

When the plural, "sins," is used, then one may assume that the word refers to acts of wrongdoing, a number of them. (The acts of wrongdoing referred to include sinful failures to act, or what we call "sins of omission.") But, when the word is used in the singular, "sin," then one should assume that the word refers to the complex condition that "sins" have brought about. In other words, "sin" refers to a complex condition that has resulted from a lot of human wrongdoing. Saint John the Evangelist used "sin" in this sense when he wrote about Saint John the Baptist and quoted him saying: "The next day, he (John the Baptist) saw Jesus coming towards him and said, 'Look, there is the lamb of God that takes away the *sin* of the world'" (John 1:29 NJB; emphasis added).

The distinction between "sin" and "sins," as I've just described it, is a rule of thumb, not an absolute distinction. There are occasions when one knows from the context that "sin" refers to a single bad act and not the mess our world is in. I can't think of an occasion in which the plural is used for the dreadful condition of our world, but there may be one. The context tells a reader or hearer which is which. There is an excellent example in the language of our theology and liturgy: "original sin." This term refers first to the weaknesses and bad inclinations we have inherited from our first parents because of the sins they committed. But the phrase can be used to refer to their sins, in which case we have the singular "sin" referring to wrongdoing. I hope from my examples and exposition that we all can see the distinction I've drawn between "sin" and "sins" is a rule of thumb for understanding how the terms are used; it is not a hard and fast rule.

But, let us bear in mind that this term, "original sin," which is singular, usually and primarily does denote a complex condition. It denotes both the wound to our human nature inherited from our first parents and the upset world order their sins and subsequent sins have brought about. Nevertheless, as I just wrote, the word "sin" in the phrase "original sin" can indirectly refer to the sins that our first parents committed, but the phrase primarily denotes the human condition that resulted from their sins and subsequent sinning. So, when in our liturgy we say that a child has inherited "original sin," we in no way suggest that the child is guilty of wrongdoing. We are saying only that the child has inherited a weakness that needs a remedy or will result inevitably in wrongdoing, and that the child has been born into a world that will encourage wrongdoing, as well as involve the child in the evils that have resulted from wrongdoing. We baptize the child in order to provide him/her with the life of Christ. This is the only life that can enable us to overcome our personal weakness; if we are baptized after we've actually sinned ourselves, then God uses the sacrament to forgive our sins. (If we sin after baptism, God uses the Sacrament of Penance to forgive us, if we just use the sacrament.) Christ's life also makes it possible to triumph over the evils of this world as they impact our lives. These evils include our actual sins, the sinfulness of others, as well as the sickness and death that God does not protect us from because the world is sinful and thereby alienated from God.

[Please remember that "alienated" as used here does not mean that God dislikes us—quite the contrary, God loves us, as he has made abundantly clear in Jesus. The word means God had to separate himself from "sin" because it is contrary to his nature. Note, I've just used the word "sin" in its singular meaning. We tend to dislike this, because human solidarity drags the innocent in with the guilty. Who we are makes us one human family. It's the way God made us, and there is no escaping the reality.]

God permitting evil is not a judgment on any individual, infant or adult. As far as we can see, God permits evil for two reasons: first, although we each are distinct individual persons, we are members of a single human race. Our very nature presumes this solidarity. So, individual wrongdoing afflicts us all, directly or indirectly, innocent as well as guilty. Secondly, sins alienate the whole human race from God, who was our protection in what for us human beings can be a dangerous world. We cannot miss the fact that God has made a developing world in which everything from viruses to earthquakes play a part, and they are dangerous for unprotected human beings. I repeat that sins alienate the whole human race, even those who have not sinned such as innocent babies. And, remember that alienation in this context does not mean God dislikes human beings; it means that God no longer protects human beings from what is dangerous in this world, such as germs, earthquakes, and the sins others commit.

The poetic story that teaches us this and other truths uses the image of a garden wherein our first parents were perfectly protected from the hazards of life on earth (cf. Gen 2:4b–25). When our first parents sinned, they were driven from the garden (cf. Gen 3, especially verses 23–24), which means we lost the divine protection we need in a dangerous world. Because of human solidarity, our first parents lost this protection not only for themselves, but also for all their progeny. Still, God immediately promised to remedy the situation! (Cf. Gen 3:15, in which verse God promises that an offspring of our first parents will strike the head of the snake that symbolizes evil.)

God's remedy, which as promised in the verse cited above, began immediately following the first sins, comes in a form our first parents did not anticipate. God's remedy did not then come and does not yet come as final judgment, rectifying the situation on the spot, permanently assigning blame, meting out full punishment, and stopping all evildoing. Instead, God's remedy comes as merciful love that asks for our love in return. God asks not only that we love him in return, but also that we love each other as he loves us, i.e., mercifully. Many people, in their heart of hearts, would prefer that God judge, thereby ending all evil immediately rather than dragging us through the struggles of this life wherein and whereby we have the opportunity to love mercifully and to believe in God's merciful love for each of us. But, these folk who would prefer that God judge us here and now assume that they'd pass God's judgment with flying colors, and that only others would be found out and punished. They really don't think they need merciful love as "wicked" people do. They have a lot to learn.

Those who want judgment now—meaning they want an immediate end to evil—often give as their principal reason the obvious fact that under the present scheme innocent people suffer. Babies die, children are blown up in wars, and good people suffer terrible deaths from cancer or in other ways. Some find this absolutely intolerable. Their attitude has been dubbed "Promethean atheism," meaning the belief system of people who do not deny that God exists, but instead defy God because of the evil God permits. These persons do not see the manifest evils of this world as God calling us to seek truth and justice and to love mercifully. They choose to become angry with God for not stopping evil now.

In order to understand why Jesus asked John the Baptist to baptize him, one must understand this distinction between sin and sins, as I've tried to sketch the distinction, as well as have some appreciation for the way God saves us from evil in Jesus through merciful love. If anyone feels somewhat embarrassed by a sense that one does not fully understand all this, please excuse yourself. It is evident to me that Matthew, Mark, Luke, and John did not understand fully when they wrote their gospels. These evangelists knew that Jesus was like us in all things except sin, which means he had not committed any sins and had no inclination to do so (cf. John 8:46; Heb 4:15, et al.). Jesus is the Innocent One. So, the four evangelists could not see how Jesus could honestly ask the Baptist to baptize him.

Saint Mark stated the matter succinctly: "John the Baptist was in the desert proclaiming a baptism of repentance for the forgiveness of sins" (Mark

1:4). Notice the plural "sins"! The people who came for baptism repented for having done what is wrong or failed to do what is right! What could Jesus repent of? Not a thing, and the evangelists knew this. Yet Jesus asked John the Baptist to baptize him. The evangelists were stuck. Saint Matthew thought he was saving himself from reporting something inherently incoherent by also reporting that John the Baptist protested that he shouldn't baptize Jesus, but instead should be baptized by Jesus (cf. Matt 3:13–14). Saints Mark and Luke reported the baptism in a subordinate or conjoined clause, so that they could immediately turn their readers' or hearers' attention to the descent of the Spirit and the voice from heaven identifying Jesus as God's Son (cf. Mark 1:9–11 and Luke 3:21–22). Our gospel for this Mass is Luke 3:15–16, 21–22. The omission of four verses is significant! Mark and Luke thought they could distract their readers/hearers from thinking about why Jesus submitted to baptism. Then, along came Saint John the Evangelist.

In an earlier homily, I erred by saying that all four evangelists record Jesus's baptism at the hands of John as the beginning of his public life. Actually, Saint John does not report that the other John baptized Jesus, although familiarity with the gospels leads someone like me to feel it is implied. Saint John the Evangelist could not make sense of Jesus submitting to what he understood was a baptism of repentance, so he omitted it. Instead, he reported what John the Baptist said when Jesus came toward him, presumably where he was baptizing, as quoted above. I repeat the quotation here: "The next day, he (John the Baptist) saw Jesus coming towards him and said, 'Look, there is the lamb of God that takes away the sin of the world'" (John 1:29, note the singular "sin"!). [*Agnus Dei* is Latin for Lamb of God (we capitalize "Lamb" in this phrase; the British don't). We sing a prayer to the "Lamb of God" at each Mass.] In using the word "sin," when quoting the Baptist, Saint John the Evangelist revealed that he was close to grasping the solution to the problem of Jesus, the Innocent One, submitting to a baptism of repentance; but he failed to connect the dots. Let us try to connect them for him.

The whole point of our Lord's life, including especially his passion, death, resurrection, and ascension, consists in identifying himself with us all insofar as we are caught up in, even implicated in, "the sin of the world" i.e., the mess of disease, disaster, evildoing, especially lying and killing, suffering in general, and death, which mess stains almost beyond recognition the goodness of God's creation. For one who is innocent—i.e., not implicated in bringing this mess about or worsening it—repentance consists, first, in recognizing our solidarity with others who are implicated, and, most importantly, by embracing God's program for dealing with this mess. Left to ourselves, we would never fully embrace the program of merciful love to which God calls us in Jesus as the solution. The proof of this assertion is two-fold: no religion in the world, except Catholic faith, embraces merciful love as the one encompassing solution to the problem of evil, although all major religions preach and practice mercy to varying degrees. The second proof is the constant effort to so distort "Christianity" that merciful love is no longer the ultimate solution, engulfing and shaping all other efforts. The efforts from the subtle to the gross that seek to undermine the centrality of God's mercy come from the evil the snake represents in the story of that first sinning.

I will not attempt an exhaustive listing of the ways in which other religions, although recommending compassion and mercy, when evaluating human behavior subordinate mercy to something else. Persons who call themselves Christian undermine God's solution to evil through merciful love, not by denying the crucifixion, but by misinterpreting it. They see Jesus as the Innocent One unjustly suffering and then dying on the Cross, and they then focus all their attention on his suffering and dying as if their sins implicated them only in his suffering and death. In this way, such persons deny what Jesus did when he came forward to be baptized at the hands of John the Baptist. They deny the kind of "repentance" that even an innocent person with no sins to repent of could engage in—namely, an explicit embracing of God's desire to redeem us from all evil through the exercise of merciful love. Such persons do not see that Jesus identified himself with every person suffering in this world, especially those suffering unjustly as he was going to do. So, instead of weeping over how their sins implicate them in what's happening, for example, to indisputably innocent children in this world at the moment because of human evil, and weeping over these children with whom Jesus has identified himself, they weep only over Jesus who unjustly suffered and died nearly two thousand years ago. This "piety" distracts them from the real effects of their present sins, especially their sins of omission, and instead allows them to feel "cleansed" when in reality they are not. Such "piety" actually allows many not to realize that they are sinning.

This "piety" especially helps many to never discover their sins of omission. They so focus on the truth that our sins caused the suffering and death of our Lord that they do not think of how their sins cause the suffering and death of those with whom Jesus has identified himself, i.e., the others who also are Jesus because *the* Jesus has identified himself with them. When a person misled by false piety focuses exclusively on the Passion of Jesus to the exclusion of those with whom Jesus identified himself, they usually think only of their personal sins, such as whoring around or other sexual infidelity, drunkenness, drugging and other excesses, and the like; in other words, they think only of the kinds of sin that make a guy or gal feel very bad about themselves when they repent, but do not make the person think of their social, political, economic, community, or often even religious obligations. Yet, their sins in these other areas, often sins of omission, may well be worse than the ones they've deeply repented. In other words, it may well be harder to be just and merciful than it is to be sober and faithful sexually to one's spouse.

The whole of the social teachings of the Church, as well as just war doctrine and related teachings, exist to call us to recognize those with whom Jesus has identified himself with by his own suffering and death. Every person killed in an unjustly fought war is another Jesus. Every child who dies of neglect because of unjust social policies is another Jesus. Every mind wasted because society does not provide proper education is another Jesus. Every person left alone and in despair because people who should care don't give a tinker's damn is another Jesus undergoing his agony in the garden. Obviously, I could go on, but I'm sure the point has been made. We should remember, too, that the obverse of each example also is true. Every person a just war justly conducted saves from evil is another Jesus. Obversely, every person harmed or killed in an unjust war or a war unjustly conducted is another Jesus. Every child rescued from neglect and educated is another Jesus, etcetera.

Whenever I think of examples such as these, I think of our Civil War. I doubt that this war was always justly conducted; truthfully, I doubt to the point of becoming certain that this war was *not* always conducted justly. For example, I'm certain that the drafting of men for the war in the northern states was not just, because the affluent could buy their way out and the burden fell unduly upon the poor. Consider the plight at the time of indigent Irish immigrants in New York. There were riots. And, I doubt that Sherman's march to the sea in Georgia was just. But, I'm certain that liberating the slaves was just. Liberating slaves was liberating Jesus! All these matters are complicated, and ultimately only God can sort them out. In order to avoid killing Jesus rather than liberating him, we always should be extremely careful that, especially when using deadly force, we're doing not only the right thing, but the *only* right thing we can do.

I grow weary of asserting that mercy does not tolerate evil. Nevertheless, I assert this truth again. Merciful love forgives evildoers, it does not tolerate the evil they do. Tolerating evil can be a way of enabling evil. Forgiveness helps the evildoer refrain from doing evil again. Sometimes more than forgiveness is needed to halt the evil. If, for example, the evil was murder, conditions may warrant locking up the murderer for the rest of his or her natural life. Nevertheless, we are called to love that murderer and to forgive him or her. Working out what this means may be very difficult.

Of course, not everything we call toleration is bad. For example, trying to restrain or punish every evil in this life would become the grossest of evils. Islamic law details a number of activities Islam regards as evil and punishes these acts vigorously. Many of these laws and the punishments they impose are gross evils. For example, Islam considers leaving Islam to become a Christian is very bad and intolerable, so the law imposes the death penalty. From this, we may learn that not all forms of toleration are bad. But, we don't have to turn to Islamic law to prove this point.

I remember a play I saw on Broadway in the 1990s by Stephen Sondheim entitled "Getting Away with Murder." I remember the play vividly. I also remember that, despite the famous author, the play flopped. I attributed this to the play's advanced moral knowledge. The play was about a therapist who ran a group. Each member of the group had been chosen for therapy because he or she represented one of the seven deadly sins. The play brought home a profound moral. The gravest sin was not one of the seven deadly sins represented by each of the men and woman in therapy. The gravest sin was that of the therapist. His was the sin of control. Controlling includes sins when it expresses a disregard of, even hatred for, the legitimate autonomy of other persons. A control freak in the sinful sense of the term seeks to suppress the legitimate freedom of others. Clever control freaks disguise what they are doing. No good therapist is a control freak.

As I look back over my life, I see the many human beings whom I have known severely damaged by control freaks. As a priest/teacher I've seen the damage most frequently in children and/or spouses of control freaks. I've even seen it in wounded pets. But, I can't imagine passing a law prohibiting most of the sins committed by control freaks. Attempts to do so would produce evils worse than the evils control freaks produce. In fact, if one wishes to think about this subject, I would suggest that a number of laws designed not to enforce justice, but only to promote social control, function as harmfully as individual control freaks. Another such law designed to punish control freaks would be a disaster. So would a number of possible pieces of legislation designed to suppress other common sins. Toleration can be less evil than what is tolerated, but this fact does not mean control freaks need not repent and seek forgiveness.

The "piety" I've tried to describe in which the believer focuses his/her attention almost exclusive on the suffering of Jesus two thousand years ago rather than on the sufferings of those with whom Jesus has identified himself today can falsify faith more than formal heresy. I've heard horrific stories of such falsified faith—e.g., Catholic guards at Auschwitz taking time off to go to Mass and receive Holy Communion while the contemporary Jesus was suffering and dying at their hands in the camp they guarded. And, my favorite example from our history, slave owners piously going to church. This is one reason I'm uncomfortable with the hymn, "Amazing Grace." The author had been a slave trader.

Our Lord's baptism at the hands of John the Baptist began his public life and stated unequivocally for those who understood what he was doing that he identified himself with all who suffer in any way from the sin of the world, and that even Jesus "repented" in the specific sense that, although he had no sins to repent nor any sin in him, he renounced all solutions to our problem of evil—i.e., the sin of the world—that were not in harmony with merciful love. The next time in his life that Jesus would submit to this kind of baptism of repentance would occur during what we like to call his "Agony in the Garden." Then, at the beginning of his Passion leading to his Death on the Cross, he would once again submit to his Father's choice of merciful love as our way to redemption from evil (cf. Matt 26:36–46; Mark 14:32–42; Luke 22:39–46; John 18:1).

We are called to love faithfully as God loves us. Faithful love, as anyone knows who's tried so to love, is essentially merciful. Without mercy no one can be faithful. We are pledged to do so "by the cleansing water of rebirth and renewal in the Holy Spirit," which was our baptism (Titus 3:5). As we pass from this solemnity commemorating our Lord's baptism, we are approaching the season during which we all should renew and deepen our own baptismal vows and invite others to join us through "the cleansing water of rebirth"!

Chapter 7

Annunciation of the Lord
God's Purpose Announced
(March 26, 2006)

Scripture Readings

Isa 7:10–14, 8:10; Ps 40; Heb 10:4–10; Luke 1:26–38.

Summary

The Annunciation celebrates Mary's cooperation with God leading to the new humanity in Jesus by which we are saved. Her Immaculate Conception prepares her for God's request. Her life of service and chaste celibacy shows sex is not essential to fulfillment. Mary's chaste celibacy offered to God to "promote the growth of the new humanity offered us in Jesus," is "indissolubly linked to the Incarnation." That is, her lifelong virginity means the new humanity of Jesus would not be inherit through intercourse. Similarly, Jesus's chaste celibacy signals his new humanity shared through baptism (not biological inheritance) incorporating us into the divine life of Christ. Opposition to chaste celibacy, as seen in a popular novel of the time, obscures how we are saved by incorporation into this life of Christ. Mary's yes to God and virginity was her cross. She and her son demonstrate that true fulfillment requires accepting the cross.

Homily

[THE ANNUNCIATION OF THE Lord is not the Sunday Mass.][1] The tidal wave of anti-Catholicism unleashed by *The Da Vinci Code* seeks to wipe from our consciousness the meaning of the event we celebrate this day.[2] This anti-Catholicism wishes to deny that God's way of saving us from evil consisted in creating a new humanity in the person of Jesus. With the cooperation of our Lady, the Blessed Virgin Mary, God created this new humanity, and joined it to the old humanity that descended from the first parents of the human race. We celebrate her cooperation today, which she eloquently expressed in response to God's messenger: "You see before you the Lord's servant, let it happen to me as you have said" (Luke 1:38). [Mary's name transliterated from Hebrew/Aramaic is Miriam.]

The new humanity is *not* handed on from one person to another, from one generation to another, by sex. One becomes a member of the new humanity, not by inheriting the humanity from parents, as one inherits the old humanity, since the new humanity, which overcomes evil and saves us from death, comes to us without sex. The new humanity changes our attitude towards sex as an essential constituent in human fulfillment. This change in evaluating sex is reflected, first, in our Lady's acceptance of lifelong virginity—a great sacrifice of the blessings of married love. This change, which sees chaste celibacy for some as a way to human fulfillment, does *not* denigrate virtuous sex. Instead, it frees such sex from the curse of seeming compulsory.

Mary's free response to God's request immediately issued in the Incarnation. She accepted all it would mean to be the mother of the new humanity, which arrives in the person of her son, Jesus. He, then, would share his humanity, the new humanity, not by sex, but by faith expressed in the Sacrament of Baptism. Immediately upon Mary's acceptance of God's request, God's Word began to develop in her womb as a human baby. Nine months from this day on which we celebrate the start of the Incarnation, we celebrate the birth of the Incarnate One, our Lord and Savior Jesus the Christ. [Incarnate means in flesh. Jesus is God's Word as human, which means in human flesh.]

Mary was a member of the old humanity, as we all are from the moment of our conception. Old humanity includes all who descend from the first parents of the human race. Although a daughter of the old humanity, Mary was and is special in that when her parents conceived her through the

---

1. This homily originally combined with a separate one for the Fourth Sunday of Lent, here omitted.

2. Brown, *Da Vinci Code*.

wholesome sexual intercourse of a loving married couple, she was especially graced in that God uniquely intervened in her conception: God's intervention meant that she did not inherit from her parents the effects of the sin at the origin of the human race, as we do. She was immaculately conceived. "Immaculately conceived" does not mean that her parents' joy in their sexual love was any way diminished. It means only that the child they conceived did not inherit from them what sin had done to human nature. Therefore, we should bear in mind that her "Immaculate Conception" was the result of healthy sex. God gave her this special gift in order to prepare her for what God intended to ask of her. The fact that she was so graced did not make her response to God any less free. We human beings never needed sin in order to be free. Who knows? Others might have been thus graced who, when the crunch came, turned God down. If there were any such women, they then lost the grace. Mary accepted, as we heard in today's gospel.

Because of the way the new humanity would be propagated, God asked a great sacrifice of this woman. God asked her to remain a virgin for life. The potboiler, best-selling novel, soon to be released as a movie, wishes to destroy all thought of the reasons God asked this sacrifice of Mary, because God's request implies that sexual activity is not essential for human fulfillment. Although less directly, God's reasons also imply that sexual sin, or at least the strong temptation to such sin, is certainly not what makes someone truly human. Our culture has brainwashed us all with the false conviction that at least virtuous sexual activity is essential to healthy living and human fulfillment. In some ways, our culture insists even that some sinful sexual activity is an essential mark of true humanity. Therefore, the culture leads us to conclude that the complete absence of any sinful sexual activity or very strong temptation would mean someone was less than truly human. Not one of us has escaped some influence from the culture in this regard.

Our sex-besotted culture nearly swamped the Catholic Church in my generation. The vast defection of priests following the Second Vatican Council is but one sign. Seemingly endless misinterpretations of the Council in part came from this "sexual revolution." A claim made even by the best-selling psychiatrist of the generation, M. Scott Peck, MD, to the effect that some sexual activity not related to faithful love could be therapeutic corrupted the counsel even of priests committed to celibacy. These ways in which our culture sought to change attitudes towards sex lie behind the dimwitted plot of *The Da Vinci Code*.

In sharp contrast to this culture, the Church from her beginning rightly concluded from God's reasoning that human beings, if God so called them, could be fulfilled human beings living chaste celibate lives. (Some temptation follows from the sin at the origin of the human race and as temptation does not violate chastity.) The possibility of chaste celibacy is a blessing for all human beings—for those who have always lived chaste celibacy; for those who have sinned sexually, even a great deal, but have repented; for those who've lived virtuous sexually active lives, such as honorably married men and women; and others not included on this list. For example, the possibility of authentic human fulfillment through chaste celibate living frees married men and women from viewing their lives and sexual love as something "compulsory." Instead, their sexual love potentially becomes a free expression of a larger, encompassing, responsible and faithful human love and love of God. Meanwhile, the chaste celibate, if celibate for the right reasons, sublimates his/her sexual energies offers the energy to God, as did Mary, so as to promote the growth of the new humanity offered each of us in Jesus. The chaste celibate, thereby, becomes a fulfilled human being.

And, very especially, those whose sexual activity has failed to fulfill them, for no matter what reason, can learn from what God offered our Lady when God asked her to remain a virgin that human fulfillment remains within their reach, too. This is true even if the sexual activity failed to fulfill because it was sinful. God in his merciful love offers them fulfillment. Human fulfillment does not depend on their sexual activity, whether successful, failed, or even sinful! The culture that has spawned such "offal" as *The Da Vinci Code* hates even the thought of what God has offered through the virginity of the Blessed Virgin Mary and the chaste celibacy of her son.[3]

The reason for what God asked from Mary should be obvious to all Catholics. Since sex would not be the instrument whereby the new humanity conceived in her womb would be passed on from one generation to the next. Instead, the Sacrament of Baptism ratified in living faith would incorporate someone into the new humanity, not descent via sexual intercourse from the person who was and is the first new human. Jesus had no children because he did not share his new humanity by sexually begetting offspring; instead, he acquired sisters and brothers through the sacrament and living faith. His sisters and brothers share his life, which is eternal in glory. Others who reject incorporation into his being do not share eternal glory.

Understanding these truths exceeds our powers in this life; therefore, believing them and holding to them is part of what we call faith. Because these truths exceed our capacity for understanding fully, we must express them in picture language and story, of which Saint Luke's gospel account is an example. Please do not permit picturing truth to put you off appreciating truth.

---

3. Thus, regardless of the example of the novel now being dated, the point is about the anti-Catholic views of the culture.

The core blasphemy of *The Da Vinci Code* consists in denying the gift of chaste celibacy, which is indissolubly linked to the Incarnation. The link is indissoluble not because one truth implies the other in strict logic, but because the truth of the Incarnation makes appropriate the truth of chaste celibacy, which the Church has understood from the moment Jesus founded her. Two alternative developments are related to affirming or denying the truth of the linkage between chaste celibacy and the Incarnation.

When, as *The Da Vinci Code* does, the link is denied by denying that Jesus lived a life of chaste celibacy, the truth that we are saved from evil by incorporation into the incarnate person, Jesus, fades and vanishes. Although not directly assaulted in the novel, the idea that God's law requires us to subordinate sexual activity to faithful love fades.

The alternative development, which results from authentic faith, leads to a profound appreciation that we each can become a true friend of Jesus the Christ and find life, truth, and love in our relationship with him. In our relationship, we find we've overcome evil in our lives, even to the point of accepting death with "the sure and certain hope of the resurrection," rather than with merely wishful thinking or despair.[4] We find we can live faithful lives and love mercifully. In this, we find joy. I find it hard to believe that people can throw this aside by taking a trashy novel as if it were the truth and feel smug thinking that Jesus wanted sex as much as they do.

The fictional Mary Magdalene is the antithesis of the Blessed Virgin Mary, and intended to supplant our Lady in the hearts and minds of those who even think about Christianity. She is imagined as the "sexual" woman, and therefore supposed to be the real hero and true embodiment of female fulfillment. A distorted devotion to the real Blessed Virgin Mary did have the effect of downplaying the dignity of married women and even led some to think women should not have sexual feelings. This distortion was always false and known to be false. The distortion perversely denies our Lady's great sacrifice. Her virginity was her Cross. And, with her son, she reveals that human fulfillment comes through the Cross, not by running from it. All this is shoveled aside by the trashy anti-Catholicism of *The Da Vinci Code*.

The Gnostics, who were simply an ancient version of today's Scientology, concocted the phony myths about Mary Magdalene. In truth, Saint Mary of Magdala (i.e., Mary Magdalene) was not the woman who wept at the feet of Jesus and washed his feet with her hair, as reported in chapter 7 of the Gospel according to Saint Luke. Instead, she was a follower of Jesus who came from a town close to Capernaum where Jesus was headquartered during his teaching life. She stood at the foot of his Cross and was the first

---

4. Words from a frequently used prayer of committal at a cemetery.

witness to his Resurrection. A great saint! The other woman may have become a saint, too, but we don't know her name.

Sadly, the Gnostics's stories about Mary Magdalene seem to have slightly corrupted the thinking of a prominent early theologian, Theodore of Mopsuestia (died AD 428). His work was posthumously condemned at the fifth ecumenical council, which was the Second Council of Constantinople held in AD 553. It sickens me that all this has been revived.

The Gnostic rejection of chaste celibacy in favor of alleging that icons of our faith engaged in sexual activity distorts various liberation movements. The most obvious distortion occurs within a branch of feminism. For example, the trial in London over allegations of plagiarism brought against the author of *The Da Vinci Code* seems to have revealed that the author's feminist wife bears substantial responsibility for the book. I surmise that she thought she was promoting women's liberation. Gnosticism also muddies the waters of other efforts to promote human dignity and liberation. To draw out these tendrils would take much longer than reasonable limits placed on this homily.[5] Suffice it to say that Gnostic mythology with its nasty attacks on faith undermines authentic human freedom wherever it prevails.

Our response should be to see in our Lady's response to God's messenger the single most important step in human liberation taken by anyone who was not also God. Her acceptance of God's will is the turning point in human history. Not infrequently, we all should say to God what Mary said to God's messenger: "You see before you the Lord's servant, let it happen to me as you have said" (Luke 1:38).

---

5. Fr. Roach explains the basic tenets of Gnosticism in "On Vanity, Humility, and Contemporary Gnosticism" in this volume.

Chapter 8

Ash Wednesday

"Consumer Catholics" and Lent (February 21, 2007)

Scripture Readings

Joel 2:12–18; Ps 51; 2 Cor 5:20–6:2; Matt 6:1–6, 16–18.

Summary

The title encapsulates the homily. Fr. Roach pointedly criticizes professed Catholics with a consumerist approach to the faith. The mindset exemplifies the spiritual hypocrisy that Jesus condemns. Fr. Roach notes, "The real hypocrisy Jesus attacked consists in falsifying what God has revealed." But importantly all of us are compromised, as Fr. Roach explains "we all need to repent of some sinfulness." The *Momento Mori* of the ashes prompts conversion to God's will. Fr. Roach reserves some of his starkest assessment for types of behavior among Catholics, here devoting an entire homily to it.

Homily

AMONG US, THERE ARE Catholics who, probably because they know no better, think of religion as a "service." They think that priests are like doctors and hair stylists, plumbers and computer technicians, etcetera, all of whom provide a service that, if we choose, we purchase. If one does not like one service provider, one chooses a different provider. The consumer who's choosing the service is in command. There are Catholics, sadly, who treat the Church as an institution providing a service. They are consumers choosing to purchase the service offered, or not. If they don't like the service at one church they go elsewhere. The "consumer Catholic" looks on the parish as one may regard a restaurant or a movie theater. If one doesn't like the fare at one restaurant or movie theater, one goes elsewhere. A "consumer Catholic" looks on the Church as a whole or the local parish in particular in this way. Yet, "consuming" Catholicism in these or any other way is as opposed to faith as overt rejection or atheism.

All analogies limp! Therefore, I should point out that the analogy I've drawn between consuming the services of a doctor and those of a priest limps in a couple of ways. In the first way, it is fine to choose one priest as, for example, one's confessor over another priest, just as it is fine to go from one confessor to another when one feels ill-advised in the confessional. This parish brings a number of priests to hear confessions twice a year in order that parishioners may have a choice of priests. Choosing a confessor is like preferring one doctor to another. It's not a bad thing. But, "priest choosing" that justifies failures to worship with the community as the faith requires is the death of faith.

Thus, the choice that turns one into a "consumer Catholic" occurs when a person does not fulfill one's Sunday obligation because one doesn't like the priest assigned to lead the community's celebration. This is equivalent to refusing all medical care because one does not like a doctor assigned to one's hospital. Medical consumers who reject all care because they dislike a doctor may simply die. "Consumer Catholics" who fail in their obligations as Catholics because they dislike something about a priest or a parish may suffer something much worse than merely dying.

A "consumer Catholic" is one who treats the faith and one's parish as a service provider whose services are consumed or rejected as one feels inclined. In larger metropolitan areas where many parishes are clustered, if the consumer does not like one parish, the consumer goes to another, or does not go at all. This is permitted, but such a consumer lacks a sense of bonding with and responsibility for the community where one is domiciled. This lack can be harmful enough to constitute sin.

Any number of things may provoke the "consumer Catholic." She might not have liked the homily, he might have thought the priest slighted him; but the most serious kind of "consumer Catholic" is one who thinks one is entitled to cherry pick beliefs that make up the faith—pick this belief, discard that one. Cherry picking Catholics often insist that an acceptable priest emphasize only the beliefs the cherry picker likes. This kind of "consuming Catholic" is like a paying consumer who thinks he or she should be able to edit the DVD or the book one has purchased. A "consumer Catholic" who "cherry picks" the Catholic system of belief and practices to fit his/her taste has thereby lost saving faith. I repeat that such a "consuming Catholic" deeply resents any priest who does not endorse the consumer's edited version of the faith.

There are still more varieties of "consuming Catholics." For example, sometimes the consumer does not like others in the parish—everything from too many old people to too many noisy and disruptive children to not enough of the "right" folk. In all cases, nevertheless, being a "consuming Catholic" is a bad thing.

Sometimes, a "consumer Catholic" claims that the Church sold him or her a bad bill of goods. This should be looked into. There are a number of possibilities. The "bill of goods" the consumer rejects may not be bad; instead the rejected bill of goods may be a list of what is true and good. Very likely, when first presented with these particular Catholic goods, the recipient badly misunderstood; for which misunderstanding the consumer holds the representative of the Church responsible rather than oneself. Sometimes a person ran into a poor or even bad representative of the Church, in which case the person should be adult enough to check in with other representatives. A "consumer Catholic" who refuses this option is like someone who has run into a bad sales clerk, and therefore never returns to what actually is a good store.

The variety of ways or issues whereby a Catholic reveals that he or she is really a "consumer Catholic" is legion. We couldn't possibly enumerate them all. Nevertheless, before leaving the topic, we should consider three categories that may not be obviously a form of consumerism.

The first consists of those who come to Mass to "get something out of it." Obviously, this is not a bad thing in itself, but should always be secondary. The first and more important reason to come to Mass is to give something—thanks to God and support to one's fellow Catholics through solidarity in worship. When this more important reason is supplanted by someone seeking merely to "get something out of it," then everything goes terribly wrong. The faith of those who do not understand their obligation to support others in worship weakens and fails.

The second reveals itself when a person comes to Mass only if one has an assigned task. This is a person who comes only if in the choir, or assigned to read, or usher, or whatever. Otherwise, this person would skip Mass. As with the first hidden variety of "consumer Catholicism," such a consumer forgets that the most important task during the Mass is to praise and thank

God; instead, such a consumer thinks that lectoring (i.e., reading), for example, is more important than thanking and praising God. It gets worse if lectoring, or whatever, is preferred because it is both visible and audible and therefore must be noticed, whereas one's praise and thanksgiving might not be noticed. We should feel sorry for such a "consumer Catholic." Our parish is mercifully spared most instances of this consumerism. We have loyal and generous volunteers who assist our worship in visible ways. I hope we will have even more.

The third variety of "consumer Catholic" is subtle and widespread. This consumer comes really only to receive Holy Communion. He or she forgets that during the Mass we are to renew our repentance, join in common prayer, hear the Word of God and learn from it, adore our Savior as we remember his passion, death and resurrection, and only then, if otherwise prepared, receive him in Holy Communion. Even that is not the conclusion. We are to engage in private prayer and again join in common prayer before a final blessing. One sees this "Holy Communion only" kind of "consumer Catholic" dashing to the parking lot before the Mass has concluded.

This "Communion-only" version of a "consumer Catholicism" is really bad news. It constitutes in practice a rejection of the Holy Sacrifice of the Mass, which is the way we in the rite of the Church based in Latin refer to the Eucharistic Sacrifice that our Lord instituted. I have known of this version of "consumer Catholicism" giving scandal to persons contemplating joining the Catholic Church, scandal of such a degree the prospective Catholic turned away.

"Lent" is a shortened version of the Middle English word, lenten, meaning spring. Long before this English term was used, the Church practiced observing a period of forty days in spring to prepare for Easter. In fact, so old is this practice that it is mentioned (and taken for granted) in the fifth canon of the very first ecumenical council of the Catholic Church known as the Council of Nicaea held in AD 325. The founders of Protestantism tried to get rid of Lent because it is a penitential season. Penance is a practice in which they did not and their followers still do not believe.

We may think of penance as the exterior expression of repentance taking place in our hearts. The official catechism [*Catechism of the Catholic Church*] describes "interior repentance" as follows: "Interior repentance is a radical reorientation of our whole life, a conversion to God with all our heart, an end of sin, a turning away from evil, with repugnance toward the evil actions we have committed."[1] Then the catechism notes two passages in the sacred Scriptures that have given rise to a traditional three-fold list of

---

1. USCCB, *Catechism*, #1431

penances: fasting, prayer, and almsgiving.² The first of these two citations is from the Book of Tobit (12:8): "Prayer with fasting and alms with uprightness are better than riches with iniquity." The second citation is today's gospel (Matt 6:1–6, 16–18) with verses 7 through 15 omitted. The liturgists omitted these verses from the proclaimed gospel because they did not want the homilist to launch into an exposition of the Our Father, which is given in these verses. The omission, unfortunately, can give the wrong impression—namely, lead one to forget that prayer is the essential penance! Let us bear this in mind when reflecting on this gospel. The liturgists wanted the homilist to do what I hope I'm doing: namely, exhorting all to do penance.

We have tried to flesh out a description of a "consumer Catholic" in the hope that if anyone finds oneself fitting the description, Lent, then, will be a special time for the "interior repentance" required to overcome consumerism. Meanwhile, if a form of consumerism does not apply to anyone of us, we nonetheless all need to repent of some sinfulness and any number of actual sins. And, if this is not enough, we all should "do penance" as intercessory prayer for our brothers and sisters who may need to "do penance," too, but are falling behind. We're in this together, as our Lord makes abundantly clear.

In today's gospel, we learn what our Lord had to say about "doing penance." Remember, his starting message was "Repent, and believe the gospel (good news)." Much of what our Lord had to say nearly two thousand years ago goes over our head today because of changed circumstances. This gospel is a perfect instance of the easily misunderstood. Take the first admonition for an example. I'll comment on two translations: "Beware of practicing your piety before others in order to be seen by them; for then you have no reward from your Father in heaven" (Matt 6:1 NRSV-CE). I would suggest that it is practically impossible in our day to "practice piety" in such a way that the pious person will be seen favorably. They might be seen, but it's most likely they'll be thought foolish.

In my judgment, the New Jerusalem Bible provides a better translation: "Be careful not to parade your uprightness in public to attract attention; otherwise you will lose all reward from your Father in heaven" (Matt 6:1). I think there are a large number of people who parade their "uprightness" in order to win approval from others. Unless I'm blind, there are a number of prominent politicians, some in high office, who do this as a matter of course. After all, if God is on one's side and one consults God, one is seen as "upright." I think the NJB translation leads us away from misunderstanding our Lord's admonition.

---

2. USCCB, Catechism, #1434 and see there note 31.

Note that in this part of his sermon, our Lord stressed the word used for the sin he most frequently railed against—hypocrisy. The NJB points out that in the gospels our Lord used this epithet principally to label some Pharisees whom he judged practiced false religion. It's petty hypocrisy to want people to think better of one than one actually is. We all do this; it's not serious. The real hypocrisy Jesus attacked consists in falsifying what God has revealed. A committed "consumer Catholic" easily becomes such a hypocrite. Jesus thought that some of his fellow Jews, especially certain Pharisees, were "consumer Jews," interpreting law and cherry picking teachings so as to falsify God's promises and blind themselves to the truth that Jesus is in person, namely, our Lord who is the Christ (Messiah). Eventually, they prompted the Roman Empire to execute Jesus, brutally. This empire was happy to crucify any Jew thought a "messiah."

Our Lord's admonition about praying in private also leads to misunderstanding in our day. (Matt 6:5–6; the NJB italicizes four words because they echo three passages in the Old Testament, which are worth looking at: 2 Kgs 4:33; Isa 26:20; Dan 6:11.) Our Lord was not attacking the public prayer that, for instance, we are engaged in during this Mass.

We have no experience of the kind of praying in public our Lord referred to. The closest most of us have come to this kind of praying would be what we may see on TV programs showing the manner in which some still practice their religion in the Middle East. We see persons praying out loud and bobbing up and down. Our Lord's point should be obvious: he attacked anyone who'd make private prayer into a public show to gain favorable attention.

The last admonition in today's gospel refers to fasting, and troubles people who receive ashes on this day (Matt 6:17–18). First, the public display of fasting known in our Lord's day is unknown in ours. Our Lord rejected these practices for the reasons given. Secondly, the ashes on our foreheads remind us that we will die and our bodies return to the "dust" from which they originally came (cf. Gen 2:7.). They're not a public declaration that we are fasting. People should see the black ashen cross on the forehead as a reminder that we all die. The Latin is *Memento Mori*. You need not run home and wash.

Our first reading was Joel 2:12–18. This book was written about 400 BC. The snippet that provides our first reading is, very appropriately, from a penitential liturgy. The words are clear even today.

We responded to this great reading with verses from Psalm 51. In this psalm, we heard the foreshadowing in the Old Testament of the truth we've learned through the Church from Jesus and would eventually, at least in the West, name the doctrine of original sin. This significant verse is the following: "... remember, I was born guilty, / a sinner from the moment of conception" (Ps 51:5 NJB). "Indeed, I was born guilty, / a sinner when my mother conceived me" (Ps 51:5 NRSV-CE). Baptism is more than an excuse for a party!

The second reading (2 Cor 5:20–6:2) calls us "to be reconciled with God." Confession is formerly titled the Sacrament of Penance and Reconciliation. Saint Paul, using intense rhetoric, said, "For our sake he (God the Father) made the sinless one (Jesus the Christ) a victim for sin, so that in him we might become the uprightness of God" (2 Cor 5:21 NJB). Despite the fact that it is mystical language, it is true; and I think it is both clear and powerful. As Jesus the Christ, God became one with us (i.e., a fellow human just like you and me). In doing so, he suffered the consequences of our sins. He suffered the consequences of human sinfulness more grievously than most of us ever will. He suffered for us so that we may through union with him become what he is—namely, God's uprightness (justice) in person. God's justice is one with God's mercy, and together they resulted in overcoming the death Jesus died on the Cross as a consequence of human sinfulness. God created the resurrection. If we do not remain united with him during this life, we'll not share the resurrection with him! I pray Lent will draw us all more closely into the life that is Jesus both on the Cross and in eternity. "Consumer Catholics" don't get this.

Chapter 9

Palm Sunday of Our Lord's Passion
Redemptive Suffering (April 9, 2006)

Scripture Readings

Mark 11:1–10 (for Palm Procession); Isa 50:4–7; Ps 22; Phil 2:6–11; Mark 14:1–15:47.

Summary

Our response to Jesus's Passion and Death indicates our chosen relation to him. Ancient prophecy anticipates Christ's kingship and divinity. Fr. Roach explains Jesus intoning Psalm 22 as central to understanding the significance of the Passion. In Jesus's death, we are called to see and repent our implication in harming others. The narrative bids deep reflection on the varied responses of those present—Jesus, Peter, John, Judas Iscariot, Pilate, the crowd, and importantly the women and centurion there with Jesus. A postscript on media treatment of the Gnostic Gospel of Judas demonstrates the frequent efforts of individuals in the academy and media to discredit Catholic faith. Fr. Roach poignantly observes in conclusion how the Gnostics avoided the Roman persecutions in which the early Christians became martyrs.

Homily

*T*HE GOSPEL FOR OUR procession reminds us that Jesus fulfilled an important prophecy by risking a triumphal entry into Jerusalem not long before he would be executed [in Zech 9:9–10].[1] Zechariah predicted that the anticipated messianic king would enter his city, Jerusalem, riding on a donkey (i.e., an ass) because nearly a millennium earlier King David, before dying, had his son, Solomon, anointed king at Gihon Spring, which was just outside the Jerusalem wall (cf. 1 Kgs 1:32–37). For this anointing, David had his son ride a mule (Zechariah probably thought the animal had to have been a donkey because later Jewish law did not accept mixed species; cf. Lev 19:19). So Jesus, who is Christ the King, rode an ass. We have a king who is God–with–us, God's very Word. Our King, Jesus the Christ, fulfills all the promises God made through prophets to David and his successors that the Davidic line would last forever.

All four gospels report our Lord's entry into Jerusalem shortly before he was executed. And all four report that the crowd shouted verses from the Psalm 118. To understand these verses, we need to know that "Hosanna" means "Save us!"

The Liturgy of the Word within the Mass of the Passion

The first reading consists of four verses from the third song of the Servant of the Lord. There are four songs, and together they form the most exact prediction of our Lord's mission. I recommend prayerfully reading them as a way into Holy Week's deeper meaning (See Isa 42:1–9; 49:1–6; 50:4–11; 52:13–53:12).

The Psalm 22 provides our response. I don't think it possible to appreciate Holy Week, specifically Good Friday, without prayerfully reading this psalm. The psalmist begins in despair and concludes in triumph in the assembly. We hear only that Jesus intoned the opening words of the despairing psalmist. We, then, are expected to remember how the psalm ends. Please read and pray!

The second reading is a hymn sung in the Church shortly after Jesus had founded us that Saint Paul copied into his Letter to the Philippians (2:6–11). This hymn, too, should be prayed in private as well as heard in the assembly. When praying this hymn, please pay special attention to this verse: "Make you own the mind of Christ Jesus: (the hymn begins) Who,

---

1. The original homily and preamble are considerably shortened here for brevity.

being in the form of God, / did not count equality with God / something to be grasped" (Phil 2:5–6).

Saint Paul wrote the Philippians not long after our Lord's resurrection. The Church was in her infancy, and the hymn he incorporated into his letter is older than his writing. Please note the clear claim in this first verse of the hymn that Jesus is divine. The mad tidal wave of anti-Catholicism swirling around us requires ignorance to be effective. Many media presentations of anti-Catholicism, including the infamous book [*The Da Vinci Code*] by Dan Brown, justify their falsehoods with a claim that the Emperor Constantine imposed "divinity" on Jesus early in the fourth century. It takes supine ignorance for a person to be taken in by this phony claim. The first verse of this ancient hymn reveals that the Church from her first days believed in our Lord's divinity.

The gospel proclaimed was the Passion of our Lord Jesus the Christ according to Saint Mark (14:1–15:47). Rather than attempt a full-fledged homily on the Passion, I will list a number of clarifying points in the hope that they will assist us in appreciating Saint Mark's brilliant account of this saving event.

To appreciate the Passion, we need first to understand that what one believes can be more important than what one does. Take as a rule of thumb, please, the adage that "As one believes, so one behaves." But, add to this adage that many of us never have the chance to carry out what we believe. Instead, we create an atmosphere in which others do the dirty deeds. Sometimes, we enable others to do what is wrong simply by voting for them. God will judge many of us principally by what we have believed and only then by what we've done or failed to do. What we believe about the Passion of Jesus the Christ will be the test of how God judges us.

The centurion provides the key to right belief about our Lord's Passion, and Saint Mark reported this key exactly: "The centurion, who was standing in front of him (Jesus on the Cross), had seen how he died, and he said, 'In truth this man was the Son of God'" (Mark 15:39). To believe rightly, a person must see God at work in the suffering and death of Jesus. Then, we must see God at work in all misery, especially in the suffering and dying of the innocent. And, we must respond to God so present by doing what God asks of us in these cases.

God's work becomes quite specific, but it remains obscure and hidden from those who do not appreciate what led up to the crucifixion or, as the centurion, was there to see what lay behind the words that Saint Mark wrote. For those of us who were not in the centurion's privileged position to realize from the lived experience what God was doing, the dying Jesus left behind a clue from the sacred Scriptures. Just before dying, he intoned

[from] Psalm 22: "And at the ninth hour Jesus cried out in a loud voice, '*Eloi, eloi, lama sabachthani?*' which means '*My God, my God, why have you forsaken me?*'" (Mark 15:34). The centurion could see that this was not a cry of despair because he was present to Jesus. We see the truth of what was happening because of what Jesus said before dying, but we know this only if we know the psalm as he did. [The translation in the NJB comes from an accurate restoration of the earliest Hebrew version.]

I recommend again that we all prayerfully read Psalm 22. It will help us if we remember that verse 30 in the Greek, which is the version our Lord's Church used from our founding, contains the proclamation, "My soul shall live forever." With or without this explicitness, the psalm proclaims the truth that God's merciful love will triumph over the evils of this world, which otherwise are reasons to despair. Our Lord invoked this psalm to remind us of this truth, as he died a miserable death on the Cross. The psalm also reminds us that God the Father did hear Jesus when he cried out before dying: "For he (God) did not despise or abhor / the affliction of the afflicted; / he did not hide his face from me, / but heard when I cried out to him" (Ps 22:24 [NRSV-CE]).

What the centurion saw when Jesus died we are called to see in all caught in misery, especially the innocent dying because of the sins of others. Jesus died; that's over! Jesus, too, rose from the dead; that's accomplished! Our remembering must not stop at past events. The past events are the keys to rightly interpreting present events. The centurion did not know what "Son of God" really meant. With this expression, he meant only that God was with Jesus; he simply did not know that Jesus actually is God–with–us, God in human form. Therefore, we must, as the centurion did, see God with every innocent human being killed, or even just dying, because of the sins of others. Jesus revealed to the Gentile centurion by the way he died that God was with him. We are expected to see God with everyone who dies similarly. (We all die because human beings have sinned.) Jesus embodies God's judgment on all misery.

Perhaps a contrast will help us understand what the centurion understood and expressed when he said that Jesus "was Son of God." A man dying as Jesus died could have cursed those who were executing him. He could have damned them. Instead, Jesus intoned the 22nd Psalm.

Early in the account of our Lord's Passion and Death, we heard about Judas Iscariot (Mark 14:10–11). Then, at the meal during which Jesus instituted the Eucharistic Sacrifice (i.e., the Mass), we heard Jesus say: "Yes, the Son of man is going to his fate, as the scriptures say he will, but alas for that man by whom the Son of man is betrayed! Better for that man if he had never been born!" (Mark 14:21; to grasp the meaning of "Son of man," read

Dan 7:13; Jesus referred to no one Scripture, but had in mind passages such as Wis 2:10–20.) It is not Judas alone of whom Jesus the Christ says, "Better for that man (or woman) if he (or she) had never been born!" This is said of every person who has betrayed Jesus.

Peter, in a lesser but nonetheless real way, also betrayed Jesus, as Jesus foretold (Mark 14: 26–31). Yet, Peter differs significantly from Judas. He repented and "burst into tears" (Mark 14:72). Although not recorded here, Peter after repenting with his tears did penance, which culminated in his martyrdom. Judas, on the other hand, seems to have committed suicide (cf. Acts 1:18–20; somewhat from the account in Matt 27:3–10). The account Saint Luke wrote in the Acts of the Apostles shows that people understood Judas's suicide in terms of the Book of Wisdom 4:14b–19. I strongly urge all to read this passage in Wisdom, which gives insight into the fate of the wicked of whom our Lord said, "Better for this man had he never been born!" (Mark 14:21).

Saint Mark's account of our Lord's Passion and Death includes an account of a devout woman who anointed him with a costly ointment (Mark 14:3–9). The ointment, pure nard, could have been sold for an amount that exceeded what an ordinary laborer would have been paid for three-hundred-days of hard work. In response to those who attacked her, Jesus praised what she had done, and said that she had anointed him in advance for his burial. He then said something that has been used through the centuries by people who want to ignore those who suffer unjustly from poverty: "You have the poor with you always, and you can be kind to them whenever you wish, but you will not always have me." Those who misuse what our Lord said don't know the sacred Scripture he was referring to (Read Deut 15:1–11). I'll quote only the last verse from this important passage that Jesus had in mind.) "Of course, there will never cease to be poor people in the country, and that is why I am giving you this command: Always be open handed with your brother, and with anyone in your country who is in need and poor" (Deut 15:11). Fulfilling this command does not prevent anyone from special generosity that does not immediately benefit the poor when the occasion demands. I think that the rest of Saint Mark's magnificent account does not need explanation for those who heard the gospel in faith.

Before closing, we should think of three persons reported in Saint Mark's account that we should react to in specific ways. These men are Judas Iscariot, Peter, and Jesus himself.

Have we betrayed Jesus as Judas did because we believed something contrary to our Lord's beliefs and teaching? On this Sunday, then referred to simply as Palm Sunday, in 1937 Pope Pius XI ordered all deacons, priests, and bishops in Germany to read from the pulpits of their churches his letter entitled *Mit brenneder Sorge* ("With burning Anxiety"). In this letter, the pope condemned Nazism as unchristian, unequivocally. How many Germans, nonetheless, betrayed Christ? I believe each of us should ask a similar question about political convictions in the U.S. today.

The second person is Peter. If we have betrayed Jesus, have we repented with tears and returned to bear witness to the faith—i.e., to all Jesus is and teaches? Are we prepared to die, if we must, in order to be faithful to him? Are we faithful members of the people he organized? The most common and easiest way to betray Jesus in our culture is through infidelity to his Church.

Then, there is Jesus himself. Do we see Jesus in those he loves especially because of the misery they suffer? Do we see the mystery of his merciful love working in them—both those who accept his mercy and even how he works in those who seem eventually to reject his love? Jesus loved both Judas and Peter. It was heart breaking for him to lose Judas. We must see his love striving in both cases and rejoice that Peter accepted his mercy.

After we've looked at these three men, we must look to our Lord's friend who came from a town close to his headquarters in Galilee—Saint Mary from Magdala, whom we also call Saint Mary Magdalene. If great saints can suffer while in glory, which I doubt, she is suffering because of the rubbish written about her.

For what happened at the Crucifixion, having failed in his effort to be present, Saint Mark recorded essentially what Saint Peter preached, who also had to learn from others who had been eyewitnesses. The one eyewitness report we have is found in the Gospel according to Saint John, which we will hear chanted on Good Friday. Therefore, when Saint Mark reports that Saint Mary Magdalene was with women watching from a distance, he probably reflects an eyewitness's report that the guards moved them away from the very foot of the Cross. Saint John, who was among them, did not regard the distance so great that he could not describe them as standing at the foot of the Cross.

There were some women watching from a distance. Among them were Mary of Magdala, Mary who was the mother of James the younger and Joset, and Salome. These used to follow him and look after him when he was in Galilee. And many other women were there who had come up to Jerusalem with him (Mark 15:40–41). Please note that when you compare Saint Mark's account with Saint John's that Mark's witnesses reported only the women who looked after Jesus as he traveled on foot in Galilee and taught. Saint John also reported the presence of his mother, who did not travel with him, probably because of age. Saint Mark intended his report to make clear that the women who cared for him stayed with Jesus until the end, not the men. I think the report reflects Peter's shame. And, at the top of the list of the women he named Saint Mary of Magdala. Her prominence reflects how hard she had worked to support our Lord's mission. She and the other women, as Saint Mark reported, also had followed Jesus to Jerusalem. They knew he was in danger in Jerusalem. They may even have learned what the men were too obtuse to learn—namely, that he would be executed and thereby save us. Mary Magdalene and the other women, therefore, are the first to whom Jesus appeared when he rose. We'll see about this at Easter. For now, we need to admire her as someone we'd like to emulate—someone who can remain present to the miserable because she knows God is at work.

Postscript

The latest attack on the Church and our faith in Jesus comes from the release in translation of a Gnostic gospel referred to as the Gospel of Judas. The text dates from the early fourth century (circa AD 300) and was found in Egypt. As are all Gnostic writings, this is a virulent attack on the faith that pretends to be a better version of who Jesus is and what he did and taught than what we find in the gospels recognized by his Church, which by the power of God the Holy Spirit preserves his memory. The authors of this ancient absurdity expected us to believe that Jesus asked Judas to betray him so that he could fulfill God's wishes and die a "sacrificial" death. I'm sure that anyone with even rudimentary faith realizes that for Jesus's death to be redemptive, as it is, he had to die as the result of sin—not a sin he allegedly committed by engineering a fraud, but as the result of the sins of others.

Furthermore, the understanding of sacrifice in this historical fiction denies everything authentic faith knows about redemption/sacrifice. The *New York Times* [recently] reports: "In a key passage in the new-found gospel, Jesus had talks with Judas 'three days before he celebrated the Passover.' That is when Jesus is supposed to have referred to the other disciples and said to Judas: 'But you will exceed all of them. For you will sacrifice the man that clothes me.' / By that, scholars said, Jesus seems to have meant that in helping him get rid of his physical flesh, Judas will act to liberate the true spiritual self or divine being within Jesus."[2]

The scholarly community is so militantly anti-Catholic that they miss the significance of what is said here. Gnosticism is a metaphysical dualism—flesh or body, bad; "spirit," good. Release spirit! This denies the goodness of God's creation and denies who we really are, a union of body and soul

---

2. Wilford, "Gospel of Judas," A18.

making one unique person. This historical fiction called a Gnostic gospel not only falsifies how Jesus died and why, but denies the Resurrection!

As I hear and read about this historical fiction, I hear the "scholars" vainly attempting to make out that the document is older than it is. Although dated around AD 300, which is the beginning of the fourth century (too old even to pretend to be an historical witness), the talking heads refer to the document as third century. They, then, unanimously claim it is a copy of an older document. Their sole ground for this claim is a statement made around AD 180 by Saint Irenaeus, who served as the bishop of Lyons. The single sentence from his writings quoted in the *New York Times* story is: "They (Gnostics) produce a fictitious history of this kind, which they style the Gospel of Judas." There's no evidence that he was referring to the document found in Egypt, which is hardly next door to Lyons anyway. The Gnostics manufactured countless documents (literally, we cannot count them), and our best source of information about what they were up to is found in the writings of Saint Irenaeus, who dedicated a great deal of time to refuting them as they were coming into being and writing prolifically.

We live in a time when all of the ancient attacks on the faith that the Gnostics mounted are being revived. This time around, ignorant purveyors of this rubbish imply that their lies come from written works that wicked Church authorities suppressed. No one can fall for such a con job, even if the person is ignorant enough to imagine that Church authorities are tyrants, if he or she knows what life was like for the Church surviving and growing under Roman persecution. The Gnostics weren't slaughtered in the persecution; Catholics were. And, the original forms of Gnosticism were rejected, not by some highfalutin "authority," but by the people who knew a religious fraud when they encountered one. What I find frightening today is the apparent lack of rank and file Catholics who are as wise as our forefathers and foremothers were.

Chapter 10

The Lord's Supper (Holy Thursday)
Real Presence (March 24, 2005)

Scripture Readings

Exod 12:1–8, 11–14; Ps 116; 1 Cor 11:23–26; John 13:1–15.

Summary

Christ washing the feet of the Apostles demonstrates humility as a central Christian virtue. Christ's Passion and Death see him identify with human sinfulness. Similarly, Christ humbly identifies with us and saves us through the Real Presence of the Eucharist. We should follow his example and be so for others. The consecration of bread and wine, Fr. Roach explains, "is that so we remember and gratefully adore Jesus as our God." True humility starts with our recognizing that God is present, and he notes that humility "can work through the effects of sin," so that persons can share in the divine life. A prior condition is our repentance. Fr. Roach closes discussing the reasons for the assembly and receiving Holy Communion in good conscience.

Homily

AT THIS SOLEMN LITURGY we celebrate two interrelated, inseparable events: our Lord washing the feet of the men who were his organization for the new People of God (i.e., the Church), and our Lord's promising his real presence in what he commanded them, and through them us too, to do in his memory. These two events are interrelated in that the washing of feet, a slave's task at the time, reveals the depth of our Lord's humility, while instituting the Eucharist reveals how in the humblest way possible he continues to identify himself with us in order to save us from evil. He humbles himself to serve as our food for living faith, hope, and love. In enabling us to consecrate this spiritual food—his own Body and Blood—he gave us a true memorial of his Passion, Death, Resurrection, and Ascension, as the prayers of the Mass make very clear.

The two events are tied together—interrelated—by the humility evident within both, and then Jesus made them inseparable in our memories by washing his disciples' feet and instituting the Holy Eucharist at one and the same supper. The humility of taking on the role of a slave relates to the humility of God making himself spiritual food for his human creatures. The first members of the Church were deeply aware of our Lord's humility, as we also should be aware of his humility today. Remember how Saint Paul recorded a hymn sung in the early Church in his Letter to the Philippians (2:6–11)? This hymn extolled our Lord's humility. Before Jesus went to that Cross to die, he taught us about his humility by washing feet and becoming our spiritual food.

In a recent homily, I reminded the assembly of the division in the Gospel according to Saint John between the wondrous signs our Lord performed in the open for the public (recorded in the part of his gospel scholars call the Book of Signs), and the wondrous signs our Lord worked for the Church and only for those disposed to become faithful members of the Church (recorded in the later part of his gospel called the Book of Glory). Our Lord washing the feet of the men he'd made into the hierarchy of his new People of God was his first act in what the scholars call the Book of Glory. Saint John's account serves as our gospel for this Mass. The disposition that enables a person to be a faithful Catholic is precisely the humility our Lord exhibited when he washed his disciples' feet. Jesus brought this out most clearly in his dialogue with the chairman of the hierarchy, the man he'd named Rock (Peter) whose successor we call the pope. As with many popes in history, Peter was the last to get it.

We often use the French *double entendre* (double meaning) to snigger over the hidden sexual content in some seemingly innocent remark. Saint John used double meanings throughout his report of this event [note John 13:6–11], so as to teach the faithful in the Church about the meaning of what had happened. First, Jesus required that Peter submit to what he was doing so that later he (Peter and his successors) would understand how they were to imitate him. Jesus humbled himself to the point of doing a slave's work so that his bishops would know that they are the servants of the servants of God. [It's one of the pope's titles in Latin, *servus servorum Dei*.] But, and this is the double meaning, Peter was in our position. He was not yet functioning as he later would after the resurrection. He had to learn, as do we, to submit to the ways Jesus has chosen to do things, even when we don't think they're right. Peter did not think it right to allow his teacher to wash his feet. Many who may otherwise be good Catholics don't think God's doing right when he allows the Church to stumble and yet insists that they go to Mass.

Jesus told Peter that he only needed his feet washed because he had bathed. The double meaning is the distinction between the Sacrament of Baptism (clean all over) and the penance we later need to wash off the dirt we've picked up after our baptisms. Of course, these disciples were incorporated into the Body of Christ before baptism became the entryway, so the double meaning does not apply literally to Peter or the others. John reported the metaphor for the benefit of us who have come after.

There was one who had not been incorporated into the new People of God, namely, Judas Iscariot, because Jesus could read hearts. This is the man Jesus referred to when he said, "though not all of you are," meaning that not all of the original Twelve had accepted the "bath" whereby they were incorporated into his Body or people, although Judas gave the outward signs of being part of the group. Sadly, we have people who have the outward appearance of being Catholic—baptized, confirmed, usually not here. They've negated the life the sacraments once gave them. This life can be revived through repentance and the Sacrament of Penance.

The gospel as proclaimed this evening ends with our Lord's admonition to his hierarchy and through them to us all [see John 13:12b–15]. Our Lord had first in mind our servants, the bishops. They are to be brothers who wash each other's feet, which clearly is a metaphor for the give and take, the correcting and supporting one another, that makes a good bishop. I'm confident that the Second Vatican Council intended this washing of each other's feet to increase greatly. The buzzword for challenging and supporting each other the Council used was "collegiality." Let's pray for the bishops.

What our Lord said to the original Twelve he also intended for you and me. There is simply no way to be Catholic without the sense of obligatory assembling, thereby forming community. And there is no real community whose members do not support and challenge each other. I'll take this opportunity to report that you all are a major challenge for me. We really wash each other's feet.

This washing of feet as the expression of communal humility is linked directly to the Eucharist, but we might not see the link as clearly as those who read or heard the original Greek of Saint John's gospel. In Saint John's Greek, the word for community and the word for communion, as in Holy Communion, is the same word. The idea that one can rightly, even safely, receive Holy Communion without being a faithful member of the community boggles my mind, it is so false!

And what we rightly refer to as our Lord's Real Presence in the Eucharist links these two events. Those who have bathed and are clean all over become the Body of Christ as really as the bread consecrated during the Mass. Yet, only those who join in the faithful challenging and supporting that washing feet symbolizes are nourished when they receive the Bread of Life, which objectively is Jesus who is our risen Lord. Others not only are not nourished, but may well be sinning by receiving. The metaphor of bread provides a way to explain why this is so. If a person suffers from gluten intolerance, he or she may not eat bread. A person who is not a faithful member of the assembly, yet receives Holy Communion, is like a person who is gluten intolerant yet continues to eat bread. Eating the Eucharist only makes the unfaithful spiritually sicker.

Obviously I'm using gluten intolerance, which literally is physical, to explain something spiritual. Many wonderfully faithful people who are gluten intolerant in the non-metaphorical sense are faithful Catholics participating fully in the Eucharistic Sacrifice. In other words, although they may not eat anything with wheat in it, they may participate fully in the Eucharist, which includes receiving Holy Communion. The change of ordinary bread into the Body of Christ, which is the Bread of Life, does not remove the effects of the wheat from which the bread was originally made. The people who are gluten intolerant, and some are wonderful Catholics, receive our Lord under the one species of the consecrated wine, which has become his Precious Blood. By receiving either species, one receives the risen Lord entirely. He can no longer be divided. So, those receiving under just the one species receive the risen Lord whole and entire.

Anyone may choose to receive our Lord under only one species; but, except one is excused by gluten intolerance or something equivalent, if one chooses to receive only one species, one must choose to receive our Lord in the species of bread, not the consecrated wine. Only those with a medical excuse may receive under only the one species of consecrated wine.

I feel the need to add something about words: "blessed" does not mean something as significant as "consecrated." During the Eucharistic sacrifice, bread and wine are consecrated, thereby becoming the Body and Blood of Christ. The dual consecration does not make our Lord more "present," since he is fully present in either species. The dual consecration is the way in which he is remembered in his Passion, Death, Resurrection, and Ascension. The distinction between the two species Jesus used to present himself as both body and blood reminds us that death took place. In death, body and blood are in some sense separated, but to the ancients it was even clearer. Where we speak easily of the soul, many at the time of Christ would have spoken of blood. For them blood was the principle of life, not soul. This is why the Law forbade eating blood. In summary, there is a dual consecration so that we may remember and gratefully adore Jesus as our God. This is the primary activity at Mass. Those who have prepared themselves to receive Holy Communion by doing so rightly confirm they have performed the primary activity of the Mass—grateful adoration of the living God.

Let us try to sum up what true humility is. At its core, true humility recognizes that God remains present and can work through all the effects of sin to win persons into sharing the divine life forever. To accomplish this end, God uses merciful love (forgiveness, compassion, pity; choose the synonym you like best). In order to share God's merciful love with others, we must be willing to do for others what they need, even if what we are called to do seems beneath our dignity. We often must humble ourselves to reach those caught in sin. But, this is not all there is to true humility; there is still more.

The humble person always recognizes the freedom proper to the other, even if the other person is damning him/herself by using freedom sinfully. Humble persons do not allow sinners to violate others unjustly. Criminal law should stop anyone from violating another person unjustly, and force may be used. Nevertheless, humble persons use only friendly persuasion (an old Quaker expression) to win those whose sin harms themselves without injustice to others, and humble persons strive even to use this friendly persuasion in lieu of force to stop those whose sins harm others. The humble turn to force only as the last resort.

This element of our Lord's humility presently resides in our discipline concerning Holy Communion. Except in notorious cases, we leave the decision to receive or not to receive Holy Communion up to the individual. Persons must decide for themselves if they have been faithful to the assembly, or have repented of their infidelity and received absolution, such that they may receive Holy Communion in good conscience. If they do not receive in good conscience, God help them. Our Lord's humility grants each of us the freedom even to sin publicly. I think it's the most remarkable and difficult part of our Lord's humility, which we are called to emulate; yet our Lord's humility is in evidence each time there are persons receiving Holy Communion.

Our first reading for this Mass introduces us once again to the Passover meal (Seder). We see in this meal the prophecy of what our Lord has done in instituting the Eucharist. We in the Roman rite, using a word derived from Latin, refer to our Passover meal as the Mass. Other rites usually refer to this meal as the Divine Liturgy. The universal term for our Passover is the Eucharistic Sacrifice, because it does more than fulfill the Passover meal. It also replaces all forms of animal sacrifice, including not only the Passover lamb but also all Temple worship. Jesus is our "sacrificial lamb." The bloodless sacrifice of the Mass replaces the bloody sacrifices of the ancient Temple.

We responded to the first reading with Psalm 116. This psalm is an excellent prayer for use in our personal prayer during the Easter Triduum. I love the opening stanza as translated in the New Jerusalem Bible: "I am filled with love when Yahweh listens / to the sound of my prayer, / when he bends down to hear me, / as I call" (Ps 116: 1–2).

In case anyone has forgotten, "Triduum" means three days, and Easter Triduum names the time from the evening of Holy Thursday to the dawn of Easter, when we celebrate the Easter Vigil Mass.

The second reading provides us with Saint Paul's report of our Lord instituting the Eucharist. Saint John chose not to report the words, I believe, because he feared abusers misusing them. Saint Paul had no such fear.

The reading as we heard proclaimed during the liturgy stopped short of Saint Paul's reason for discussing the Eucharist at this point in his letter. He wanted to admonish those who were sinning when they received Holy Communion. Here are his words: "Therefore anyone who eats the bread or drinks the cup of the Lord unworthily is answerable for the body and blood of the Lord" (1 Cor 11:27). If the family members or friends whom you bring to Easter Mass haven't been faithful to Sunday Mass, you may remind them of this verse.

Chapter 11

Good Friday

A Forensic Metaphor (March 21, 2008)

Scripture Readings

Isa 52:13–53:12; Ps 31; Heb 4:14–16, 5:7–9; John 18:1–19:42.

Summary

The homily uses a legal metaphor reflecting on repentance and salvation in Christ. Christ identifies with all who suffer the consequences of our sins. This implicates us in his crucifixion. We need to look where our sin harms others in this "indictment." So too, in venerating the bare wood of the cross, we are "kissing all with whom Jesus has identified himself." Fortunately, our repentance leads to receiving God's mercy and a share in resurrected life. This share in Christ comes through fidelity to his Church, made difficult by contemporary anti-Catholicism.

Homily

*T*HE *AMERICAN HERITAGE DICTIONARY of the English Language* defines "forensic" as follows: "1. Relating to, used in, or appropriate for courts of law or for public discussion or argumentation."[1] More simply, one

---

1.. *American Heritage Dictionary*, 4th ed.

may understand "forensic" to mean "legal." Using a forensic metaphor to understand our Lord's Passion and Death means likening what happened to a court case. The gospel narratives report the facts. In the metaphorical court, then, the facts as presented become an indictment of those who perpetrated the crime. For this Holy Week, beginning with the Palm Sunday of the Lord's Passion, I chose to use a forensic metaphor in expounding the proclamation of our Lord's Passion and Death. I hope the metaphor helps. God is the judge in this metaphorical court, and in reality. God's judgment is not pronounced until Easter.

To prepare us for hearing the proclamation of our Lord's Passion and Death according to Saint John (18:1–19:42), which is the high point of the Good Friday liturgy, we heard the fourth Song of the Servant from the Prophecy of Isaiah. The four Songs of the Servant are embedded in the Prophecy of Isaiah. Early on, theologians and other scholars recognized that these poems predicted with awesome accuracy the way in which Jesus the Christ (i.e., Messiah) would save us. The fourth and last song was reserved for this Good Friday liturgy. [The NJB lists the four songs as follows: Isa 42:1–4 (5–9, disputed); 49:1–6; 50:4–9 (10–11 disputed); and today's first reading, 52:13–53:12.]

We responded to the fourth Song of the Servant with verses from Psalm 31. This psalm is a great prayer to use when one is distressed. The opening stanza sets the theme: "In you, O Lord, I seek refuge; / do not let me ever be put to shame; / in your righteousness deliver me" (Ps 31:1 NRSV-CE).

Our second reading had two parts. The first used a metaphor likening our Savior to the high priest in the ancient Temple who mediated between God and human beings. We're advised to seek our Lord's mediation because he guarantees to bring us God's mercy and grace when we are in need. The words of the reading, at least in the NJB, are simply beautiful.

The second part referred us to our Lord's Agony in the Garden (cf. Matt 26:36–40, et al.). In fact, it is an account of his agony outside the gospel narratives. The account should remind us that we too are called to obey the living God. The foundation of this saving obedience lies in our fidelity to worship according to Church law based on the third commandment— Remember to keep holy the Lord's Day. In our Holy Thursday homily, we repeated the passage in the catechism that makes our obligation clear and mentions that it is sanctioned. I hope all read this passage. As Jesus was "perfected" by obeying his Father, there is no salvation for any of us without "the obedience of faith." (This phrase comes from Saint Paul, e.g., Rom 1:5 and 16:26, and has been developed and explained repeatedly in previous homilies.)

Reference to Melchizedek is an historical metaphor. The brief mention that introduces Melchizedek occurs in Genesis 14:18–20. No ancestry was given, so he came to be thought of as an eternal high priest—no beginning. Since Jesus is God-with-us, as God our Lord he has no beginning. Only as Incarnate has God's Word a beginning: "for us humans and for our salvation he came down from the heavens and became incarnate from the holy Spirit and the virgin Mary, became human and was crucified on our behalf under Pontius Pilate . . ."[2] As simply God's Word, he is eternal. Hence, Jesus, God's Word Incarnate and our high priest, was referred to as a priest according to the order of Melchizedek.

The Passion narratives in our four gospels, including the glorious one we've heard proclaimed today, hold up a mirror before our eyes in which we see ourselves as members of the sinful human race desperately in need of salvation, a salvation which only God could bring. Although our Savior suffered and died nearly two thousand years ago, we did this to him. We may say that we did this evil to him although he lived two thousand years ago because he chose to identify himself with all who suffer, in particular with those who are innocent and nevertheless are tortured and killed. These injustices and wanton cruelties happen everywhere today.

Our Lord made this identification clear when, after his resurrection and return to glory, he manifested himself to the man known as Saul of Tarsus as Saul was en route to Damascus to persecute Christians and even have some killed. The risen Lord did not ask Saul why he was persecuting Christians; instead he asked, "Saul, Saul, why are you persecuting me?" (Acts 9:4c). Jesus had made himself one with the victims of Saul's persecution. He continues in our day to make himself one with all who suffer from our sinfulness, and then even with you and me as sinners in our misery that sin brings. By this identification, Jesus asks the "Sauls" of this world—i.e., any one of us—to become another Saint Paul. (As I'm sure we all know Saul's name changed to Paul, and he became our Saint Paul.)

Hence, we all are implicated in the evils that reached their apogee in the crucifixion of Jesus, the Innocent One. Some among us might even have been active in such evils. We see these evils all around us. Our world is filled with lies, often called spin. I, for one, feel guilty in this regard.

Recently, I sat in the waiting room on the fourth floor of the Seattle Cancer Care Alliance (SCCA) quite recently while [a parishioner who had driven me there] engaged in conversation a woman who manifestly needed

---

2.. From the translation of the Nicene-Constantinopolitan Creed in Tanner, *Decrees*.

to talk.³ Although not engaged in the conversation, I heard everything. The poor woman's insurance was running out. For a while, she could mortgage her assets and make a stab at paying, but the stopgap would not last long. She'd run out of money soon, and treatments would end. Then she would simply be allowed to die prematurely. The injustice cut me to the quick. My insurance won't run out. Why? How guilty am I for the manifest injustices of our health care system? How guilty are you? The narratives of the Passion hold a mirror up so that we can see what we're implicated in. That woman should not die prematurely; she should not die without proper treatment.

What about war as we "celebrate" the fifth anniversary of the preemptive strike on Iraq? How many have been maimed? How many have died? And to what end? Is anyone guilty of anything? Who contributed politically to the preemptive war? Look in the mirror. Read the indictment. Hear the narrative of the Passion. Where is Christ in all this?

Are we stewards of God's creation or destroyers of the environment? God did not give us this good creation to pollute and destroy. Are we implicated in the destruction? Look in the mirror! Listen to the indictment! Does environmental degradation kill innocent people?

Are we implicated in people losing their homes and savings? A person who gulled an unsophisticated person into purchasing a mortgage he/she could not possibly afford and who now is without a home should look into the mirror and read the indictment. Did any of us make money on these scams? Did investments that benefitted any one of us come from this mortgage chicanery? Do we believe ideologies that excuse this greedy and destructive behavior? Look into the mirror! Read the indictment!

The Sacrament of Matrimony is under siege in our culture. Look at the divorce rate. Have we contributed to this disaster by our sexual behavior making a mockery of the fidelity that authentic marriage requires, perhaps especially in sexual matters? Do young people look at us and decide the way to go is sexual activity outside a sacramental union and without reference to such a union? Do we contribute to a sex saturated culture and endless advertisements about erectile dysfunction that have the subliminal message that successful sexual intercourse is essential to living successfully from the cradle to the grave? Does anyone think civilization can stand when holy matrimony is thoroughly undermined? Does anyone care about the consequent abortions? Talk about the slaughter of innocent human life that belongs to God. Then, does anyone help care for such life so that mothers

---

3. Fr. Roach was diagnosed with non-Hodgkin's lymphoma some years prior. He was now beginning treatment. In late August 2008, doctors found inoperable pancreatic cancer leading to his death on November 7.

may choose not to abort? Is anyone paying attention? Look into the mirror! Hear the indictment!

How many among us were seduced by the sexual revolution and its psychological supporters? Certainly, the psychology that endorsed and justified this revolution influenced a substantial number of clergy and religious to exempt themselves from their commitments. God alone knows how many abandoned their commitments improperly (some left quite properly) because of this revolution and the ideologies that justified it. The number of priests who left priestly ministry during this revolution was greater than the number who left upon the rise of Protestantism. How many who stayed remember with sorrow and repentance their confusion induced by this revolution? God alone knows. God's mercy is great. The mercy of others toward the confusion of clergy and religious (priests, nuns, and brothers) has been paltry. Both those who have good reason to beg mercy and those who deny mercy need to hear God's indictment. How else can any of us enter into God's judgment at Easter?

How many consider themselves guilty of murder for having purchased illicit drugs, the profits from which are supporting armed forces that kill our fellow Americans here and abroad? Afghanistan now has bumper poppy crops. There's been a long, slow civil war in Colombia, largely over drugs. Who's buying those drugs? Who's using them on Vashon? How have drugs purchased in the U.S. corrupted Mexican law enforcement and the wider Mexican government? On and on it goes. Read the indictment! Gaze on what happened to Jesus, the Innocent One!

I believe I could continue for some time, but I think the point has been made. When we venerate the bare Cross and kiss it, we are kissing all with whom Jesus has identified himself. If we understand this, the "Saul" in each one of us may become a "Saint Paul." Without accepting the indictment, we do not come under the judgment. Accepting the indictment is called repentance leading to "the obedience of faith." God's judgment is mercy leading to peace and joy in this life and unimaginable joy in the resurrected life, a share in which is offered each of us. We celebrate the resurrected life on Easter. Reject the indictment and one misses the judgment of mercy that is embodied in the resurrection. God's mercy is greater than all our sins put together. In sum, the Passion narratives in the gospels are not simply about Jesus; they're about you and me. If we believe this and make it our own through repentance, we will be able to receive the mercy that is God's Easter judgment.

Chapter 12

Easter

Resurrection (March 27, 2005)

Scripture Readings

Acts 10: 34a, 37–43; Ps 118; Col 3:1–4; John 20:1–9.

Summary

Recognizing God as the creator of all else illuminates the nature and significance of the resurrection. "Resurrection is the name for God recreating," Fr. Roach notes, our bodily and individual personal existence. Participation in it requires our prior cooperation of repenting and accepting shared life in Jesus. This asks us to accept God's grace and guidance through Christ and his Church. Adherence to the Catholic faith founded by Christ is nowadays made difficult by the false individualism and skepticism of the surrounding culture.

Homily

THE TEENAGE SON OF a loyal friend of the parish inquired through his mother what Catholics believe about resurrection. This homily provides the answer.

Catholic faith rests on the conviction that God is the Creator. We believe that one can know this truth without faith, but with the gift of faith comes precision and confidence that even a sound philosophical conclusion does not provide. With Catholic faith, what it means to identify God as the Creator becomes sharper and clearer than reason alone can provide.

The Old Testament records for us how as the people God had chosen to receive his guidance and promises came to understand better who God is, they realized that their tribal God was the only God because God is the Creator. But, they did not at first understand that the very existence of everything that is not God depends upon God. The Latin phrase that Western philosophers and theologians have used for centuries to encapsulate this truth learned late in the history of the chosen people is *creatio ex nihilo* (creation from nothingness). This truth did not become clear to God's chosen people until about 150 years before the birth of Jesus. You may find the full truth about God as Creator in the Second Book of Maccabees (7:28). This book was written just over 130 years before Jesus was born, and is one of the last books written for our Old Testament. Regrettably, the founders of Protestantism in the sixteenth century removed this book from the canon of the Bible. Of course, it is found in the Catholic Bible.

If one clearly understands that God is the Creator and that it is as the Creator of everything else that God is God, then one can begin to understand the event we celebrate in a special way this Easter Sunday. Obviously, the Creator of everything else can re-create, if God so chooses. Resurrection is the name for God re-creating.

You and I were created. There, of course, were a number of other created realities, especially other persons, that God used in bringing you and me into existence. These secondary causes, as philosophers like to refer to them, are not of concern here. What does concern us is bringing fully to mind the simple truth that we weren't around somewhere for God to ask if any one of us wanted to exist. Therefore, you and I did not have to cooperate with God in becoming created. God, using other creatures, brought us into existence without our consent. In sharp contrast, God's re-creating act that we call resurrection is not like this. We are not re-created without our cooperation and consent.

Although we were created without our cooperating and consent, we will not know resurrection without co-operating with God. Resurrection names God's act of re-creating a person who has come to the end. In other words, resurrection means that God re-creates a dead person. If some part of us enters into the so-called "life force," or whatever makes us up physically returns to nature's cycles, this would mean nothing to us as the persons we are in this life, since what it means to be a person would have dissolved.

These myths only cover the fact that, if the myths were true, when we die the person we are would come to a final end. If God does not re-create, death is the end, simply and completely the end of one's personal existence.

Death is the great equalizer. Without God re-creating, we're all equally nothing when we die. With God's re-creating, which we call resurrection, we are constituted anew as the same persons we are in this life. Adding the word "bodily" to the word "resurrection" indicates we understand that we are re-constituted as the kind of creatures we are now—a strange and wondrous union of matter and spirit, i.e., of body and soul. We Catholics do not believe that resurrected life is merely the life of a disembodied soul, whatever that would be. We believe in bodily resurrection, i.e., the resurrection of the whole person.

First, as a promise to God's chosen people, and then as the realization of that promise in Jesus, God offers re-creating us upon our deaths. As I've now said repeatedly, this re-creating we call resurrection. We are re-constituted with our personal identities intact, but we do not return to the kind of life we presently live. Instead we live directly from God's own life. We can't even adequately imagine what this means. The glory and joy of this new existence is beyond what we can know in this life.

The resurrected life following death is no more nor less than a share in the life Jesus took up when he rose from the dead that first Easter dawn. In one sense, there is only one who has been raised, that is Jesus. We who will be raised are raised with him as members of his Body. We died with him in baptism, thereby becoming a member of his Body; we rise with him after death, thereby coming to share the resurrected life he now lives. This sharing in the life that belongs to Jesus by virtue of who he really is (i.e., God's Word Incarnate) begins during this life. Sharing in his life is a principal reason for the existence of the Church he founded, in which you are worshipping this morning. Here through Word and Sacraments we begin, while living this life, to share his life that lasts forever.

While living this life some persons begin to share, without knowing they are sharing, in the life that belongs to Jesus. These persons are men and women of good will who through no fault of their own do not know what God has asked us to believe and do through the Church Jesus founded. Those who have been given the opportunity of knowing God's will and have refused or neglected to follow what God asks of us are not innocent and may well relinquish any share in our Lord's life by their neglect of his will.

This observation should make clear how being re-created (i.e., resurrected) differs from being created. We will not enjoy resurrection except we cooperate with God in this life. Our cooperation usually is referred to as doing God's will. In the most famous Catholic prayer, we say to God,

"Thy kingdom come; thy will be done, on earth as it is in heaven." We either mean it, or we don't; and if we don't mean what we pray, we won't share in his resurrection.

God created us without asking us if we wanted to exist. God won't raise us from the dead without in one way or another asking us if we want to share his life. If we don't want to share his life and show that we want to share his life here and now, we won't share his life eternally.

What it means to cooperate with God, i.e., to do God's will, has been the topic of everything we have accomplished in this parish during Lent. We need only review what has been proclaimed in the homilies of Lent—the five Sundays and the major solemnities of Holy Week—in order to know what God asks of us. Follow their lead and one will most certainly be cooperating with God in becoming a new person of the resurrection. Jesus, who is God's Word sharing our human life fully as one of us, set the pattern for our cooperation with God the Father while living in this world. What has been proclaimed in this parish spells out how our Lord's sharing in our human life reveals to us what God asks of us so that God may bring us to the Easter dawn, sharing God's own eternal life after our worldly life ends in death.

There are two principal obstacles standing in the way of people like ourselves doing God's will. They are contemporary expressions of the sin that has dogged human existence since shortly after God created the first human beings. The first obstacle is the individualism that permeates the American culture in which we live. This individualism is not an expression of authentic individuality, which Catholic faith embraces. Rather, this individualism is an isolating distortion of our individuality. Under the influence of this individualism, people who are captured by the limitations of our culture believe that they can make up for themselves whatever they choose to call God's will. When they make up God's will for themselves, they usually choose to believe, quite falsely, that God requires no "organized religion." They don't like "organized religion"; so, of course, they decide that God could not possibly have been serious about it. For them, it's an intolerable bother to participate in the Mass each Sunday, so why do it?

The second obstacle is scandal. Not only have the real sins of members of the Church, including, even especially, clergy, created scandal, but also distorted and exaggerated reporting of these sins and even just allegations have created scandal. There has as well been a media blitz of unprecedented proportions that falsifies just about every aspect of Catholicism. In addition to this propaganda or falsification and distortion, there's been the well-publicized behavior of people claiming to be Christian who in fact are fanatics. Fanaticism turns even people who are strongly called to faith away from the Church. As a result of sins, propaganda, and fanaticism, the media are able to portray the Church as a cult led by an aging and dying man in Rome, who patently is no longer able to fulfill the duties of his office, and has not been able to do so for some time. We have dealt with these subjects in our Lenten homilies. These earlier homilies, among other matters, have proclaimed clearly that for an authentic Catholic the pope is the Bishop of Rome, not a cult leader.

Ironically, the propaganda machines have trashed even a saint of the Church who is closely linked to our Lord's resurrection that heralded the first Easter dawn. Of course, I'm referring to Saint Mary of Magdala, often called Saint Mary Magdalene. This wonderful woman was the first and most privileged witness to our Lord's rising. The propaganda machine misidentifies her with a woman who according to Saint Luke was regarded as a public sinner. The propaganda machine then goes on to elaborate fiction about a relationship between Jesus and this woman falsely named Mary of Magdala. The fiction is a direct attack on the very heart of the faith which Jesus seeks to impart to each of us. In the seventh chapter of his gospel, Saint Luke reported what really happened between the unnamed woman and our Savior. The fiction would have been impossible if Saint Luke had only been able to tell us that woman's name. Because he could not, evil imagination has taken over and done the rest.

I remain amazed and deeply impressed by the wisdom of those who remain faithful despite this propaganda barrage, which does far more than merely amplify the sins of our fellow Catholics. I think the manifest fidelity of good Catholics, among other things, represents a profound humility expressed in the recognition that we all are sinners. So recognizing our sinful human condition is an essential part of doing God's will.

As we recall with joy God's gift of eternal life proffered us in the resurrection of Jesus the Christ, who is God's Word become one of us, we renew our determination to do God's will in all we do. We're encouraged and prompted to embrace God's plan for us in this life, a plan God lived as Jesus, by the love revealed in the resurrection of our Lord. This is the merciful love that conquers all sin and evil, including the evil of death. There is one and only one symbol of the resurrection. It is the dawn. With the first Easter, a new day dawned for us all. All that is asked of us is to live this new life that Jesus the Christ seeks to share with us. And, by asking us to live sharing in Christ's life, God is asking for our all. When we have given our all, we will know for all eternity what resurrection is. Happy Easter!

Chatper 13

Second Sunday of Easter: Divine Mercy Sunday
Mercy is Judgment (March 30, 2008)

Scripture Readings

Acts 2:42–47; Ps 118; 1 Pet 1:3–9; John 20: 19–31.

Summary

Awareness of God's mercy aids us in responding to his offer of salvation. Our Lord's resurrection is also God's mercy. We seek both at Easter. Saint Faustina Kowalska was God's instrument reminding us of the Divine Mercy. As God shows us merciful love and forgiveness, we are called to repent and show mercy to others. God's mercy does not conflict with his justice; it is his just judgment. Seeing this frees us from resentments and other impediments to forgiving others as we must. A final reminder notes that the Church and its sacraments mediate God's grace.

Homily

POPULAR PIETY CAN DISTORT devotions such as the one Pope John Paul II attached to this Sunday, which is the octave of Easter. This tendency undermined devotion to our Lady growing out of her appearances at

Fatima in Portugal. Thus far, the tendency has not undermined the devotion to Divine Mercy. This devotion stems from the profound mystical experiences of then Sister, now Saint, M. Faustina Kowalska (1905–1938), a Polish nun who died on the 5th of October 1938.

Sister Faustina, daughter of a poor farming family that had suffered greatly during the First World War, was God's chosen instrument to remind the human family again of Divine Mercy. Divine Mercy is boundless, but requires repentance. Those who would distort this devotion omit the requirement. They would give the impression that God's merciful love is what the German Lutheran theologian Dietrich Bonheoffer (1906–1945), a contemporary of Saint Faustina's, referred to as "cheap grace." Hitler executed Dietrich Bonheoffer. God graciously called Saint Faustina home before the Nazis could get their hands on her. They did execute her contemporary and fellow Pole, the great Franciscan saint, Maximilian Kolbe (1894–1941). The Nazis who ignored the requirements of Divine Mercy have since faced the judgment that follows.

In blunt terms, in the period leading up to Saint Faustina's immensely beautiful and important mystical experiences, the world ignored God's offer of mercy. The result was the Second World War with the attendant Nazi and Stalinist horrors. This had clearly been predicted by Our Lady when she appeared at the end of the First World War to three beautiful children of very modest means at Fatima in Portugal. Very few took her message seriously. Therefore, the dire consequences she predicted came true. Saint Faustina, in many ways, is an update of Fatima. In this devotion, we're called not only to accept Divine Mercy offered us boundlessly, but also live what this acceptance requires—namely, loving others mercifully as we have been loved. Our fellow parishioners who are promoting this devotion are offering us a great opportunity.

What mercy did the victors in the First World War show the defeated? Then, in response, what mercy did the Nazis show Jewish people? What mercy had been shown by rapacious capitalists and large landowners to those who worked for them? Then, what mercy did Stalin's communists show peasants and many, many others who did not fit into their plans? What mercy did Hitler's rocket campaign show the English, or the Japanese show those they conquered, especially in Shanghai, China? Then, what mercy did the Allies show with saturation bombing and use of atomic bombs? Were these horrors unleashed because ordinary people were unfaithful and did not live the merciful love God has so generously offered us? Are present horrors unleashed because of our loss of the faith that requires showing mercy?

SECOND SUNDAY OF EASTER: DIVINE MERCY SUNDAY

In many places, Saint Faustina's diary records how Divine Mercy works as God's judgment. In her mystical experiences, the Good Lord told her the following: "I am prolonging the time of mercy for the sake of sinners. But woe to them if they do not recognize this time of My visitation."[1]; "Before the Day of Justice, I am sending the Day of Mercy."[2]; "He who refuses to pass through the door of My mercy must pass through the door of My justice."[3] Our Savior clearly stated the door of God's mercy in his Sermon on the Mount. Immediately after Jesus taught us to pray the "Our Father," he said: "Yes, if you forgive others their failings, your heavenly Father will forgive you yours; but if you do not forgive others, your Father will not forgive your failings either" (Matt 6:14–15).

The Church uses a number of criteria to evaluate the authenticity of private revelations, such as the mystical experiences of Saint Faustina. Among these criteria, perhaps the most important is perfect conformity between what allegedly was revealed privately and the public revelation the Church proclaims. The content of Saint Faustina's mystical experiences conforms perfectly with what God has revealed and the Church proclaims. Only the "single sacred deposit of the Word of God" commands the assent of faith, while authentic private revelations both confirm God's revelation and remind us of specific contents. A person would distort the devotion to Divine Mercy if one would downplay or ignore the truth that God's mercy also is his judgment in the sense that mercy precedes and forestalls God's judgment; but God's final judgment will come.

Pope John Paul II notwithstanding, I am disinclined to substitute a devotion for what the official liturgy asks us to celebrate on this the Second Sunday of Easter, which is the octave of Easter. Fortunately, the full significance of Saint Faustina's mystical experiences fits perfectly with today's Liturgy of the Word, so endorsing the devotion does not substitute for the Liturgy of the Word, but complements it. We find a not insignificant link between the devotion and the liturgy in today's gospel. In this gospel, we hear our Lord instituting the Sacrament of Penance and Reconciliation (Confession): (The Resurrected Lord said the following to the original hierarchy) "Receive the Holy Spirit. / If you forgive anyone's sins, / they are forgiven; / if you retain anyone's sins, / they are retained" (John 20:22-23). There's more suggested by these words than establishing the Sacrament of Penance and Reconciliation.

---

1. Kowalska, *Divine Mercy*, #1160.
2. Kowalska, *Divine Mercy*, #1588.
3. Kowalska, *Divine Mercy*, #1146.

The words imply an essential of Catholic faith: God's graces are mediated. The Good Lord has chosen that his merciful love should come through the community (i.e., the *ecclesia* or Church) that Jesus founded. This further implies that all of us who belong to the Body of Christ are called upon to forgive one another as the instruments or mediators whereby God forgives us individually. Remember, our community includes those who have gone home to God in eternity–the saints. We ask them to beg forgiveness and other blessings for us, and promise implicitly with our request that we too shall forgive others. The saints' intercession prepares us to see God. Thus, we call upon the greatest of these saints: "Holy Mary, Mother of God, pray for us sinners now and at the hour of our death." In addition to praying the "Hail Mary," each night before going to sleep, I call upon my favorite saint. Her forgiveness in my regard expressed through her prayers for me consoles me greatly and mediates God's inestimable graces. In Jesus, God has called you and me—each of us—to forgive one another.

Each of us may detect sin in our lives by asking ourselves if we hold on to grudges. Holding on to a grudge is resentment in the sense expressed by the French word from which our English term comes–*ressentiment*. The French suggests re-feeling a sentiment over and over again. Holding onto a grudge recycles the unforgiving feeling directed against the person one believes is responsible for the perceived or real slight or injury. By refusing the true forgiveness God expects us to offer those who actually or seemingly offend us, sin holds us in thrall. As our Lord said in his Sermon on the Mount: "Yes, if you forgive others their failings, your heavenly Father will forgive you yours; but if you do not forgive others, your Father will not forgive your feelings either" (Matt 6:14-15). If one holds on to resentment because of a perceived slight, real or imaginary, the "holding on" blocks the forgiveness God offers.

Perhaps in response to Saint Faustina's message, Pope John Paul II wrote the dissertation required for his secular doctorate on *ressentiment* as analyzed by the German philosopher, Max Scheler. Clearly, *ressentiment* opposes God's mercy. I believe only those who have accepted God's merciful love are capable of mercifully loving others as the gospels require. For others, forgiveness is selective and self-serving.

Merciful love is therapeutic in that showing mercy frees one from the grip of evils past and present. In a culture in which mercy or true pity has been forgotten, people look for a substitute to free them from the evils they have experienced. We're also capable of using military force in this way. Presently, in the U.S. we use the courts and talk a great deal about closure in the effort to exorcize past evils. Actually, for the most part what people seek in this way is revenge. I think it also significant that a great deal of contemporary psychology advocates what amounts to revenge, disguised as "justice," rather than mercy as a way to healing having been hurt. This is another failure of contemporary psychology, of which there have been many. But, if only authentic faith makes loving mercifully possible, no wonder that our culture is in this situation.

Our condition reminds me of a passage in the Gospel according to Saint Luke. Upon completing a parable about an unscrupulous judge and an importunate widow, our Lord said: *"But when the Son of man comes, will he find any faith on earth?"* (Luke 18:7; emphasis added). I fear that if our Lord were to come presently, the answer may be, "Not very much." Alarmingly, the answer may apply particularly to those who claim to believe, yet refuse to let go of their grudges.

Today's gospel proclamation provides other instances of God's mercy as judgment. First, Jesus told the original hierarchy: "As the Father sent me, / so I am sending you" (John 20:21). God the Father sent the Son on an errand of mercy. The Son, then, sends the Church he founded on the same errand. With these words, our Lord set the standard against which every bishop from then to the present is judged. The judgment extends to priests and deacons as well.

Our gospel proclamation contains a touching example of mercy as judgment in the way Jesus dealt with the disciple we call Doubting Thomas. Thomas was a man of faith, but overwhelmed by our Lord's Passion and Death. Because Jesus loved him mercifully, he was able to judge the truth of Thomas's faith, despite the doubt that demanded special proof. Jesus acted on his judgment of Thomas and provided the proof. This was a great mercy and led to Thomas making the clearest possible profession of faith. After Jesus had graciously and mercifully offered Thomas tangible proof that he had risen bodily from the dead, Thomas addressed him with these words of pure faith: "My Lord and my God" (John 20:28). Then, prompted by merciful love for those of us who come after Thomas, Jesus said: "You believe because you can see me. / Blessed are those who have not seen and yet believe" (John 20:29).

Although Thomas's declaration of pure faith saying to the Resurrected Lord, "My Lord and my God," required understanding, the demands on his understanding at that moment were not as challenging as those on us who enjoy God's blessing because we "have not seen and yet believe." Traditionally, we speak of the seven gifts of the Holy Spirit. They are: "wisdom, understanding, counsel, fortitude, knowledge, piety, and fear of the Lord."[4] When understanding is taken as an encompassing term, then wisdom, counsel,

---

4. USCCB, *Catechism*, #1831.

and knowledge are developments of understanding. It takes these components of well-rounded understanding in order to profess faith and remain faithful. It also takes fortitude (i.e., courage). I would say that for the young in our day it especially takes fortitude. Piety and the fear of the Lord are really one and the same gift, which comes with understanding, in particular with wisdom.

We believe because we understand the testimony entrusted by witnesses, such as Thomas, to the Church Jesus founded. I find great comfort in the survival of this organization, unlike any other, for two millennia. Only God could have made this possible. In this way, we join the blessed "who have not seen and yet believe." Our believing is a work of God's mercy.

Our proclaimed gospel concluded with the words Saint John wrote as the conclusion to his original text. What now is marked off as chapter 21 in our Bibles is an epilogue, and most probably was written by one or more of John's students (disciples) following his death. The Church knows the epilogue too is inspired text as well as what Saint John wrote. The epilogue ends with a second conclusion that builds on what John hinted at in his conclusion. The second conclusion makes quite clear why we believe that the sacred Scriptures do not provide all that God has revealed and we are called to believe. We need sacred Tradition as well, because as the words in the second conclusion remind us, "There is much else that Jesus did; if it were written down in detail, I do not suppose the world itself would hold all the books that would be written" (John 21:25). Fear not! Sacred Tradition sorts it all out and provides us with the essentials.

Our first reading (Acts 2:42-47) provides an instance of how what started in loving mercifully did not work out practically. The poor local church founded in Jerusalem, possibly the first of the Church's fully organized local churches, dealt with straightened circumstances by sharing everything (Acts 2:44-45). When not long after our Lord's Resurrection and the founding of the Church, the Romans conquered Jerusalem multiple times crushing the Judean insurgency led by false messiahs against Roman rule, the local church was caught up in the disaster and communal living virtually ended. Fortunately, many Catholics escaped because they took seriously our Lord's prophecies about what would happen to the city. Their attempt at communal living was not in vain. It has continued in a number of ways. The most prominent way consists of organized monasteries, convents, and other religious orders, such as the one to which I belong.

We responded to the first reading with verses from Psalm 118. After checking other translations, I decided that the New Jerusalem Bible provides the best, because it uses the term "faithful love." "Alleluia! / Give thanks to Yahweh for he is good, / for his faithful love endures for ever. / Let the House of Israel say, / 'His faithful love endures for ever.'" (Ps 118:1-2 with opening "Alleluia!") God's faithful love is mercy until death and, for those who receive him, beyond.

Our second reading opened with a sentence that made clear our Lord's Resurrection is God's mercy (1 Pet 1:3-4). What glorious words! The great saint who first held the office in the Church now held by Pope Benedict XVI wrote in a clear and succinct fashion. The reading requires no explanation. I would observe only that God did not have to show mercy. Surely, as our history demonstrates, God had ample reason to give up on the human race and pronounce a summary judgment of condemnation. Instead, God offered us mercy. Have we accepted his mercy? The sure sign is in loving others mercifully, too. As Saint Faustina wrote in her diary what she believed were our Lord's words come to her in a great mystical experience, "He who refuses to pass through the door of My mercy must pass through the door of My justice."[5] She did know the truth about Divine Mercy!

---

5. Kowalska, *Divine Mercy*, #1146.

Chapter 14

Solemnity of the Ascension

The Two-fold Meaning of Ascension
(Celebrated on Sunday, June 4, 2000)

Scripture Readings

Acts 1:1–11; Ps 47; Eph 1:17–23; Mark 16:15–20.

Summary

Christ's Ascension concludes Christ's post-resurrection appearances, and points to our own destiny. The homily connects together Christ's Ascension, glorification, and resurrection. "Ascension" refers to Christ's glorification concluding his post-resurrection appearances. The risen Christ makes clear to his Church he, according to Fr. Roach, "entered with his humanity into his divine life," the common humanity he shares with us. Christ's Resurrection and Ascension in this way suggest to Fr. Roach "two sides of the same coin—human life transformed into divine life" beyond our imagining. Resurrected life is thus not just this life improved. Finally, Fr. Roach notes that we begin sharing in this divine life here, especially through the Real Presence in the Eucharist. Understanding Christ's Ascension for Fr. Roach implies "the transformation of human living into God's life." This all in all gives us a truer image than merely "Jesus floating upward."

Homily

ONE MAY NOT SEPARATE the term "ascension" from the term "resurrection," if one wishes to use the term "resurrection" to denote what happened to Our Lord, Jesus the Christ, upon dying. The event that we celebrate upon concluding our Lent actually was a process taking three days according to our way of counting. We celebrate this event with our Sacred Triduum (Sacred Three Days)—Good Friday, Holy Saturday, Easter Sunday. These days commemorate Our Lord dying on the Cross, which includes his descending among the dead, rising from the dead, and his glorification. "Descending among the dead" is a poetic way of saying both that Jesus actually died and that he briefly shared the lot of the just dead who awaited his resurrection. Glorification denotes the conclusion of the resurrection; it is simultaneous with resurrection. Saint John in his gospel uses this term more clearly than any of the other New Testament writers. Saint Luke, composing the Acts of the Apostles, comes in second. To catch on to the meaning of "glorification" I recommend that you prayerfully read the seventeenth chapter of the Gospel according to Saint John. This chapter often is called Our Lord's priestly prayer. In a moment, we will see that "ascension" means glorification with an additional and subordinate signification. The bottom line is that the term "resurrection" can mislead if it is not joined to another term, such as "glorification" or "ascension." To appreciate this solemnity, we must understand why.

Through history, sadly including in our own day, human beings have believed in a phony resurrection, the result of our human tendency to wishful thinking. This false belief makes out that when we die we transfer from this life to an improved version of what essentially is this life. The Egyptians held this phony concept of resurrection. The life we supposedly were going to was so similar to this life that the Egyptians packed their tombs—the big ones were pyramids—with supplies from this life for use in the next. Some think that the Koran's description of paradise after death is much the same—an earthly garden of delights in the heavens. I fear that some people in our country who call themselves Christians hold much the same belief. One thing is for sure: it is not what Jesus taught! It is not what he lived in dying and rising from the dead. In order to make this clear, we attach the word "glorification" and/or "ascension" to "resurrection" in order to denote what we believe as followers of Jesus the Christ and members of his Body, the Church.

The second person of the Blessed Trinity, God's Word, became human as Jesus born of the Blessed Virgin Mary. In doing so, God shared our life. He continues to share our life through his Church by identifying himself with those whom he loves. We see this sharing in all of the sacraments. Through his Church, Jesus incorporates us into his very life. Having been incorporated into his life here, we may see Jesus as our representative with God. So, when as human Jesus died on the Cross, he began to live the divine life, the life of the Blessed Trinity, as human—i.e., as our representative. Previously, he had lived this life only as God, not also as our human representative. As our representative, he offers us the opportunity to share the divine life with him as human. We are only human, whereas he is God and human. By uniting our humanity to his divinity, Jesus opened the possibility of our sharing in God's life. So, if we die with Jesus, we rise with him. After death, therefore, we do not simply continue to live an improved version of our present life. Instead, we begin to live, directly and with greatly expanded consciousness, a new kind of life—the life of the Blessed Trinity. We cannot even imagine it; it is so glorious!

We should remind ourselves that we have begun to live that divine life here and now. We were baptized into the death and resurrection of Our Lord—i.e., into the life that belongs to Jesus as God. In baptism, we were incorporated into Jesus—i.e., became members of his body. We were confirmed (anointed) so that we would have the strength to fulfill the duties of this divine life during our present life. We nourish the divine life in us with Holy Communion. We receive Holy Communion after we have properly remembered Our Lord's Death-Resurrection-Ascension—i.e., prayerfully celebrated the Eucharistic Sacrifice we call the Mass.

Worthily receiving Jesus by receiving his resurrected body into our very selves strengthens his divine life in us while we are living this life. Since his life has begun in us here, the big difference between life here and hereafter is that here we don't fully see, or experience, or feel, or know God's life that we actually are beginning to live here. If here, we hold on to God's life that Jesus gives us by living as his friend, then we will one day know fully and immediately what it means and feels like to live the life of the triune God, which, I repeat, we begin to live here. Again, the bottom line is what we really mean by resurrection. When we profess our faith with the Nicene Creed and say: "We look for the resurrection of the dead, and the life of the world to come," we don't mean we anticipate an eternal golf game or endless life on the beaches of Maui with beautiful bodies. What we do mean is that we are looking forward to a new life with God. For this resurrected life, God newly creates, or re-creates, us. This new creation makes our living the new life into what the creed calls, "the life of the world to come." Mummification and pyramids are not appropriate preparation for living this new life hereafter. Living this life in such a way that Jesus can call us "friend" is appropriate, even requisite, preparation.

Jesus faced a problem in making these realities known to and through his Church. He first had to make his chosen witnesses know for sure that he had risen from the dead the same person and as fully human—no ghost—as he had been when he was crucified. Then, he had to make clear to them that despite meeting him as Resurrected Lord in this life, his human life as the Resurrected Lord would be quite different from the life he had lived with his friends here. As I said above, by rising from the dead he, as it were, had taken our common humanity into divinity. To live humanly within the Blessed Trinity differs radically from living humanly on the shores of the Sea of Galilee. Somehow, Jesus made this difference clear to his Church, so her official recorders—Matthew, Mark, Luke, and John—make clear that after appearing to his Church upon his resurrection, he entered with his humanity into his divine life. To accomplish this task, the evangelists attached the second term, either "ascension" or "glorification," to the term "resurrection."

In our first reading from the Acts of the Apostles, we hear Saint Luke's elaborated account of this entrance into divine life. Of course, the human entry into the divine took place immediately upon the resurrection, but Saint Luke underscores it by proclaiming it as if it were a second event that occurred when Our Lord had completed the series of appearances he used to make known the fact that on our behalf he had conquered death. "Ascension" adds to "glorification" the subordinate idea that at some point Our Lord brought his resurrection appearances to an end. Please *do not* be literal about the "forty days." As with Our Lord's time in the desert, upon which we build our Lent, "forty days" is symbolic and stands for a length of time that is neither too short nor too long. Please *do* note that Luke identifies the ascension with the resurrection by using the following literary device: When he reported the resurrection, Luke wrote that when the women discovered the empty tomb and were puzzled, "two men in dazzling garments appeared to them." As the terrified women bowed to the ground, the two men asked them, "Why do you seek the living one among the dead?" (Luke 24:4–5). Later, when Luke wrote the Acts of Apostles, which opens with his report of the Ascension, he wrote: "While they (the chosen apostles) were looking intently at the sky as he (Jesus) was going, suddenly two men dressed in white garments stood beside them. They said, 'Men of Galilee, why are you standing there looking at the sky? This Jesus who has been taken up from you into heaven will return in the same way as you have seen him going into heaven'" (Acts 1:10–11).[1] By portraying whatever messengers God actually used to convey his truth first to the women at the tomb and then

---

1. Fr. Roach in these three quotations from Luke and Acts appears to use the translation in the *Lectionary for Mass*. See the fourth note in the First Sunday of Advent in this volume.

to the chosen apostles at the Ascension as two remarkable men dressed in white, Luke lets us know that the events are inseparable, two sides of one coin—human life transformed into divine life. Luke uses these "men" also to remind us that just as the time came when the series of appearances of the Resurrected Lord were deemed enough to convey the truth that he had conquered death, so the time will come when our human drama will have gone on long enough and then Jesus will return as he left, with a difference. One will not have to be disposed to receive God's grace to know that he's come back. His return will be the end of all creation as we now know it; his return will make us all aware—both those sharing his life and those who have rejected it—of what he began while he lived this life with us.

I hope that I've conveyed the truth that life after death is not this life jazzed up. When we die, we really die, as Jesus did; yet, if we are ready, we begin a spectacularly new kind of life, again as Jesus did. We begin to live as God lives. It boggles our imaginations. We must never mistake what we look forward to with sure and certain hope for what some religions and our pop culture, especially Hollywood, propose is life after death. In sharp contrast to this illusion, we know that this life really ends when we die. Something spectacularly better begins for us in Christ.

The lectionary required that we choose one of two readings to serve as our second reading—either Ephesians 1:17–23 or 4:1–13. In both passages, Saint Paul refers to Our Lord's Ascension. I choose the first selection to serve as our second reading because it is less complicated literarily, and makes the essential points as well as the second selection. The key sentence makes up the two verses that close the reading; see Ephesians 1:22–23. What Paul says by describing Jesus as "head over all things" Saint John said by describing Jesus as God's Word and writing that "All things came to be through him, and without him nothing came to be" (John 1:1–3, 3 quoted) These expressions are ways of affirming that Jesus is one with God, the Creator. In Paul's context, the expression underscores the fact that as Resurrected Lord, Jesus as human is living God's life, and God the Father has assigned him to serve as the head of his extended human body, which is his Church that we belong to. This life that belongs to Jesus and that he offers to share with us fills everything, because the Father initiated creation through his Word. In his Church to which we belong, we may find the fullness of this life. We should seek this fullness while we live here so that we may share in it hereafter.

The gospel for this solemnity is part of what scholars call "The Longer Ending" of the Gospel according to Saint Mark. The essential point seems to be, as I said in an earlier homily, that in its original form Mark's gospel reported only events that essentially were public. The truth of events, such as the resurrection, revealed only to those who were disposed to belong to

Our Lord's Body, his Church, Mark kept private. Sometime after his death, a Church writer, also inspired by the Holy Spirit, added a conventional account of the private events. This longer ending reports the Ascension. (Mark 16:19)

Unfortunately, and this misfortune needs at least a study group to explain, the longer ending includes a list of signs that will accompany those who believe (Mark 16:17–18). This list alone is proof that the Bible must have authoritative interpretation if it is to serve as a way to God's Word, Jesus. And it is not enough to say only that a reader should not be a literalist. This brief list mixes what should be taken literally with what is figurative. The tragedy of some few of those who recognize no God-given authority to guide them in interpreting the sacred Scriptures may be found in small Protestant sects in the United States. These are the sects whose members prove that they are believers by handling poisonous snakes. Andrew Lloyd Webber's latest musical, *Whistle Down the Wind*, portrays these snake handlers. I think he made a mishmash of the Gospel in *Jesus Christ, Superstar*. I don't like what he has done with believers in this latest offering. I mention the musical here to remind us of how widely known are those who misinterpret the two verses in the longer ending to Mark's gospel. I think that it should prompt us who have the grace to know his Church to thank God that we belong to his Body that interprets the Bible under the guidance of the Holy Spirit. The Holy Spirit not only prevents us from trying to prove ourselves by handling poisonous snakes; it also leads us to understand Our Lord's Ascension as the transformation of human living into God's life, rather than thinking only of Jesus floating upward.

Chapter 15

Pentecost

The Uniqueness of Faith (May 15, 2005)

Scripture Readings

Vigil: Ezek 37:1–14; Ps 104; Rom 8:22–27; John 7:37–39.

Sunday: Acts 2:1–1; Ps 104; 1 Cor 12:3b–7, 12–13; John 20:19–23.

Summary

Pentecost shows that the Catholic Church founded by Christ is guided by the Holy Spirit, is the unique repository for us knowing who God is, and how God saves us. Our consciously lived faith through the Church is our distinctive response to the human condition. The Christian and Catholic faith is both universal and unique to the Church. Church teaching thus denies that all ways to God are equally valid. In fact, faith is a notion proper to the New Testament. Fr. Roach then discusses the "obedience of faith," as a free and total submission to God so that we may (in Saint Paul's words) "have the mind of Christ." Thus, faith is believing *in* Christ, not just believing *that* certain things are true. Seeking our full relationship with Christ includes membership in Christ's Body, the Church. A postscript from another homily contrasts the Church as the unique deposit of faith with modern syncretic views of spirituality.

Homily

Our celebration of Pentecost coincides with a media frenzy designed to discredit the guidance God the Holy Spirit provides the Catholic Church. The media frenzy intends specifically to discredit Catholic faith, specifically, the belief that the Catholic Church which Jesus founded and that on Pentecost God the Holy Spirit animated is the repository for the unique truth about who and what God is and the way God has chosen to save us from sin, from all other evil, and ultimately from death. In sum, the frenzy desires to discredit the claim that Christian and Catholic faith is the unique truth about God, encompassing all truths professed in any other religion or quest for the divine, as well as rejecting all errors found therein.

So that no one will think that what follows in this homily is some abstruse theological discussion of interest only to those who happen to like a theological head-trip, I will compare Christian and Catholic faith with one other major world religion and show how only one of the two can possibly be true.

Christian and Catholic faith includes as an historical fact essential to everything else Catholics believe. We believe that approximately two millennia ago, outside Jerusalem, soldiers of the Roman Empire acting under orders crucified a Jew by the name of Jesus. The Church sees God in the crucified person and understands the death as his personal sacrifice offered for us as part of saving us from sin, evil, and death. The sacred writings that the Church compiled and calls the Bible includes the writings of the Hebrew people before the birth of Jesus (the Old Testament) as well as writing about Jesus (the New Testament). The Church believes that some writings in the Old Testament predicted what happened to Jesus, whereas all the writings that make up the New Testament either provide a report of his death on the cross or refer to it. I believe firmly as truth that Jesus my Savior died on the cross. Let us compare this to what a Muslim believes.

The sacred book of Islam known as the Koran (Qur'an) denies that Jesus was crucified. The Koran is divided into chapters or books that are called Sura. The denial that Jesus was crucified occurs in the fourth Sura near the end. Close to the denial of the historical fact that Jesus was crucified, a reader finds a distinction between Jesus and the Word of God. In other words, the Koran says that Jesus is not God's Word but a prophet whom the Word of God used. Finally, in this section referring to Jesus as the Son of God and believing that God is triune, the Koran calls blasphemy.[1] If

---

1. The original text of the homily quotes the following passage regarding the denial Jesus was crucified: "That they [the Jews] said (in boast), / 'We killed Christ Jesus / The son of Mary, / The Apostle of God'; / — But they killed him not, / Nor crucified him,

faith is a matter of truth, then what the Christian and Catholic faith holds about Jesus and what the Koran teaches cannot both be true. In the face of this evident contradiction, the prevailing religious "group think" of our day sets aside the question of truth and says that both religions are equally valid ways to God.

By pointing out error in the Koran, I do not say there is no good in Islam. I think there is both truth and goodness in Islam, but neither the full truth nor goodness of Christian and Catholic faith. I further insist that mixed in with the goodness and truth that one may find in Islam there is error. This is not the kind of error that comes from trying to apply true principles and making mistakes. The kind of error that comes from interpreting and applying truths exists within Catholicism. The error (i.e., untruth) that exists in Islam exists in the Islamic system of belief itself. I can repeat this analysis with any of the world's religions. They simply are not equally valid ways to God.

As the unique truth about God, the Christian and Catholic faith in all its components is God's instrument through which God seeks to bestow on us his saving, merciful love that comes through the Passion, Death, Resurrection, and Ascension of Christ. God seeks a free response from us to his initiative. God prompts this favorable free response from us by loving us mercifully before we even think about God and responding to him. Then God uses our favorable free response, which God has prompted, to deliver us from all sin and evil, including death. All saving action is the work of the triune God, i.e., all God's saving action in our regard is the work of the Trinity, even when we perceive the action as that of just one person, not all three. We attribute the work of the triune God to one person of the Trinity when in the process of our salvation we experience that one person particularly. Thus, when Jesus said to his Father when he was in agony in the garden of Gethsemane, "My Father . . . if this cup cannot pass by, but I must drink it, your will be done!" (Matt 26:42b), what Jesus as human prayed does not imply that he wanted something different from what his Father wanted. The prayer was our Lord's way of bringing his human nature in line with his desire as one with Father and Holy Spirit to redeem us from evil, even if redemption meant suffering and dying. All salvation is summed up in these events, which we refer to as the Paschal (Easter) mystery.

Even persons who, through no fault of their own, do not know our Lord or are blamelessly prevented from following him in this life, if they

---

/ But so it was made / To appear to them, / And those who differ / Therein are full of doubts, / With no (certain) knowledge, / But only conjecture to follow, / For a surety / They killed him not: - / Nay God raised him up / Unto himself; and God / Is Exalted in Power, Wise; . . . Sura 4: 157–158 in Ali, *Holy Qur'an*.

are saved from sin and evil, their salvation comes through Jesus. Saint Paul expressed this truth in his First Letter to Timothy: "For / there is one God; / there is also one mediator between God and humankind, / Christ Jesus, himself human, / who gave himself a ransom for all–this was attested at the right time" (1 Tim 2:5–6 NRSV-CE).

The phrase "Christian and Catholic faith" has come into use in order to say both that our faith comes from Jesus the Christ (i.e., is Christian faith) and that the Catholic Church he organized is the repository and preserving agency of the faith our Lord imparts intending this faith for all, which makes it Catholic. True and complete Christian faith necessarily is Catholic in precisely the sense the Church is Catholic wherein God the Holy Spirit preserves the full memory of Jesus, so the shorter expression, Catholic faith, states the faith is Christian as well, even when the word Christian is not expressed.

All of the authors whose writings make up our New Testament report this claim that Christian and Catholic faith is the unique truth about God intended for all. After receiving the power of the Holy Spirit on Pentecost, the first pope, a millennium before this term of endearment was used as his title, bore witness to this claim before the Sanhedrin (the Senate of the Judean people). Peter and John had been arrested for proclaiming our Lord's resurrection within the Temple precincts. In fact, Peter had just delivered his first sermon. They were hauled before the Sanhedrin and ordered to give an account of themselves (cf. Acts 4:8–12 in NJB). The account begins, "Then Peter, filled with the Holy Spirit, addressed them, . . . " His witness ended with this famous statement: "Only in him (Jesus) is there salvation; for of all the names in the world given to men, this is the only one by which we can be saved."

I repeat that if, through no fault of one's own, one does not know this name and the unique person who bears the name, then Jesus can save the person without the person knowing who's saving him/her. But, the salvation will be the work of Jesus.

I also repeat that the Church Jesus organized before his death, which is the Church animated by God the Holy Spirit after his death, resurrection, and ascension, is the sole repository of his unaltered, undiluted memory and the appointed dispenser of the sacraments of his saving merciful love. God the Holy Spirit who animates this Church is the Spirit of Jesus. The Church is the chosen instrument of the action of the Triune God whereby we human beings are redeemed from all evil and invited to all truth.

I assume that all parishioners know and understand this summary of Christian and Catholic faith. Many times, and in many ways throughout our long history, the human component of the Church has made it very difficult to see the truth I've just restated. To understand how bad human judgments and sin have infected our history as well as the present, we need a distinction. We need to distinguish between what is merely human and can therefore err and sin, and what is God-given. We need this distinction to understand our personal lives of faith as well as the life of the Church Jesus organized, and his Holy Spirit animates in which our faith lives. Before we can describe this distinction, we must be clear about what our faith is.

God prepared human beings for faith in his Word before God's Word became incarnate. This preparation took place everywhere people strove to know God and do God's will, but the preparation took place in a very special way within the history of the people God chose to be the vehicle of his promise. We find this history as a record of preparation for Jesus in the writings collected as our Old Testament. These writings are the record of what served as faith before God's Word became incarnate. Then, Jesus so transformed or fulfilled what had served as faith before he came that I've said faith is a New Testament concept, implying that Jesus invented faith. In the sense of fulfilling what went before, Jesus did invent faith; but through inspired New Testament authors he referred to what had gone before and prepared for him as faith as well. To grasp what I'm saying, please prayerfully read the eleventh chapter in the Letter to the Hebrews. The chapter reviews the history of those whose belief in God prepared the way for Jesus. Thus, the chapter ends with the following sentence: "These all won acknowledgement through their faith, but they did not receive what was promised, since God had made provision for us to have something better, and they were not to reach perfection except with us" (Hebrews 11:39–40). Although this famous passage in the sacred Scriptures refers as faith to the obedience offered God before the coming of Jesus, this same passage makes quite clear that in Jesus God gives us something better than what served as faith before God became one of us. In Jesus, God gives us the fullness of faith. To underscore this fulfillment, I've referred to faith as a New Testament concept, because faith's full meaning is a New Testament concept.

Using the words of Saint Paul, the Church describes faith as obedience, but the obedience of faith differs significantly from most ordinary obedience. Ordinary obedience occurs when we obey someone because the person has the authority to command us. For example, on Wednesday when I was working on this part of the homily, the television news reported that an airplane had flown into restricted airspace over our capitol buildings in Washington, DC. The television showed pictures of police ordering people to leave capitol buildings, and go as far away as possible as quickly as possible. The people shown were obeying the police. Despite special circumstances, this was a case of ordinary obedience. It turned out that the plane was a small private plane that flew into restricted airspace. At the time I wrote this, it had not as yet been determined whether the civilian pilot was just stupid or had some malicious intent. Air Force jets and a helicopter forced the plane to land at an airfield in nearby Maryland. When the plane was secured, people were told they could return to the capitol buildings.

Notice that obedience requires recognizing an authority. If this Wednesday an unknown person without uniform had ordered people to leave a capitol building, there would have been questions before anyone obeyed. If the person had no authority to give such a command, he/she would have been arrested. With this example in mind, we are reminded that even the most ordinary obedience requires recognizing the authority of the one commanding. Furthermore, if all the person commanding has is brute force or intimidation, then obedience is not ordinary; instead it is coercion.

Jesus praised a Roman centurion for recognizing his authority and said of the man, "In truth I tell you, in no one in Israel have I found faith as great as this" (Matthew 8:10b). The Roman centurion's faith was that of the Old Testament variety approaching fulfillment because he recognized God's authority in Jesus (cf. Matt 8:5-13; Luke 7:1-10; and the same or a similar incident reported in John 4:46-54). Laudatory as the centurion's faith was, it represented only the beginning, an essential beginning but only a beginning.

Faith, which Saint Paul and the Church following him describes as obedience, requires more than recognizing God's authority. The language that Church documents use is both precise and accurate, but I fear does not convey to everyone the full emotional meaning of what the Church solemnly affirms is true. Nonetheless, let us hear again what the Church affirms as solemnly as she can teach. I say that these words are taught as solemnly as the Church can teach because the quotation that follows is from a principal document of the Second Vatican Council about divine revelation promulgated on the 18th of November 1965. Vatican II was an ecumenical council, the 21st, whose documents were confirmed by papal authority. This is the Church's most solemn teaching. The document referred to as *Dei Verbum* (*Word of God*) refers explicitly to earlier teachings of the same truth about faith beginning with Saint Paul's Letter to the Romans. I will quote from the best translation I know, which is found in the second volume of *Documents of the Ecumenical Councils*.[2] The English is British with British spelling as well as following their rules for punctuation and capitalization:

> 5. In response to God's revelation our duty is "the obedience of faith" (see Rom 16, 26; compare Rom 1, 5; 2 Cor 10, 5-6). By this

---

2. Tanner, *Decrees*.

a human being makes a total and free self-commitment to God, offering "the full submission of intellect and will to God as he reveals," and willingly assenting to the revelation he gives. For this faith to be accorded [given] we have need of God's grace, both anticipating and then accompanying our act, together with the inward assistance of the Holy Spirit, who works to stir the heart and turn it towards God, to open the eyes of the mind, and to give "to all facility in accepting and believing the truth." The same Holy Spirit constantly perfects faith by his gifts, to bring about an ever deeper understanding of revelation.

6. By divine revelation God has chosen to manifest and communicate both himself and the eternal decrees of his will for the salvation of humankind, "so as to share those divine treasures which totally surpass human understanding." (I have omitted footnotes.)

Saint Paul described himself and those who also have accepted their duty, which is "the obedience of faith," as follows: " . . . we are those who have the mind of Christ" (1 Cor 2:16c). In other words, "the full submission of intellect . . . to God as he reveals" means we think like God and want what God wants. We know how God thinks and what he wants by knowing Jesus, God's Word. We give "the full submission of . . . will to God as he reveals" when we do what God wants because we too want what God wants. We don't just do what God says because God is infinitely more powerful than we. We do what God says because we've come to want what God wants, or in Saint Paul's words, "we . . . have the mind of Christ." Faith, then, presents us with challenges, and this is where the big distinction between what God gives and what is merely human comes in.

Faith is our relationship with Jesus whom we recognize as God's Word, and in whom we find freedom from sin and all other evil. But, our friend and savior Jesus does not give us a detailed plan of life. Instead, along with his merciful love (grace) which transforms us, he gives us himself as an example, and he also imparts basic principles. We've an enormous amount of work we must do to convert his example and principles into specifics here and now. This is where the merely human enters and we can err. Jesus does not guarantee that we always will get it right, but our Lord does send God the Holy Spirit into our lives. Neither does Jesus guarantee that no one of us will ever sin and mess things up. Our Lord does promise to forgive us when we repent, but he does not guarantee we will never sin. Instead, we're left to work out what his example and principles should mean in our lives. And we should promptly repent and ask for his forgiveness if and when we sin, which then we follow up by doing penance. This grappling with our Lord's example and his principles while trying to work them out and apply them, even when we are inspired by God the Holy Spirit, is an opportunity for the merely human to enter. As a result, both as individuals and as Church, we become embroiled in what turns out to be mistakes, in what needs to change, and even in what is sinful. This does not for one moment mean that God the Holy Spirit has ceased to preserve the faith both in the Church and in her individual members. It does mean that life as a member of the Body of Christ, which is his Church, always presents challenges.

Faith is a highly personal relationship with Jesus the Christ in whom dwells the fullness of divinity. Yet, we need to remember that we are unable to have a personal relationship with Jesus except we accept all of who he is. Therefore, we must accept his Body, which is his Church. We must love his Body, the Church, and recognize by the power of God the Holy Spirit that Jesus continues his mission of redemption through his Body, the Church he organized. This is an enormous challenge, because of what I've mentioned repeatedly above: the Church is made up of human beings like you and me who are being transformed, if we cooperate, more fully into his Body. Meanwhile, we err, often. The "we" includes men from all ranks of the clergy as well as women religious. Hilaire Belloc (1870–1953), the French-born British writer and famous Catholic apologist, once remarked that hell is paved with the bald pates of clerics. (A bald pate is a bald head.)

Despite our capacity for human error and sin, God the Holy Spirit guides the Church and protects what God has revealed. The Second Vatican Council in the document promulgated on the 18th of November 1965 [speaks of what God has revealed] as a union of sacred Tradition and sacred Scripture, which together "form a single sacred deposit of the word of God, entrusted to the Church."[3] God the Holy Spirit makes certain in every age and every place that this single sacred deposit of the Word of God is never corrupted nor ever lost. We are called to believe what the deposit contains implicitly, and this despite questions around the margins as to whether this or that teaching is within the deposit.

For example, it took us centuries to realize that charging interest on loans is not necessarily sinful. Charging interest on a loan has for centuries been called usury, although today some use the term to mean charging only excessive interest. If one simply looks up the word "usury" in a concordance of an older English translation of the Bible, one discovers the Old Testament is replete with condemnations of people who take interest on loans. Using a

---

3. Quotation is from the Vatican II document, *Dei Verbum*, section #10, in Tanner, *Decrees*. The sentence appears incomplete or corrupt in the original text of the homily. The bracketed phrase suggests a possible interpretation.

classic concordance for the Authorized Version (popularly known as King James), I found twenty-one negative references to the practice of usury. My favorite is in Psalm 15. This psalm answers the question the psalmist posed in its first verse: "O Lord, who may abide in your tent, / Who may dwell on your holy hill?" In the last verse of the psalm, the inspired author answered the question by saying that those "who do not lend money at interest" may dwell with God. The Authorized Version used the very word: "He that putteth not out his money to usury."

Remember that "the single sacred deposit of the word of God" includes the sacred Scriptures, although joined with sacred Tradition, which means among other things that the Scriptures must be rightly interpreted in order to reveal the "Word of God" to us. Faced with this question as to whether we were interpreting the sacred Scriptures correctly, we were puzzled by a New Testament mention of usury. Please read the parable found in the Gospel according to Saint Matthew (25:14–30) and the very similar parable in the Gospel according to Saint Luke (19:11–27). Note two almost identical verses (Matt 25:27 and Luke 19:23) and ask yourself if they endorse usury. Historically, answering this question was not the catalyst for our change of teaching regarding usury. The change came about as we, the merely human element of the Church, realized that money functioned differently in the modern economies we were creating from the way money functioned in the economies known by all whose writings are included in the Bible. The truth was the principle that lay under specifically prohibiting usury: namely, that it is sinful for anyone of us to exploit our fellow human beings for personal or corporate gain (i.e., treat persons unjustly in economic matters thereby increasing our own wealth), especially sinful when they are in need. Nevertheless, since not all interest on all loans is unjust, usury as such may not be condemned as sinful. [The teaching about usury provides a pristine example of what is called the development of doctrine.]

Unfortunately, I think there is a great deal of sin in our economy around interest rates, and I think our bankruptcy laws may well prompt God's wrath. The development of our doctrine with regard to the taking of interest or usury was not a license for economic injustice. The history of this development does illustrate how great is the challenge facing us as we assent without reservation to "the single sacred deposit of the word of God" while recognizing that those in authority in the Church as well as we ourselves face an enormous challenge of interpretation and application. On this Pentecost, we celebrate the truth that God the Holy Spirit is with us even in the doubtful areas, and that God will bring great good from our struggles. We must always remain honest, committed to God's Word and Church, open, and in good conscience. Then, God the Holy Spirit can work within us.

Postscript: A Note on Spirituality[4]

What popularly many call spirituality today usually is not faith. Some of what is called spirituality is quite good. For example, a parishioner described to me how he feels close to God when skiing on Mount Rainier and referred to this as spiritual. What he described can be quite good, and since the human spirit soars on such an occasion, one may call the experience spiritual. What it means to feel close to God on such occasions is less certain. For some, it may mean a combined feeling of how glorious our lives can be, and yet how fragile and mortal they are. Some skiing can be dangerous and remind the skier of his/her mortality. One feels close to God when such a reminder is in play. On the other hand, feeling close to God can consist in rejoicing in the wonder and beauty of his creation. And, there is an indefinite number of other possible meanings. Great and good as this, and like spiritual experiences are, they are not faith! Furthermore, they are no substitute for faith.

The centurion who as Saint Mark reported stood at the foot of the Cross on which Jesus died and said, "In truth this man was Son of God," probably was as fit and athletic as the parishioner who skies on Mount Rainier. The sport in which he exulted certainly was not skiing, but I'm confident that he too had a spiritual life in the sense that on special occasions his human spirit soared and he felt close to God. I hesitate to guess what the sport was. Furthermore, he might well have been a monotheist who explained the multiple gods of paganism as diverse manifestations of the divine, as Hinduism does. So, when his human spirit soared he too could feel close to God even in the sense our parishioner described. But, after he stood at the foot of the Cross, he knew that his previous spiritual experiences were not faith. They were good, but they were not what he discovered while at the foot of the Cross on which Jesus had just died. We need to make this distinction today when talking about spirituality.

Some of what is talked about as spirituality today is actually quite bad. There is no easy way to characterize phony or bad spirituality. The most common form I encounter rests on ignorance of specific systems of belief and how they differ. The person then blends the differing systems basing the blending on superficial similarities. This practice is referred to as syncretism. The result is a hodgepodge that initially seems to meet the blender's psychological needs. Over time, the blending usually breaks down. A great deal of bad syncretistic spirituality has been shaken by the manifestations of fundamentalism, especially in Islam. These manifestations have shaken the

---

4. The postscript complements the above discussion on the uniqueness of the Catholic faith. It is a postscript from Fr. Roach's homily on the Ascension from June 1, 2003 (not included in this volume).

assumptions of much bad spirituality. This observation notwithstanding, there really is no way to characterize bad spirituality. Its name is legion, and it most certainly is not faith.[5]

I repeat that much called spirituality today is quite good and, although not faith, it goes well with faith. On the other hand, faith founds a truly spiritual life in the precise sense that faith brings a life that lasts beyond death. I urge people to have as much good spirituality as they can, but never to cultivate it at the expense of growing in faith.

---

5. A passage from a sermon on the Epiphany from January 7 of 2007 (not in this volume) amplifies the point: "Phony ecumenism, which is quite distinct from authentic ecumenism, and secularism join in providing many with misplaced certainties. Phony ecumenism has come up with fuzzy ideas about inclusiveness. In one way or another, this phony ecumenism comes down to asserting that all religions are at base essentially the same and really equal one with the other. To arrive at this erroneous view, the phony ecumenists cherry pick from the belief systems of a wide variety of religions those ideas they like and add to what they have picked the popular convictions they already hold about what religion ought to be. Then, they regard the resulting mix as certain. From their personal certainty they think nothing of judging the Church, Christian faith in general, and all believers, especially clergy."

Chapter 16

Holy Trinity Sunday

(June 10, 2001)

Scripture Readings

Prov 8:1–4, 22–31; Ps 8; Rom 5:1–5; John 16:12–15.

Summary

The first line aptly summarizes: "The Catholic belief system flows from the interlocked doctrines of Creation, Incarnation, and Trinity." Each illuminates the others. The unity of the Trinity ensures that the Incarnation is unique. The love among the three persons points to the Incarnate Christ's love for us, which calls us to, in Fr. Roach's words, "join an eternal communion of equals in love" that is the life of the Trinity. Creation *ex nihilo* shows how remarkable and unique the Incarnation is, where, quoting him again, "God built a bridge uniting the divine, which is uncreated, with the human that is created." A concluding discussion of the Trinity reaffirms it as a central doctrine at once mysterious and magnificently inspiring. The last third of the sermon discusses our language for the Trinity. An addendum of selections from a homily on God's oneness complements the Trinitarian discussion. In these selections, Fr. Roach crucially notes that monotheism itself "says nothing about how God exists internally," and so makes way for God as triune.

Homily

THE CATHOLIC SYSTEM OF belief flows from the interlocked doctrines of Creation, Incarnation, and Trinity. The doctrine of the Trinity is the crown of this fountain of faith. In the Latin liturgy we set aside this first Sunday following Pentecost, otherwise a Sunday in Ordinary Time, to remind ourselves of this crowning belief. When I say that the Catholic system of belief "flows from" these interlocking doctrines, I am thinking first of a logical connection. Yet it also happens that the sequence—first Creation, then Incarnation, and then Trinity—is the historical sequence in God's revealing something of himself to us, as well as the logical sequence in the revelation.

In my opinion, setting aside a special Sunday to commemorate the Trinity is of special importance for us in the Latin rite of the Catholic Church, because our liturgy, in my opinion, is not sufficiently Trinitarian. The other rites of the Church—especially those that use the "Liturgy of Saint John Chrysostom"—emphasize the Trinity more effectively than we Latins do.

[Saint John Chrysostom (c.347–407) did not compose the liturgy, only honorifically attributed to him. The liturgy that bears his name was developed in his diocese. Our liturgy, on the other hand, is called the "Roman Liturgy" or, after the Second Vatican council, the *Novus Ordo* (new ordering) of the Latin Liturgy.]

I believe that the references to the Trinity in the prayers of the Latin rite are too muted. For example, few people who pray the Greater Doxology (i.e., the "Glory to God in the highest" or "Gloria") in the Latin rite, as we do every Sunday except in Advent and Lent, realize that the prayer concludes with a Trinitarian formula of words: "For you alone are the Holy One, you alone are the Lord, you alone are the Most High, Jesus Christ, with the Holy Spirit, in the glory of God the Father." If we take the pronoun "you" in the phrases "you alone" to refer to Jesus, we must understand two things: first, just as there is one and only one God, there can be one and only one God Incarnate, who is Jesus the Christ. Even God cannot multiply incarnations, precisely because there is one and only one God. Either Jesus is God Incarnate, or he is not. If he is God Incarnate, as I firmly believe he is, then he is unique just as and because the Creator is unique. Another so-called incarnation would mean either that there are many gods or that "god" is not the Creator and everything else a creature.

Someone might respond to what I've just written by saying, what about the Father becoming incarnate, and the Holy Spirit? This question would reveal that the person asking the question had not as yet grasped the unity of the Trinity. God became one of us as Jesus the Christ. And, it is God's Word who has become one of us as Jesus, but God's Word is God. The triune God is one and only one. We often make this point by saying that God is Trinity in Unity. So, if God the Father, or God the Holy Spirit, would have become one of us, there still could have been only one God with us, or God Incarnate. The unity of the Trinity is such that God becoming one of us could have united only one human nature to the divine nature. God is three in one. In the language of Latin theology, God is three persons in one divine nature. Human nature differs from divine nature. One cannot have three persons in one human nature. Each person requires a distinct human nature. Among us humans, human nature is multiplied; each person is another individual human nature. The divine nature, God's nature, cannot be multiplied. So, once God's Word, one nature with God his eternal Father, became human, the one and only God had become human. The Incarnation, therefore, is as unique as God himself.

We also could take the phrase "you alone" to mean that in this stanza of the "Gloria" we are addressing God without reference to persons. Either way, it is God we refer to as "alone" when we address God as "Jesus Christ, with the Holy Spirit, in the glory of God the Father."

So, one can understand the conclusion to the Greater Doxology as referring to Jesus Christ—i.e., Jesus "alone"—as divine. In this understanding, Jesus the Christ is alone as God and in the glory of the Father with the Holy Spirit, because he cannot be God other than as a member of the Trinity. My point is that the reference to the Trinity is so muted that many people miss it. One does not miss the references to the Trinity in the Liturgy of Saint John Chrysostom. We, therefore, need Trinity Sunday in a way that other rites of the Church do not.

The Catholic system of belief is a logical whole. If one gets a major part of the system wrong, one misunderstands the whole system, even if one repeats the words exactly. The most common misunderstandings begin with the doctrine of Creation. Yet, this is the doctrine that is the logical foundation of our faith. It is the doctrine that makes us monotheists. And, our identification of God as the Creator has led many scholars to classify Christianity as a (mono)theistic religion, usually along with Judaism and Islam, as distinct from, for example, Hinduism and Buddhism. (Hinduism and Buddhism have creation stories, but do not identify the divine exclusively as the Creator.) Of the three religions classified as theistic, I would argue that the Catholic Church is the oldest continuous organization—continuous meaning without a discontinuity or break in the organization that changed its character. The unbroken succession of bishops of Rome (i.e., the Popes who are successors to Saint Peter) is the sure sign of this continuity.

Because of the presence of the bishop of Rome, now called the Pope, from the beginning until now, the Catholic Church is older than all other forms of Christianity. The next oldest are the Orthodox churches, who at various times and in various ways broke with Saint Peter's successor. Protestantism is very recent. Luther and Calvin invented it in the sixteenth century.

Catholic faith, I believe, is even somewhat older than Rabbinic Judaism, which acquired its present form only sometime after the destruction of the Temple in AD 70. By this time, the Church was already underway with a successor to Saint Peter as bishop in Rome. Some would insist that the destruction of the Temple did not introduce a discontinuity in organized Judaism or its system of belief. I respectfully would disagree. Finally, many secular scholars would insist that one can prove nothing definitive about either Judaism or the Catholic Church until the second century. This is a strictly secular position that denies credibility to Church records if secular corroboration is lacking. The first secular corroborations of our existence are records of, or references to, the bloody persecutions the Roman Empire mounted against us. As one would expect from persecutors, they depict us in wildly distorted ways. For example, some persecutors thought our Eucharist was cannibalism. So, the secular record corroborates virtually nothing that was true about us except our existence. Using this exaggerated standard, the very existence of Jesus becomes at best doubtful. The third theistic religion is Islam, which Mohammed invented in the late sixth to early seventh century of the Christian era.

Every religion I know anything about has a creation story. But, only the three religious traditions classified as (mono)theistic identify God as the Creator, exclusively. "Exclusively" means that not only is God identified as the Creator, but also only the Creator is God. Creation stories found outside the major theistic religions might identify the Creator with the supreme divinity, although not always. But they do not insist that only the Creator and nothing else is divine. I would insist that Catholicism as a system of belief has the most developed exposition of the doctrine of Creation. We see all of reality divided into two parts—God who always was, is, and always will be; and everything else that God creates and sustains in existence. We protect the doctrine of God as exclusively the Creator from corruption by insisting that God created from nothing. [The sacrosanct formula for this protection of the doctrine of Creation is the Latin phrase, *creatio ex nihilo*.] Without this protection, it becomes possible to imagine two ultimate realities—God who creates and the stuff he used to create. Then, one can imagine that the stuff is a kind of second "god," whereas there is one and only one God upon whom everything else depends for its existence.

Thanks to our active imaginations, the phrase, *creatio ex nihilo*, can give rise to another misunderstanding. We can imagine the creation as an event in a temporal sequence: first there was nothing, and then God created, so something other than God began to exist. The difficulty of imagining "nothing, God creating, resulting then in something else existing" as a sequence lies in the fact that time measures only what God has created. Apart from creation there is no time. God is eternal. As a result of this truth, our imagination simply can't cope with creation. This is just one reason why we are not meant to read even our creation story in the Book of Genesis literally.

If we grasp the meaning of *creatio ex nihilo*, we can understand why there cannot be a conflict between science and our faith. Science can ask questions only about what happens in time. Scientists can push those questions back as far as possible, but they can't get out of time. Scientists can and do ask what factors in time bring about events, including the Big Bang, in time. When the question arises, is there something more than what we find in time? Science provides no method for putting the question or means for trying to answer it. In other words, science has no method for asking the question of classical philosophy and/or faith about creation—who outside of time makes what happens in time possible? So, to ask and answer this question, the scientist has to take off his hat as scientist, and become an ordinary person capable of asking the questions that lead to what we have classically called philosophy, and on to what we call faith. The question about the Creator outside of time arises because what happens in time can be explained only by something else that happens in time. Nothing in time can explain the whole, i.e., everything that happens in time, i.e., the very existence of what time can measure. So, we reasonably conclude that there is a Creator outside of time, whom we call God. Then, what God has revealed about himself and we believe with faith makes this all much more precise.

If one does not get it clear in one's mind that God is the Creator and only the Creator is God, then one understands nothing of Catholic faith! By the way, protecting this doctrine by insisting that God created from nothing began with one verse in a book in the Old Testament found in a book that the Protestants threw out of the Bible—2 Maccabees 7:28: "I implore you, my child, look at the earth and sky and everything in them, and consider how God made them out of what did not exist, and that human beings come into being in the same way."

If we have the doctrine of Creation clearly in our minds, we can appreciate the doctrine of the Incarnation. ("Incarnation" means that Jesus is God in the flesh.) If we do not appreciate that God is the Creator and only the Creator is God, then 'god' becoming human is not at all remarkable. In other religions, "gods" of this sort have allegedly been walking the earth from time immemorial. If we understand the doctrine of Creation, then the Incarnation is remarkable. For, in the person of the Creator's Word, Jesus, God built a bridge uniting the divine, which is uncreated, with the human that is created. For our part, as soon as we realized that Jesus the Christ was more than human, although he is perfectly human, and we heard him talk to God his Father, we knew that there was some kind of multiplicity in the one and only God. (Perhaps I should add that the human Jesus is united to the divine in the divine person or reality that God's Word is from all eternity. In the Incarnation, the human does not become divine; instead, the human is united inseparably to the divine in the person or individual reality that is God.)

The next and final step in understanding this multiplicity in God comes with Jesus promising to send the Spirit, as we commemorated he did last week by celebrating Pentecost. Without dividing God into three gods, we now know that the one and only God is triune. This strictly speaking is a mystery, but I hesitate to say this because few words used in expounding Catholic faith are as commonly misunderstood as "mystery." Please read and pray over Ephesians 1:3–14. The word "mystery" as it is meant in Catholic faith, appears there in the ninth verse: "God has let us know the mystery of his purpose, . . . " "Mystery" also is used with the same meaning in Romans 16:25, and again in Ephesians 3:3. (The concept was introduced into the Old Testament in the Book of Daniel, cf., 2:18.) Essentially, the concept means something that God knows and that we may know only if and when God tells us (revelation). Even when what God tells us is something that seems to be just about God, as in God revealing that God is triune, the information also clues us into what God intends or what his purposes are in our regard, which again we can know only if God tells us (revelation).

For us, mysteries are a challenge, because what God tells us usually gives rise to more questions than the ones the mystery (revelation) answers. For example, we now know that God is triune, but we don't know how. But, from knowing that God is triune (i.e., internally multiple), we know enough to grasp something of God's purposes in our regard. God's purpose expounded in the section of Ephesians that I've recommended you read and pray over is to bring everything in creation under the headship of Christ.

We may see many other purposes for us in God being triune. I think that nothing teaches us more about love than the doctrine of the Trinity. The three—Father, Son, and Holy Spirit—are equal as God. Yet, they are hierarchical as persons or individual realities. Their love rests on their equality, and is reciprocal. From this, we learn that true love is between equals, even if they have hierarchically related roles, and also is reciprocal, not one-sided.

We also learn that God's love for us and God's desire that we love God in return is not a needy love. God does not need our love. God eternally is fulfilling love. So, God's love for each of us is free (i.e., grace) over and above the love that God is. So, God has no "need" to win or earn our love in order to find fulfillment in love. From this, we learn that true love must be free, not coerced, not even manipulated.

Against this backdrop, we can understand what the sacred Scriptures say about Christ's love for us—"No one can have greater love than to lay down his life for his friends" (John 15:13). Jesus did not need to earn our love by doing something heroic for us, although he did do something heroic for us. He died for our sakes. So, gratitude is an essential part of our love for Jesus. But notice: his sacrifice (Passion, Death, and Resurrection) is our Thanksgiving (i.e., Eucharistic) Sacrifice to God the Father. (Synonyms: Eucharistic Sacrifice, Divine Liturgy, Mass.) As you hear these words, we are in the process of offering that sacrifice. Therefore, our gratitude actually is deeper than thanking Jesus for what he has done for us. The gratitude expressed in this sacrifice is simply the way God has given us to recognize that God is the source of our existence, and we are grateful for being. In Jesus, particularly in his sacrifice, we are reconciled to the source of our being, and this is further reason for gratitude. But, Jesus as our representative (remember he is human as well as divine) is our thanksgiving. It is he who truly recognizes the goodness of human existence as God created it, and he who restores what has been tarnished in our existence to its original goodness, if we just let him forgive our sins by accepting through repentance the mercy in his love for us. But, Jesus goes way beyond merely restoring the original goodness of human existence; he elevates it to a sharing in divine existence, which is eternal. Going beyond Job, who refused to curse God because of the evil in God's creation, Jesus, by overcoming all obstacles and rising from the dead, turns the original goodness into eternal joy. In the Eucharistic Sacrifice, we join with Jesus in thanking God the Creator of all not only for our existence, but also for eternal joy. If Jesus had not overcome what sin and death have done to human existence, I don't think that I could always thank God for my existence.

The language we use to speak about the triune God always is limited. At this time in our history, we are discovering limitations in our language that our forefathers and mothers in the faith never suspected. I cannot say how we will eventually handle these limitations, but on this Trinity Sunday I think we should at least look at some of them.

The language coming from the sacred Scriptures that we traditionally use for the triune God is problematic. "Father" and "Son" are used with a meaning they had in the human understanding of reproduction prior to modern science. People commonly understood human reproduction as similar to reproducing plants. For example, the oak tree (father) produced a seed (an acorn; by the way Latin for "seed" is semen) or "son", which even as an acorn was the whole oak tree in miniature. Then, the seed fell onto the ground. If the soil (i.e., the mother) was good, the acorn, which was the tree in miniature, grew into a mature tree. If people understand reproduction in this way, then "Father" and "Son" are appropriate metaphorical terms for referring to the first two persons of the Trinity, because the "Father", or source of divinity, begets the "Son", which replicates God's Being, as one oak tree replicating itself, i.e., as human beings understood reproduction, in which understanding the father was seen as "replicating" himself in his son. The mother contributed only nurturing soil.

Our theology always has recognized that the gender specific language is merely metaphorical. So, for example, Saint Thomas Aquinas spoke of the three persons of the Trinity as *ingenitus*, *genitus*, and *procedens* (ingenerated, generated, and proceeding). These theological terms are very helpful. God whom we address as "Father" is rightly seen as the Source of divinity. We bear in mind that there is one and only one divinity identified as the Creator. Then, this one and only one divine Being replicates his Being as reality generated. Finally, their Spirit of truth, justice and love, goes out from them as the third divine replication. As with God generating, so with the going out (*procedens*), the process is eternal. God always was, is, and will be triune.

Metaphors can help, if we admit they always are limited. I help myself think about the Trinity by thinking of God traditionally called the Father as the Author (source) and his Word, who became Jesus, as the autobiography God continuously writes in which he puts himself and through which he plans creation. Finally, I think of the Holy Spirit as the spirit emanating from the author and his autobiography, a spirit of truth, justice, and love. (I owe this metaphor either to G.K. Chesterton or Dorothy Leigh Sayers, or both.)

Saint Patrick tried a metaphor when he was converting the Irish. He used a cloverleaf—three in one. I'm not too fond of this metaphor, because the three parts of the leaf are not each the whole leaf, which they must be to fit the Trinity. This introduces a common problem today. In a search for language without the problems inherent in "Father–Son" some people come up with words that do not imply a relation between the terms. I have heard trendy people make the sign of the Cross, saying "In the name of the Creator, the Redeemer, and the Sanctifier." Very bad! Creator relates to creature; Redeemer to the redeemed; and Sanctifier to those who are sanctified. Creatures, the redeemed, and those sanctified are not God. In other words, all three terms, if used of God as in making the sign of the Cross, relate God to what is not God. The terms do not relate among themselves, as within one Being, so the three terms could be the names for three "gods." Therefore, the terms do not necessarily indicate the Trinity, which terms used in making the sign of the Cross should. The terms could indicate tritheism (the word for three god-ism). Furthermore, many religions have triads, either by giving three distinct names to God without implying a specific and limited multiplicity in the one and only one God who creates everything else that exists. Or, they have a triad that links three gods. Trinity is not a triad, nor does it mean tritheism. Trinity is unique in world religions.

The term "Son" presents problems of its own. When used of God's Word for all eternity, "Son" has the same limitations as "Father." There's no gender or sex in God. It seems less problematic when used of the Word become Incarnate as Jesus, because Jesus was male. But, could the Word Incarnate have been a daughter rather than a son? Given the time during which the Word of God chose to become one of us, the answer is No. As a woman, he could not have functioned as he did. Nevertheless, ultimately Our Lord's gender/sex makes no difference. Our principal creed guards this truth very carefully. Although the councils of Nicaea (AD 325) and Constantinople (AD 381) used the traditional language to denote God the Source as "Father" and the Word as the eternally begotten "Son" of God, when proclaiming the Incarnation they carefully used a word without gender–*anthropos*, which means an individual human of either sex. Unfortunately, we have no English equivalent for this term. We can use "man" with this gender free meaning, but "man" also means a male. So, our translation of the creed used at Mass can be misleading: "For us men (the plural of *anthropos*, so it should be translated "us humans") and for our salvation he (a separate pronoun is not found in the original, so the pronoun could be rendered "it") came down from heaven: by the power of the Holy Spirit he (again, no pronoun in the original) was born of the Virgin Mary, and became man (*anthropos*)." If the council fathers had wanted to point out Jesus's gender/sex, there is a perfectly good Greek word they could have used, a word that means a male human. The word is *aner*. They deliberately did not use it. What I've said here of the Greek original also is true of the official Latin translation. The Creed as presently translated misleads many. The Incarnate Lord is as closely identified with women as "he" is with men. The truth used to be so clear to people that the famous mystic of fourteenth century, the Lady Julian of Norwich, could speak of Jesus our Mother, as did other medieval saints. Catholics should bear this in mind as we wait upon the development of understanding, as well as developments in our language and translations. While waiting, we should work at understanding the language we presently use.

I feel that I've failed in this homily to do justice to the Trinity. In a final push, I'll simply testify to what the doctrine means to me. If God were not triune, I doubt that I would bother worshipping God. The triune nature of God teaches me that God does not want a master–slave relationship with me. Instead, he wants me to join an eternal communion of equals in love, whose union in love does not obliterate their unique individuality. I see in this communion to which I am called and which I celebrate at each Eucharistic Sacrifice a paradigm for my human relationships—union in equality with individuality. I also see that each person is a unique, everlasting reality in God's sight, and that each person belongs from conception until death to God and no other. As the Mother in Second Maccabees put it, "that human beings came into being in the same way" as the whole of creation (2 Macc 7:28). In other words, each of us is as unique and special as the whole of the universe. This changes how I feel about myself, and dictates that I respect others as well. I hope the Trinity inspires you as much, or even more, than this doctrine has inspired me.

Addendum[1]

The world's religions may be classified as one of the following "isms": polytheism—there are many beings called gods; pantheism—everything taken as a whole is god; panentheism (this is a technical term that Microsoft spell check has not as yet discovered)—god, whatever that is, is in everything, but might not be identified with the sum of everything, as many understand pantheism, nor may god be identified exactly with what the divine stuff is in; henotheism—as far as this people is concerned there is only one god, but there may be more gods for other people, although this people's god is the strongest; atheism—there is no god, but there is something "religious" or "spiritual" about human beings that they need to work on, and that some refer to as "god" without realizing there is no such being (some scholars think that Buddhism is atheistic; I agree); anti-theism—a conviction that people who believe there is a god, especially if they believe there is only one god, are dangerous, because they will do wicked things claiming that god told them to (anti-theism is acquiring followers rapidly); and finally, monotheism—there is one and only one God identified as the Creator of everything else that exists.

There is another term related to the preceding list, "agnosticism." Agnosticism used to mean not knowing that "God" exists while not denying

1. Augmenting the discussion of the Trinity here are brief selections from the homily for Sixth Sunday of Easter, May 16th, 2004, "What God-One-Ism (Monotheism) Means for Us" (not included in this volume).

that "God" may exist—in other words, an agnostic claimed not to know if any god existed, but an agnostic also claimed not to know that no god existed. (The word comes from the Greek for not knowing.) Being an agnostic meant that one was neither a believer nor an atheist. Among the older generation who are uncomfortable with the position identified as anti-theism, agnosticism substituted for anti-theism. So, being an agnostic came to imply that a person not only did not know if any "God" existed, but also implied that the person believed belonging to religious organizations is harmful.

One system of monotheism—One-God-Ism—treats the "one" simply as a numeral. Actually, "monos," which is the Greek word joined to the Greek word for "god" to form the term monotheism, means "one and only" or "unique." The word is not treated in Greek as a numeral and is not used in counting. The Greek word for "one," if we were counting, as in one, two, three, is "hen." Please look back to the beginning of this homily where I presented some vocabulary. Notice again, please, the word "henotheism." Scholars coined this word to say that the very ancient Hebrew people had one god (*hen theos*), but did not necessarily deny the existence of other gods for other people. These scholars theorize that Yahweh was the one god for the chosen people, but in very ancient times these people had not as yet recognized that Yahweh was the one and only God. They had not as yet recognized that the gods of other people did not exist.

Monotheism is the claim that there is one and only one God. A true monotheist denies that any god exists except the One and only God. To make this claim accurately, one must recognize that the one and only God is the Creator, who has created everything else that exists and sustains what has been created in existence. All reality either is the Creator or created. If we understand monotheism, we understand that monotheism says nothing about how God exists internally. We know that the one and only God exists, but not how God exists.

God clearly is one reality, because God created anything that is not-God. But, is God's oneness the same as our oneness as a single human being? If you or I, for example, have multiple personalities, we're crazy. And, evidently, no one of us is more than one person. I'm one being and one person, not one being and three persons. Of course, poetically, one might say he is a different person from the person he was thirty-years ago. We know that he's trying to say, but if he weren't one and the same person through it all, he wouldn't even know the difference he's referring to. But, is it necessarily true that the one and only God has to be only one person in order to be the one and only God? I think not! In fact, the one and only God is not one person; the one and only God is triune—i.e., three persons.

Chapter 17

Solemnity of the Transfiguration

Our Lord's Transfiguration and, We Hope, Ours (August 6, 2000)

Scripture Readings

Dan 7:9–14; Ps 97; 2 Pet 1:16–19; Mark 9:2–10.

Summary

Christ's transfiguration reveals the power of his divinity and its transforming effects on his humanity. Daniel prophesizes Christ's divinity, revealed in the transfiguration to strengthen the Apostles. Christ's transfiguration recalls us to who Jesus is as our law and teacher (prophet). It points to Christ's life within us that we must cultivate. Early Church references to Christ's manifestation of his divinity reigned in false speculation. We also need to guard against our false images of God.

Homily

"TRANSFIGURATION," AS WE USE the word in the sacred Scriptures and in our liturgy, denotes a metamorphosis—i.e., a radical change of form and appearance—in Jesus, that took place before Peter, James, and John, whereby they saw something of his otherwise invisible reality. They saw some transforming effects on his humanity of the power of his invisible divinity. Our Lord granted them this vision in order to strengthen them for the trials ahead. His Passion and Death on the Cross he knew would test their faith. His transfiguration before them was meant to help them face their testing. He was successful with one out of the three. John stood at the foot of his Cross. One out of three was not too bad. The account of the Transfiguration we hear this Sunday comes from the Gospel according to Saint Mark (9:2–10).

There are at least two other truths that Our Lord wished to teach with his transfiguration. Moses and Elijah joined them on the mountain in order to make clear by a mystical, symbolic action that Jesus is the fulfillment of the Law (Moses) and the Prophets (Elijah, although Moses, the lawgiver, was also a prophet). God the Father also used the moment to make clear that Jesus is his beloved, and that we are to listen to him. In these ways, God intended the Transfiguration not only to strengthen Our Lord's first disciples to face his Passion and Death, but also to teach us through the ages that Jesus is our law and our teacher (prophet).

The first reading from Daniel was chosen to open the liturgy of the Word for this Mass in order to remind us that this book from the Old Testament pointed prophetically to the truth that Our Lord is divine. The Book of Daniel is an apocalypse. "Apocalypse" means "uncovered" or "revealed." The writing is cryptic or coded and symbolic. The writing "reveals" something if the reader knows the code. Apocalyptic writings appeared when God's people were being persecuted. The writers encoded their messages, often using reports of mystical visions, so that the persecutors, if they found a copy, would not understand it. The Book of Daniel was written during the persecution of the chosen people that took place during the second century before the birth of Jesus. In our Old Testament, the Books of First and Second Maccabees provide excellent accounts of this persecution. Saint John used the Book of Daniel as a model for his apocalyptic writing, often called the Book of Revelation, which in the traditional way of compiling the writings of the New Testament appears as the last book in the Bible. Saint John wrote his apocalypse when the Roman Empire had begun to persecute Catholics and he was in prison. So, he encoded his message to his churches. The overarching message usually found in apocalyptic writings is: "Hang on! God will destroy the wicked and save the upright, even if it means ending the world."

The author of the Book of Daniel assured the people of his day that God would destroy the monarchs based in Syria who were persecuting them. God did. In the course of getting his message across, the author of Daniel reported a vision in which God seems to have a heavenly being with him who looks like one of us (i.e., a son of man, to use the Old Testament term used elsewhere simply to denote a human being). This "son of man" comes from heaven and is brought into the presence of God, described as the "Ancient of Days," or the "Ancient One," or the "one most venerable"—however translated, the image is meant to make us think of a wise old king on a throne. God then gives the heavenly "son of man" power to establish a kingdom that will never end. Jesus alluded to this vision whenever he used the term "son of man" to point to himself. He wished for people who heard him to begin to suspect that he was more than a mere man.

In addition to these truths of faith for the ages, the experience of the Transfiguration itself was intended not just for the first disciples to strengthen them for their coming trial; it is meant also for us in many ways. I have learned both from my pastoral work and from personal experience that it is easy for us to acquire toxic images of God. Sometimes children project onto God their painful experiences of authority. Even good parents, and not all are, inadvertently do a few things that their children perceive as arbitrary, painful, and/or unjust. Since we address God as "Father," it is easy for the child within us to project onto God the feelings associated with these memories. Simply irrational fear of punishment for wrongdoing—i.e., for sin—can cause some to imagine God as a kind of monster. These toxic images, no matter where they come from, often lie at the base of our consciousness and cause us discomfort when we try to pray. They very often are the reason persons refuse to go to church. God intends the Transfiguration as an antidote for these toxic images. He invites us whenever we are at Mass or praying in other ways to feel as Peter did when he said to Jesus: "Rabbi, it is good that we are here!" If anyone of us has difficulty saying with Peter to Jesus whenever we are at Mass or at any other prayer that "it is good that we are here," we should check to see if we have allowed toxicity to creep into our images of God. There are things one can do about toxic images of God. I, perhaps, can be of some help. I do say that we all must rid ourselves of this toxicity, or we will not pray as we ought.

Some toxicity in our imagining God is almost comic. Some imagine God and everything connected with the divine as incredibly boring. Boredom is toxic, but in a somewhat comic sense. If one imagines that God, knowledge of him, and prayer are boring, one just doesn't understand. As with other forms of toxicity, this ignorance can be overcome.

The Transfiguration also teaches us that, as we have been incorporated into the life of Jesus, there is something glorious about each one of us that usually lies hidden. We should cultivate an awareness of this glory within us, if we haven't chosen to throw it away, and we should look for opportunities to let it shine forth. The glory of the Lord's life within us will draw others to him. And, being aware of how glorious we are should console us and strengthen us always.

Our second reading comes from the pseudonymous Second Letter attributed to Saint Peter. As we know until quite recent times—beginning around early Modernity—pseudonymous writing was an established and accepted practice. It still exists in the sense of some authors choosing to use a pen name. In other ages and cultures, disciples or successors within a tradition who were furthering the tradition used the name of the originator when writing. So, for example, in the Old Testament, King Solomon never wrote the Wisdom of Solomon—it was written centuries after his death in his name (i.e., pseudonymously) as if he were writing it, because he was the founder or best representative of ancient Israel's tradition of wisdom. The Prophecy of Isaiah had at least three authors—the original prophet named Isaiah, and at least two successors who continued his work and wrote in his name. Saint Peter probably commissioned the first letter written in his name, and then after his death, still writing in his name as if he were doing the writing, a successor who was carrying on his work of teaching wrote the Second Letter of Saint Peter. It might even have been one of the first bishops of Rome (i.e., Popes) who succeeded Peter. This practice was accepted as quite legitimate—everyone understood it—and the Holy Spirit inspired the Second Letter, so the Church includes it in the canon.

The author of Second Peter wishes to correct misunderstandings of the *Parousia* that were disturbing some members of the Church. "*Parousia*" is a Greek word meaning "presence" or "arrival." The early Church used the term to denote Christ's second coming or the general judgment. The Church had barely been founded when a gaggle of fantastic heresies that historians lump together and call Gnosticism tried to make use of Catholic beliefs in their mythological speculations. Instead of viewing Christ's glory seen at the Transfiguration as a manifestation of the divinity of a real, but unique man, their speculations either denied that he really is human and/or falsified what it means that he also is God. In their fantastic speculations, "glory" would usually become something we should achieve by using their mythological speculations rather than an attribute of God that belongs by right to Jesus, and which he shares as a gift with us. They also indulged in weird speculations about what we call the Second Coming, the *Parousia*, which had the effect of denying the meaning of our history, which actually comes to its climax in the *Parousia*. These speculations discredited the truth revealed at the Transfiguration that will be revealed even more fully when Christ comes again. So, the inspired author of Second Peter, who knew the truth from the man who had been there, writes in his name to set the record straight, and to counteract the Gnostics.

A contemporary form of Gnosticism is Scientology. Many scholars, and I agree with them, judge that Mormonism is another form of Gnosticism. I would go even further and say that all of the religions invented in the United States in the nineteenth and twentieth-centuries, including Fundamentalism, either are fully Gnostic or have Gnostic elements. Fundamentalists vigorously deny that they are Gnostic in any way but their "fantastic" use of the Bible, I believe, is an element of Gnosticism. Their fantastic use of the Bible is popularly called literalism.

The antidote to Gnosticism is to know the truth about Christ and his glory, as the inspired author of Second Peter wants us to. We begin to know this truth when we begin to realize that as a member of the Body of Christ, his Church, God makes us also be his beloved.

Chapter 18

The Solemnity of the Assumption
(August 15, 1999)

Scripture Readings

Rev 11:19a, 12:1–6a, 10ab; Ps 45; 1 Cor 15: 20–27; Luke 1: 39–56.

Summary

Mary's Assumption teaches us about our own redemption. A lengthy opening section explains the Creationism controversy. In Mary, God restores humanity to its original integrity, and according to Fr. Roach "transformed the original creation into something more glorious than before sin." In Jesus, we are redeemed from that loss of our nature's integrity. This redemption sees God's creativity shine more gloriously than in the rest of the universe. Mary thus shows how redemption unfolds in the rest of us. Mary's fullness of grace means her passing from this life was unlike our dying. From this, we get the image of her taken into heaven. In Mary, God's grace is fully triumphant over all effects of sin. Her assumption points toward our share in the divine life awaiting the faithful.

Homily

BEFORE WE TURN TO the truth that this great solemnity commemorates, recent events have made it necessary to treat a serious matter of faith. The Board of Education of the State of Kansas recently removed the theory of evolution from the list of subjects the science classes of the public schools in the state are required to teach. Commentators and critics have said that removing this topic opens the classrooms to the teaching of what is called "Creationism." This apparently is the desire of those who brought about the change in the state's requirements. Whatever the details of this political act, the media have given the impression that what is called "Creationism" is what we call "the Doctrine of Creation," which we profess in the first line of all of our creeds. It is a matter of great importance, spiritually and politically, that all Catholics know that our belief is *not* creationism! Instead, "We believe in one God, the Father, the Almighty, maker of heaven and earth, of all that is, seen and unseen."

There is no authority formulating creationism, as there is with our doctrine, so I can cite no formula to sum up creationism, as I just cited our creed. Instead, creationism is usually characterized by a literal reading of the opening chapters of Genesis, despite the fact that these were not written to be taken literally. It also is characterized by a remarkable obscurantism with regard to the data showing that our universe developed over great lengths of time and space. Creationism has a long and sad history during this century in our country. Before the recent action in Kansas, the most memorable event in this history was the so-called "Monkey Trial" held during the summer of 1925 in Dayton, Tennessee. The trial also is known as the Scopes trial after the teacher who was charged with the crime of teaching evolution. [What I believe is far and away the best book about this trial is entitled *Summer of the Gods.*][1]

There are a number of reasons why all of this is important to us as Catholics. I have time to deal with only a few of these reasons. First, authentic Catholic faith is afraid of no truth, and in no way opposed to science. In the sixteenth century, this truth was nearly undone by a handful of clerics who, misled by the academic establishment, condemned Galileo. The Holy Spirit made sure that their stupid actions were not part of the infallible teaching of the Church. Nevertheless, they left behind the pernicious impression that science and faith were in conflict. To correct that impression in a definitive way, the present Pope, John Paul II, established a commission in 1981 to re-examine the entire history of this matter. The commission attributed the

---

1. Larson, *Summer.*

injustice done Galileo to the "subjective errors" of those who judged Galileo. Pope John Paul II made the commission's conclusion the official judgment of the Church on the matter. The Church is committed never to allow such an error to be made in her name again.

The doctrine of creation rests on the reasonable conclusion that our vast universe does not explain either its own existence or its evolving design. The doctrine does not assume that God merely started the universe; the doctrine, rather, implies that creation is on-going. Creation is a continuous process. God always is creating as long as something other than God exists. It is as a part of his on-going creation that God created each one of us.

What today we call science cannot discover God. It cannot ask the question, Does God exist? because as science it has no way to answer the question. In more formal terms, the question about God is beyond the scope of scientific methodology. This was true even in ancient science. Aristotle wrote a work on physics. Then he asked the question about God. That later work is called his metaphysics. "Meta" means after; the work about God came after physics.

One might use a corny example to understand what I'm saying. If something goes wrong with my car, I turn to [an] auto-mechanic and ask him to repair it. If something goes wrong with the great little poodle who serves as my vicious guard dog, I ask a veterinarian. I don't ask a Vet to repair my car, unless she happens also to be an auto-mechanic. Being an auto-mechanic and being a veterinarian are both self-limiting activities. Science also is in principle self-limiting.

A little less corny example may be the following: scientists report the discovery of a star. They tell us that the light they have identified as the new star has been traveling from its source for millions of years. Don't ask if the star, the source of the light, exists now. The question is meaningless to the scientists. They may reply by asking, whose *now* are we asking about? We have only our *now*. Only God can "know" both the now of the source of the light, the star itself, as well as the now of the observer, our now. And science cannot establish that there is such an observer anymore than a person working as an auto-mechanic can repair a dog. This does not mean that a person who is an auto-mechanic is limited only to what he or she can do as an auto-mechanic. No, a scientist can become more than a scientist and ask as a person if it is reasonable to believe that the universe explains itself. But, he or she asks that question as a believer or theologian or philosopher, not as a scientist.

In this way, evolution is related to our faith. A scientist as such can tell us as much as his science enables him to say about the development of our universe. As scientist, he or she cannot say whether it is created or not.

If a scientist, or anyone else, tries to answer a question that science cannot answer and make it look as if the answer is scientific, the result is called scientism. Scientism is phony. So is creationism. Creationism is the attempt to pass off a pseudo-scientific description of creation, wrongly attributed to the sacred Scriptures, as if it were part of faith. As Catholics, we want no part of scientism or creationism. We believe in the doctrine of creation, and praise God who is our on-going or continuing Creator. We're perfectly content to learn that he created a developing or evolving universe.

Before closing this topic, I must say something about the Bible and the doctrine of creation. A fully correct understanding of the doctrine does not appear in the written record of the history of faith, which we call the Bible or sacred Scriptures, until the second century before the coming of Jesus the Christ. The only mention in the Bible of this adequate understanding of the doctrine appears once: 2 Maccabees 7:28. Protestantism rejected this book; it is not included in their Bible. None of the earlier texts state *creatio ex nihilo* (creation from nothingness), as the correct doctrine is denoted. Yet, this is the only doctrine that is compatible with science. It simply affirms that God is the reason there is something, anything, rather than nothing. Causing everything to exist, to continue to exist, is what I called above the on-going creation, or the continuous process of creation.

The mythic ways in which the doctrine of creation is first expounded in the Bible still leads many to believe that creation consists of an action that took place, as it were, at the beginning. Even in the fourth/fifth-centuries, Saint Augustine could see that this idea wasn't right. He tried to correct it by saying that creation takes place with time (*cum tempore*), not in time (*in tempore*). "In time" would mean that God started it all with, for instance, the Big Bang; then, he doesn't act again until he starts something new, like life. "With time" means, for instance, that God is creating with the Big Bang, with everything that existed before the Big Bang, and in all of the developments that come after the Big Bang. One can easily see which understanding is more compatible with evolution. God always is creating when there is something rather than nothing. For this and other reasons, the correct affirmation of *creatio ex nihilo* in Second Maccabees is of singular importance. I hope all of this also helps people understand why I steer children away from Bible camps and Bible schools that are non-Catholic. I don't want our children told that the stories at the beginning of the Bible teach creationism.

By the way, we should be clear that the doctrine of creation tells us that God creates everything else that exists; it does not even hint at how he does it, except to affirm that he does it in his Word that became Jesus.

Our Solemnity today, the Assumption into heaven of the Blessed Virgin Mary, further honors God the Creator. First, we need to understand this doctrine. It was solemnly defined on the first of November, 1950, as follows: "the Immaculate Mother of God, Mary ever Virgin, when the course of her earthly life was finished, was taken up body and soul into the glory of heaven."[2] (In this definition which was written in Latin, *Deiparam* is the word translated into English as "Mother of God." *Deipara* literally renders the Greek, *Theotokos*, the term the third ecumenical council, AD 431, used to affirm that Mary gave birth to a person, not merely a body, and the person is God. *Theotokos* means God-bearer.) The words of this definition of the ancient belief could be as misleading and open to misunderstanding as the way in which the sacred Scriptures initially teach creation. The words of the definition seem only to paint a picture of the Blessed Virgin Mary sailing off into heaven. This picture is not what the doctrine means.

The doctrine affirms that in the Blessed Virgin Mary, God the Creator, who is person of Jesus the Son, not only had restored humanity to the original integrity in which he created us, but also transformed the original creation into something more glorious than before sin, shared this new creation with one of us, a woman who is merely human, not also divine. God had never withdrawn his creative power from us, or we would have ceased to exist; but, after sin, we have not in this life enjoyed his creativity to the fullest extent. In redeeming us through Jesus from our loss of integrity and justice, God reveals his creativity more gloriously than he does in the whole of the universe. But, in Jesus, the human and the divine are one person. So, it is in Mary that we can see how the redemption plays out in the rest of us who are only human.

In sum, then, we may say that in Jesus, God not only restored the fullness of created human existence, but enhanced it by offering us all a share in his uncreated existence. The first to accept his gift fully was his mother. Complete realization of this enhancement, this sharing in his life, does not begin for us who are only human until we leave this life. And, during this life we could freely refuse his merciful love, thereby rejecting a share in his divine life. So, he has given us in the person of the Blessed Virgin Mary an example of one from among us in whom Jesus's gift of divine life is fully and abundantly victorious. God did this to encourage us to join her.

Our brothers and sisters in the Eastern churches presently separated from Rome hold the same belief, but give it a different name. They call it the Dormition. They recognize that the grace of Jesus triumphed fully in his mother, so her passing from this life was different from our dying. Our dying is part of the misery that came into God's good creation with sin.

2. Fr. Roach is quoting from an English translation of *Munificentissimus Deus* (Latin for "The most bountiful God"), the Apostolic constitution of Pope Pius XII defining the dogma of the Assumption.

Her passing from this life was just going to sleep, which is what the word "Dormition" means. We both, despite the different way in which we state our belief, are affirming that in Mary the grace of Jesus the Christ is totally triumphant over sin and all of its effects. She is the pledge that our share awaits us, if we do not reject it.

We should rejoice in Our Lady in something like the way we rejoice in a great athlete's achievements. The great athlete enjoyed special gifts which he or she developed by working very hard. Mary enjoyed special gifts which she developed by working very hard. Sadly, some of us are tempted not to rejoice really, but to engage in a bit of resentment. "If I'd just had his body, I too could have been a great athlete." Resentment! Jealousy! Sour grapes? The equivalent with Our Lady is to think: "Well, if I'd been immaculately conceived and had given birth to Jesus the Christ, I too could sail into heaven." Resentment! Jealousy! Sour grapes? I wonder if anyone of us, if given the gifts she was given, could have been one half as compassionate as she was and still is. Her sanctity truly is an achievement, and I for one am convinced that I could never have made it. I could never have borne the suffering that her compassion entailed. So much for my resentment. I'll just admire and ask her to help me. I find great consolation in knowing that a woman who is just as human as I am, and most certainly not also God, has made it into an intimate sharing in God's own life. Awesome!

Another way we may state this truth is to say that in the person of Mary, the *Theotokos*, as the Council of Ephesus proclaimed her, the Church is fully and finally triumphant. This way of stating the truth also consoles me.

Finally, as the Immaculate Conception, Our Lady is the patron of the United States. Although we celebrate this solemnity on the 8th of December, the definition of the Assumption, as we saw above, refers to Our Lady as the Immaculate Conception. So, let's take this occasion to ask her to pray for our country. We need her prayers!

Chapter 19

All Saints Day and All Souls Day
Three Preparatory Notes[1]

What is a "holy day of obligation?"

One answer is that Wednesday, November 1st, the Solemnity of All Saints, is a holy day of obligation. The next day, November 2nd, which is All Souls' Day, is in some cultures referred to as "The Day of the Dead." November 2nd is not a holy day of obligation.

Of course, we need an answer for the question that tells us what the phrase "holy day of obligation" means. If we understand that God loves us freely, not from obligation; and if we understand that God saves us from evil, freely, and not from obligation, we then realize that we owe him a debt of gratitude. We offer him thanks through the sacrifice that in the person of Jesus God made on our behalf, i.e., through offering the Mass. (In other words, we discharge our debt of gratitude to God by participating in the Mass, in particular on Sundays and holy days of obligation.) If we appreciate the need to offer thanks as well as sacrifice for sins, then we will in effect be asking, "Rabbuni, let me see again!" (Mark 10:51).

---

1. The three notes precede the homily (not included in this volume) for Thirtieth Sunday of the Year, October 29, 2000. The notes seem an apt introduction to the included sermon for All Saints Day.

Homily

To help us fulfill our obligation, God first gave Moses the third commandment. Then, with the advent of the Church, the commandment became, Keep holy the Lord's Day. The Church, then, tried to set out for our welfare a minimum standard for fulfilling our obligation: participate in the Mass on all Sundays, which begin on Saturday evening, and on other special days, such as All Saints' Day, The Solemnity of the Immaculate Conception, Christmas, and so forth. It's really quite simple, although some seem to find it very hard to fulfill.

How do we gain an Indulgence for All Souls' Day?

An indulgence is an ancient spiritual expression of our human solidarity with pre-Christian roots in the Old Testament. By an indulgence, we through the Church avail ourselves of help from what Our Lord and his saints have achieved. By accessing these achievements, we can help ourselves do the penance we need. We can even access this help for those who are doing penance after death so that they can enter into God's eternal joy. This help is called an indulgence. If you do not understand what this practice means and how it developed, please first read Second Maccabees 12:38–45. This book from the Catholic Old Testament shows that our practice of praying for the dead, as we do on especially All Souls' Day, antedates the birth of Our Lord. The practice of praying for the dead came into existence as soon as God revealed that there would be a resurrection. After this piece of history is clear, please read sections #1471 through #1479 in the official *Catechism of the Catholic Church*.[2] An indulgence applied to the dead—the indulgence we can gain on All Souls' Day—amplifies our prayer for those who have gone before by adding to our prayer some of what the spiritual achievements, sacrifices, and other good works of the saints and of Our Lord have merited. It is a practical expression of our solidarity with those who have gone before.

All Hallows' Eve. (a.k.a.) Halloween

Please ask yourself and then ask a young person who is or should be in faith formation what it means to say: "Our Father who art in heaven; *hallowed* be thy name." If you get the right answer, you will be on your way to understanding, rightly, what "Halloween" means.

---

2. USCCB, *Catechism*.

The other name for All Saints' Day is All Hallows' Day. A hallowed person is one whom God has made holy, which is the same as made saintly. On the first of November, we celebrate in memory of all of the saints, but in particular those saints whose names do not occur on the list (canon) of recognized saints. (Canonization means adding a person's name to the list—i.e., the canon—of persons the Holy Spirit not only made holy, but also prompted the whole Church to recognize in the full public manner that comes with canonization, i.e., the adding of the person's name to the list.) All Saints' Day is the time to remember and to request the prayers of the innumerable saints whose names are not on the list and therefore are not widely known. All Saints' Day is an intense concentration of holiness (i.e., sanctity). Catholics who know that all wickedness has been ultimately defanged know that we can make fun of evil from within the security of the love of Our Lord. So, the evening before we celebrate the sum of holiness, we make fun of the evil God has conquered through Our Lord Jesus and in the lives of the saints. We turn evil into mischief and mock all creatures who have turned themselves over to evil, including mythic creatures who represent evil. This is Halloween.

Making fun of evil on Halloween replaced more than one European pagan celebration. These pagan gatherings usually celebrated witches (e.g., a gathering known as the witches' sabbath). Since entrance into organized witchcraft usually required ritualized sexual intercourse, debauchery was associated with the celebrations. These celebrations commonly took place the evening before the first of May. In Germany, the debauched celebrations were named after Saint Walburga (c. 710—c. 777/9) because people began celebrating on the evening of her feast. (In German, although she came from Dorset in England, her name is spelled Walpurgis and the night before her feast is called Walpurgisnacht.) She was a great nun of the eighth century. She also was a medical doctor, and her contributions to the missionary activities in Germany came to a climax when she became the abbess of a dual monastery. (A dual monastery is one in which the men are in one set of buildings and women in another. She was the head honcho over both.) The monastery still exists, although today I believe it is all women. It is an insult to her memory that her name is associated with witches' revelry. It is this kind of witches' revelry that the Catholic sense of humor tried to replace by mocking evil on All Hallows' Eve.

In my opinion, a parent should help a child understand what I've tried to explain and encourage a child to mock evil as something that has lost its hold over those who are living parts of the Body of Christ. At the same time, since there are many in our culture who are trying successfully to re-paganize the celebrations that take place on Halloween, it is advisable, I think, to alert the young person to the evil, especially debauchery, that he/she may find associated with this evening later in their lives. I mean nothing more than this: a young person in high school now may go on her own to college in a year or two. She should know before she goes that not all of the Halloween parties she might be invited to when she gets there will be innocent. A little suspicion and a little caution probably is all she needs.

We should all know that evil has been defanged in precisely this sense: Evil can have no hold over us except we allow it, if we avail ourselves of the power of Our Lord. By conquering death, Jesus the Christ has conquered evil. Evil cannot hold us forever. Death was evil's ultimate weapon, and Jesus has broken the weapon. Happy Halloween!

Chapter 20

All Saints Day

*O Many Witnesses in a Great Cloud Around Us
(November 1, 2007)*

Scripture Readings

Rev 7:2–4, 9–14; Ps 24; 1 John 3:1–3; Matt 5:1–12a.

Summary

Fr. Roach offers a succinct account of the feast. True witnesses for the faith suffer for Christ in one way or another. On All Saints Day, the Church recognizes the many saints who are not on the official list (canon). On this day, the Church celebrates the vast cloud of witnesses to the faith sharing in God's eternal life. We should strive to imitate them and ask them to pray for us.

Homily

RATHER THAN EXPOUNDING THE Scriptures assigned for this solemnity, I thought we might hear a homily about all the holy ones (all saints) found in the Letter to the Hebrews. Here it is: "With so many witnesses in a great cloud all around us, we too, then, should throw off everything that weighs us down and the sin that clings so closely, and with perseverance keep running in the race which lies ahead of us" (Heb 12:1). The great cloud of witnesses all around us are the saints. Remember that "martyr" means "witness." "Martyrs" is precisely the word the Greek original used, which here is translated "witnesses." All who truly witness to the faith are inevitably martyred, in one way or another, which should sadden no one of us seeking to be true to the faith because the reward is so unbelievably great. We may state this another way: all who adhere to the truth in this world of lies suffer, in one way or another. And those who are faithful to the truth and live the truth join the great cloud of witnesses.

Please remember that "sin" has many meanings. Actual sins are our personal sins, deliberate, free acts either of commission or omission for which we are responsible and which upon repenting we confess in the Sacrament of Penance and Reconciliation. "Sin" also names the dreadful situation in the world that the actual sins of countless numbers have brought about, and which, thanks to the Evil One, usually even exceeds the total of human sins. In the verse quoted in the preceding paragraph, "sin" first refers to the mess in our world.

The inspired author continues in Hebrews 12:2–4 [please see the text]. Those who in their fight against sin had to shed their blood, or suffer through other heroic acts, make up the great cloud of witnesses who surround us. They are our prayer chain each day of our lives, if we but call upon them. In addition to calling upon the Blessed Virgin Mary, I ask for the intercession of at least one other saint each day. I recommend the practice.

On this great day, the Church officially recognizes what we surely know: namely, the names of all the saints are not on the list (canon) of those we celebrate publicly. We simply do not know who all or how many are saints, but we are sure there're a great many more than those canonized (i.e., whose names appear on the list, which is the canon.) Each of us may know of someone we are reasonably sure is a saint. Today is the day to remember this person especially and in private ask for his or her prayers.

The first reading celebrates in cryptic, symbolic terms the vast cloud of witnesses assembled before God's throne (i.e., the saints sharing God's eternal life in praise and joy). We responded to this first reading with verses from Psalm 24. The third through the sixth verse offer an Old Testament description of those who are counted among the saints.

Our second reading consisted of three verses from the First Letter of Saint John. In my judgment, the reading begins in the wrong place. It should have started three lines earlier. Here it is, as I believe we ought to have heard it: "If you know that he (i.e., God) is upright / you must recognize that everyone whose life is upright / is a child of his" (1 John 2:29); this verse is essential to understanding everything Saint John wrote in this letter!

Our gospel for this great solemnity consisted of the Beatitudes from the Gospel according to Saint Matthew, with the last half of the twelfth verse omitted. The complete verse reads as follows: "Rejoice and be glad, for your reward is great in heaven; *this is how they persecuted the prophets before you.*" ([NJB] The omitted half of the verse is emphasized.) This omitted half of verse 12 tells us that those whom Jesus declared "blessed" bore the characteristics of the persecuted prophets, who are now all saints.

Repeatedly, I've urged our faith formation people to require, if possible, all our children to memorize the Beatitudes. They are listed, ready for memorizing, both in the *Compendium* of the *Catechism of the Catholic Church* in that section labeled "Formulas of Catholic Doctrine"; and they also are listed in the *United States Catholic Catechism for Adults*.[1] The Beatitudes are described briefly in the Glossary. Finally, the American version of the official catechism, just mentioned, virtually closes with this sentence: "In Part Three of this Catechism, we have learned how the Beatitudes and the Ten Commandments guide the consciences and lives of the members of the Church so that they make alive, in the midst of humanity, the power of God's love to transform society by the wisdom, compassion, justice, and fidelity that flow from God himself."[2]

We should know the Beatitudes and live by them so that we may join the great cloud of witnesses when our time comes. Meanwhile, I think it wise for us to call upon members of that cloud to pray for us.

---

1. USCCB, *Compendium*; USCCB, *Catechism for Adults*.
2. USCCB, *Catechism for Adults*, 500.

Chapter 21

All Souls Day

Life After Death (November 2, 2003)

Scripture Readings

Wis 3:1–9; Ps 23; Rom 5:5–11; John 11:17–27.

Summary

The homily explains intercessory prayer for the dead. It does so by examining Christ's death for us and his offer of resurrected life. Christ dying for our sins does not mean Christ took our place in receiving retributive punishment from God, and that we somehow get off, in Fr. Roach's words, "scot-free if only we have faith." To say Jesus "justified us by his death" (in Saint Paul's words) means that in dying Christ teaches and enables us to act justly toward God. Being just toward God requires giving him what is due, particularly gratitude for his mercy. Salvation is our receiving a share in Christ's resurrected life and the life of the Trinity. But before that, we may justly be asked to complete penance after death (Purgatory). However, God can forgive deserved penance, and this forgiveness may happen through another's intercession. This is why on All Souls Day, we pray for the dead who need our intercessory prayers.

Homily

*I*N MY JUDGMENT, THE reading from the Book of Wisdom (3:1–9; a.k.a., The Wisdom of Solomon) says most of what needs to be said on this solemn day: " . . . the souls of the *upright* are in the hands of God, / and no torment can touch them" (Wis 3:1; emphasis added.) Neither this reading nor any other part of our faith offers the slightest consolation regarding life after death to those who are not upright and remain unrepentant.

Since few, if any, of us are fully upright, we may take consolation in what Jesus has done for us as reported in the second reading: e.g., "So it is proof of God's own love for us, that Christ died for us while we were still sinners" (Rom 5:8).

As members of this parish have heard repeatedly, no statement in the New Testament gets more profoundly misinterpreted than "Christ died for us." I refuse to try again to explain the penal theory of atonement,[1] which says that Jesus took the rap for us, enduring God's punishment that should have been ours, and let us off scot-free if we have only faith: "How much more can we be sure, therefore, that, now that we have been justified by his death, we shall be saved through him from the retribution of God." (Rom 5:9) [In this reading what I've referred to as the consequence of sin was translated in the NJB as "the retribution of God"; many other translations use the word "wrath" rather than "retribution."]

In truth, Jesus died for us in the specific sense that he died on account of our sins. Suffering the consequence of our sins, which in our Lord's case consisted of torture and judicial murder. Jesus suffered in an intense way the universal consequence of sin, i.e., death. But, he did not suffer this universal consequence of sin as a punishment. God punishes only the guilty; Jesus was completely innocent. The fact that the consequence of sin, in general, as well as specific sins profoundly affects those who have not sinned reveals human solidarity. We are one human family. On the positive side, our solidarity enabled Jesus, having joined our family, to save us. On the painful side, our solidarity means that the consequences of sin affect us all, the innocent as well as the guilty, simply because we are all human. And the bad effects of sin in this life are not distributed as just retribution for specific wrongs done. Yet, again on the bright side, Jesus conquered the principal, universal consequence of sin, which is death, by rising from the dead; and it is possible for us to share in his victory over death because of the human

---

1. Fr. Roach offers a broad, non-technical summary here of what is often called the penal substitution theory of atonement. Those further interested may consult scholarly sources on theories of atonement.

solidarity whereby we share willy-nilly in the consequences of sin, including the ultimate consequence, which is death.

"Justification" is a word that mystifies most people in our day. It probably always has. When Saint Paul wrote, as quoted above, that Jesus "justified us by his death," he was saying that through his sacrifice Jesus both taught us how to act justly toward God and *enabled* us so to act. The word "justification" and related terms come into our language via Latin from the Greek. The root meaning at the source of the word is "to act justly towards." A person who has been justified is a person whose sins have been forgiven and who, *enabled by Christ*, can now act justly towards God. The most basic just act—i.e., doing what God deserves from us—consists of gratitude, especially for God's mercy. This is why we assemble at least once a week to unite ourselves to our Lord's sacrifice really remembered, which has become our Thanksgiving sacrifice and which we call the Mass. Failure to thank God results in the loss of justification. Thanking God is not incompatible with struggle, questioning, incomprehensible suffering and pain, as well as many other things we do not see as blessings, except as we receive the grace to appreciate the Beatitudes (Matt 5:1–12). Through it all we are thankful for God's mercy, or all would be lost for us.

Saint Paul went on to say, "For if, while we were enemies, we were reconciled to God through the death of his Son, how much more can we be sure that, being now reconciled, we shall be saved by his life. What is more, we are filled with exultant trust in God, through our Lord Jesus Christ, through whom we have already gained our reconciliation" (Rom 5:10–11). Note well! Saint Paul said that "we shall be saved by his life."

Salvation consists in sharing Christ's life, which is eternal. He shared our life; now he offers us a share in his life. But, a share goes only to those who accept and practice what Saint Paul preached as "the obedience of faith" (cf. Rom 1:5 and 16:26). By this obedience and only this obedience, we give God what he deserves. No other obedience counts, except it somehow is the obedience of faith. (Some obedience not to God is evil.) With the obedience of faith, we thereby respond to God's abundant mercy with love and trust. And, by being obedient to God, we share his mercy with our fellow human beings.

The gospel is the middle section of Saint John's report of Jesus raising his friend, Lazarus, from the dead. This raising was resuscitation, not resurrection. Lazarus had again to die, finally, before his resurrection in the Lord. Nevertheless, this raising from the dead predicted our Lord's resurrection, and revealed his power to rise. So, in replying to Lazarus's sister, Martha, Jesus said, "I am the resurrection and the life. Those who believe in me, even though they die, will live, and everyone who lives and believes in me will never die" (John 11:25-26 NRSV-CE).

[I've used the New Revised Standard Version in this quotation because the *New Jerusalem Bible* follows a different manuscript tradition, which sees the words "and the life" that follow the word "resurrection" as a redundancy a scribe added to repeat the meaning of "resurrection. Nevertheless, since "and the life" has been so frequently heard, I thought it best to use the more traditional translation.]

Life after death, if it is something to look forward to, is a share in our Lord's resurrected life. What the final alternative is, we really do not understand, except to say it is horrible. If we are destined to share fully in our Lord's life, and we leave this life without finishing the penance God justly asks of us, we are enabled to finish this penance after death. Somewhere around the twelfth century, Catholics using Latin began to refer to penance done after death as Purgatory. The other linguistic branches of the Church avoid this word. I blame Dante for making it a fixed term. But, a word should not distract us from the truth.

From before the founding of the Church, around the time God made it clear to his chosen people that there would be a resurrection, believers began praying for the dead. The Second Book of Maccabees, from the second century before Christ and written in part to attest to the truth that resurrection was coming, witnesses to the practice of praying for the dead who died with pardonable (venial) sins on their consciences (cf. 2 Macc 12:38-45). Praying for the dead implies that some of the dead can benefit from our prayers. Those who fully share our Lord's life need no help from us; so, we don't pray for the saints. Instead, we ask them to pray for us. But those who weren't fully upright (i.e., were not yet saints) when they died may still need our prayers as they work out their penances after dying. On All Saints' Day (a.k.a., All Hallows' Day) we remembered all the saints, known and unknown, and asked them to pray for us. Today, All Souls' Day, we pray for those who can still benefit from our prayers because they need our help doing their penances.

Note in the gospel how Saint John reports what Jesus said: " . . . and everyone who lives and believes in me will never die" (John 11:26 [NRSV-CE]). The word order, "lives and believes," implies that believing shapes our living, in the sense that we live in order to believe. If what we believe does not shape our living, what we believe is a dead act; or in the words Saint James used, "As a body without a spirit is dead, so is faith without deeds" (Jas 2:26 NJB). "For just as the body without the spirit is dead, so faith without works is also dead" (Jas 2:26 NRSV-CE). Or, if Saint Paul were writing, instead of "lives and believes" the sentence would say something about the failure to obey in faith, or an absence of "the obedience of faith." No matter whose terminology, our Lord clearly taught that we have something to fulfill in this life. We don't even want to talk about what it means to fail to fulfill our task of believing completely. We have various names for complete failure. One is "mortal sin." "Mortal" means deadly. Praise God that until our last breath forgiveness is available, if we but repent! But, receiving God's forgiveness may still mean we have a lot to do.

Some might find what follows to be a very crude example or analogy, but I can think of none more exact. The example compares God's retribution upon deadly sin to a court sentencing a criminal to death. When we really sin mortally, God's punishment is like the death penalty. (When following this example, do not dwell on trivial or easily forgiven sins. Especially don't dwell on sexual sins in which no one was hurt, although there are plenty of such sins in which people are badly hurt. Think instead of sins in which people are really hurt and especially think of real injustice and killing.) Then, after receiving our sentence of death, we repent and seek forgiveness for our sins through the Sacrament of Penance. Through the sacrament God truly forgives us, completely! By forgiving us, God commutes our death penalty to life, but the life to which our sentence has been commuted requires that we perform the penance our sin deserves, just as a court that commutes a death sentence to life in prison thereby substitutes imprisonment for the barbaric death penalty of our criminal law. After forgiveness, we are obliged to do our penance—i.e., serve the life sentence—here or hereafter. It's much harder hereafter, so I for one will be very grateful if people will please pray for me when I die. I doubt very much that I've yet done all the penance my sins deserve.

When the founders of Protestantism rejected the notion of penance—and they all did, denying that "confession" was a sacrament—they called God's justice into question. For those who were "saved," justice was severed from mercy. A person received either mercy or justice (i.e., salvation or damnation), not both. They believed that faith took care of all matters of justice. On the other hand, historic Christianity, which is preserved in the Catholic Church, remembers that God is as just as God is merciful. The two, justice and mercy, are one in God. Therefore, we are not surprised by a complication in "being saved." The complication is the penance we may owe God.

Yet, we are also aware that God's mercy is so overwhelming that God can and does forgive the penance we owe, as a very wealthy person may forgive the debt someone owes him/her. And, just as God grants forgiveness through a sacrament, which we call the Sacrament of Penance or Reconciliation, so God also uses his Church, although God is not constrained to using only his Church in granting additional forgiveness from deserved penance. We call applying for this additional forgiveness an indulgence. All Catholics, of course, know how to apply for an indulgence. At the end of this homily, I will print the specifics for obtaining indulgences for the dead who may need our help at this time of year.[2] These indulgences function as powerful intercessory prayers. We no longer follow the example set in Second Maccabees (12:38–45), which involved taking up a collection because of the perceived abuses in the late fifteenth, early sixteenth centuries stemming from the practice. These perceptions, more than actual abuses, occasioned some of the early successes of the Protestant movement. At the ecumenical Council of Trent in the sixteenth century, we abolished all use of donations or collections with reference to indulgences and restricted indulgenced acts to prayers, pilgrimages, and the like. The directions found at the end of this homily describe the prayers, and so forth, as a "work."

The practice of indulgences and praying for the dead powerfully express human solidarity. Because of human solidarity, God grants his graces always through some form of intercession whereby we show our solidarity one with the other. (This is just another reason why we are obliged to assemble for some essential prayers.) We ask the saints to pray for us, especially the Blessed Virgin Mary. We look to the protection of angels. We recognize as above these saints and angels, our Lord as human interceding on our behalf with his Father, our God, especially through the Eucharistic sacrifice. And, we pray for our brothers and sisters who are dead and not as yet fully sainted. Finally, we pray for each other in this life. It is a sadness of our day that some make praying for each other in this life, which is the last on this list of prayerful expressions of solidarity, into the only expression of human solidarity. Doing so gravely weakens the full sense of our true solidarity.

All Souls' Day, therefore, is not only a day to pray for our dead who may still need our prayers, but it also is a day to reflect on the penance God may deserve from each of us.

---

2. The following passages were printed after the homily, from the *Enchiridion of Indulgences* that came out of the Second Vatican Council: "The faithful who devoutly visit a cemetery and pray even mentally for the dead are granted an indulgence applicable only to the souls in Purgatory—plenary from November 1 to 8, partial on other days of the Year (#13). On the day on which the Commemoration of the Faithful Departed is celebrated (i.e., All Souls' Day) or, with the consent of the Ordinary, on the preceding or following Sunday, or on All Saints, in all churches, public oratories, and for those who legitimately use them, semipublic oratories, a plenary indulgence may be gained, applicable only to the dead. The work prescribed for gaining this indulgence is a devout visit to a church, during which the Lord's Prayer and the Creed are recited, together with sacramental confession, Eucharistic Communion, and prayer for the intentions of the Pope (#67)."

Chapter 22

The Solemnity of Christ the King
The Meaning of Christ's Kingship
(November 26, 2000)

Scripture Readings

Dan 7:13–14; Ps 93; Rev 1:5–8; John 18:33b–37.

Summary

Understanding Christ's authority and kingship point to how we are saved, and how the faith views authority in the secular order. Christ the King means that Christ embodies and rules his Church as a king does his nation. Christ invites us to share in his divine life and ultimately to be citizens of his Heavenly Kingdom. Our life joined to God's does not mean that our individuality disappears. In God, we fully become who we are as persons. Christ as King also calls us to recognize God as above and behind all legitimate authority. This guards against illegitimate authority or idolatry of merely human causes, as Fr. Roach holds, "We should invest in good causes but never make them our idols" as if they could fulfill our deepest needs. Baptism grants us a share in our Lord as priest, prophet, and king—to worship and witness Christ as God-with-us. Christ as King gives us the truth. The First Part of this volume appropriately ends with Fr. Roach urging us to seek the truth in a spirit of gratitude and penance.

Homily

As we know, this Sunday is the last o+f the liturgical year. Next Sunday, our liturgical cycle begins again with the First Sunday of Advent. Advent prepares us anew for Our Savior coming to us. This, obviously, is the right way to begin our year's liturgical commemoration of Our Lord. The question before us today is why we close the year celebrating his kingship.

I fear that the significance of Our Savior as our king is largely lost on us, because we live in a democratic republic. Perhaps the British, because they have a monarch, Queen Elizabeth II, understand this solemnity more easily than we; but, perhaps not! A monarch represents his/her people in ways an elected official, like a president, does not. The monarch embodies the spirit of the nation. He/she is the people or nation in person. In the early sixteenth century, King Henry VIII, a merely human embodiment of England, declared himself the head of the Church. Thus began the ecclesial organization that in England calls itself the Church of England, and since our Revolutionary War calls itself here in the U.S. the Protestant Episcopal Church of the U.S. There are few things that I am absolutely certain about. One of them is that Henry VIII never embodied the Church. Sorry, Henry! But the Church has only one King, and we are celebrating him today. (In British law the monarch, Queen Elizabeth II, is still head of the Anglican Church, which is separated from Rome. This establishment requires placing the state over the church.) The Catholic Church can never accept state control.

The concept that is hard for us Americans to grasp is a person embodying a greater reality. A king (or queen, if reigning) embodies the state, the nation, the people. The infamous King Louis XIV of France famously said, "*l'état, c'est moi!*" (*the state, it is I!*) Many have thought this a declaration of great arrogance. I don't think it was. The king simply said that he embodied the state. What he said means "I am France in person." Louis may have been, and probably was, an arrogant son-of-a-gun. Nevertheless, this is how kings were understood. I think that, at least in principle, Queen Elizabeth II, a reigning queen, still is understood this way. She personifies Great Britain.

Do you think our presidents embody the United States? I don't. I think of them as our most important elected official, but not as the embodiment of America. Those who think of them as the embodiment of the U.S. have proposed that we call the solemnity we are celebrating this Sunday, The Solemnity of Christ the President. It doesn't work for me. So, for me, the challenge remains to recapture the feeling of seeing someone as embodying in his/her person who I am as a citizen, so that I may better appreciate what it means to call my Savior, Jesus, my King. So, I can see in Jesus who I am as a child of God, a citizen of heaven.

This vision expresses the truth that for our lives to be fulfilled we must mingle with the life that is Jesus Our Lord. For one of Our Lord's ancestors during, for example, the reign of King David, the man or woman felt that his or her life was intertwined with the life of the King. He embodied the nation. In turn, since ancient Israel was a theocracy, the person felt his or her life was thereby joined to God's life. In Jesus the Christ, if our lives are mingled with his, we are truly joined to God's life. It is to this end that we are active members of his Church and worship together as his people. This intertwining of lives is what participation means. It is this participation that enables us to realize who we really are.

We citizens of the United States are so individualistic that we have great difficulty feeling real participation at all. We sense that we are unique persons, but we do not have strong feelings that our being real persons requires that we participate in what is greater than ourselves. Yet, God made us for this participation. We fail to be who we really are if we do not participate. As I've said repeatedly, this is why we are worshipping as a people in his Church rather than just as individuals in our homes. If we worship only as individuals, never as a people, we never become who we really are—the persons God created us to become!

This need to participate is so much a part of us that Jesus spent most of his public life calling his Church into being. This was for our benefit. The Church as locus for participation saves us from idolatrous participation in organizations that by their nature cannot meet our deepest need—e.g., political movements or causes, self-defined and sometimes enclosed community organizations, and the like. Our recent history provides us with many examples of people engaged in idolatrous participation—for example, during the Great Depression many people of good will joined a communist party under Soviet domination, only to find that they had submitted themselves to a monster, i.e., an idol. Some people of good will thought they could "participate" in Nazism, innocently. They became monstrous idolaters. Less seriously, some people in our country throw themselves into causes—defend the environment, find a cure for breast cancer, whatever—as if the cause can save them. We should invest ourselves in good causes, but never make them into our idols. Primary investment in the Church saves us from treating merely human movements as if they were divine. By this primary investment, we recognize Jesus the Christ as our King.

Until I did some serious thinking for this homily, at baptisms I have inadequately described our participation in Our Lord's kingship. I'd like to remedy that now. When we are baptized, we take on a share in Our Lord's three offices (duties)—priest, prophet, and king. In confirmation, we receive strength to carry out these roles. We share in his priesthood by prayer and sacrifice, in particular, by joining with the rest of his Church in prayer at the Eucharistic Sacrifice on the Lord's Day. We share in his work as a prophet by witnessing to the truth all through our lives. When speaking of our sharing in his kingship, I used to address only the truth that we are called to exercise authority as he would. This is true, but not the only point of sharing in Our Lord's role as King. We share in his kingship by embodying all through our lives the truth that he is—namely, God-with-us. So, you and I are called to live so that we extend the Incarnation. God, by coming in the flesh, which is what the word "Incarnation" means, became one of us—God present in our midst, in our history, in the world he created. We are commissioned by our baptism into Christ, and by our Confirmation to continue his presence in our world. A British person makes his/her queen present by his attitude toward her—for example, a man bows and a woman curtsies. An American may make his/her nation present by, for example, wearing a flag pin or showing patriotic devotion or saluting the flag. These are pale and paltry metaphors for what we as Catholics are called to do in order to continue the presence in our midst of Christ our King! We are called to live a life animated by Our Lord's spirit, the Holy Spirit. So whether others recognize it or not, in meeting us they can in some measure meet Jesus our King.

Our two readings and gospel for this Sunday confirm that Our Lord is our King! The first reading uses an expression that Our Lord used to designate himself—Son of Man. The expression is common in other writings in the Old Testament, but in the other places it means simply "man," as in common American jargon, "Hey, man!" But, as used in Daniel, the expression designates one like a "Son of Man" who is a heavenly being (Dan 7:13b). This is as close as one can come to an expression in the Old Testament that describes Our Lord—true God and true man in one person. So, Our Lord used it. By using it, Our Lord invited his disciples to think and pray, perhaps thereby to begin to realize that he was more than a mere man.

The passage in Daniel also provides images that help us distinguish imaginatively between Father and Son or Word in the Trinity. Finally, the passage proclaims that God the Father makes the "Son of Man" king of the world.

Our second reading teaches us that our Resurrected Lord is "the ruler of the kings of the earth" (Rev 1:5 [NRSV-CE]).[1] The NJB translates this phrase as *"the highest of earthly kings."* I think that the phrase "king of kings" captures the point. Our Lord is the king we are called to see behind and

---

1. Fr. Roach explains below his favoring the NRSV-CE for this homily.

above all legitimate kingship—i.e., all legitimate uses of authority and the symbols of peoplehood. If we see him "behind and above" all legitimate kingship, we accomplish two things: first, we avoid making something merely human into an idol; second, we have criteria to distinguish between legitimate and illegitimate authority. This is why totalitarian states hate us Catholics.

We are called to participate in his kingship, because he has forgiven us our sins: "To him who loves us and freed us from our sins by his blood and made us to be a kingdom, priests serving his God and Father, to him be glory and dominion for ever and ever. Amen" (Rev 1:5c–6 [NRSV-CE]). You and I are priests, prophets, and kings. Remember?

"The Revelation to John" (Rev 1:5–8) also reminds us that Jesus will come again in glory. This is something we can look forward to, as long as we are not among those who deliberately ignored him when he first came.

Finally, "'I am the Alpha and the Omega,' says the Lord God, who is, who was, and who is to come, the Almighty" (Rev 1:8 [NRSV-CE]). Alpha and Omega are the first and last letters of the Greek alphabet. Our Lord is saying that he is both the beginning and the end, which means that he is eternal, i.e., God. These symbols are emblazoned on our Book of the Gospels. In case we missed the significance of the Greek letters, the eternal Lord is described as one "who is and who was and who is to come"—an excellent way to describe being eternal. Finally, just in case, the text says simply that he is "the Almighty." John makes the same point in three ways, all in the eighth verse.

Our gospel records a famous exchange between Pilate and Jesus, in which Jesus acknowledges that he is king (John 18:33b–37). At the time, Our Lord is suffering and about to be crucified. He stands before the man who sends him to his death. He says: "My kingdom is not *from* this world. If my kingdom were *from* this world, my followers would be fighting to keep me from being handed over to the Jews (i.e., Judean authorities). But as it is, my kingdom is not *from* here" (John 18:36 NRSV-CE; emphasis added). Many are familiar with translations that render the underlined preposition not "from" but "of." The translation chosen by the NRSV is better, and takes us back to the imagery in our reading from Daniel. Jesus the Christ, our King, is not from this world; he came into this world from God, and became part of this world. Still, he is not from this world; he is directly from God.

Pilate was not satisfied with the answer, and demanded that Jesus be more specific. He asked: "'So you are a king?' Jesus answered: 'You say that I am a king. For this I was born, and for this I came into the world, to testify to the truth. Everyone who belongs to the truth listens to my voice'" (John 18:37). Jesus the Christ was born a king to testify to the truth! One cannot follow Jesus the king and live lies! Anyone who claims to follow Jesus the Christ does so if and only if he/she seeks the truth, wherever it may be found. The Truth! Pilate typifies those who reject Our Lord. He feigned skepticism and asked: "What is truth?" (John 18:38). Every hypocrite who has turned his/her back on Jesus and his Church has pulled this stunt in one way or another. They have denied the truth, the ability to know the truth, or have refused to seek it out, or whatever. This question is the skeptic's dodge: "What is truth?" as if there were no answer. We should all kneel and thank God for letting us know the answer—Jesus the King is Truth in person. I said kneel because we should thank God penitentially, since I doubt that any one of us has sought the Truth and lived it quite as well as we might have.

Part II

Thematic Homilies

Chapter 23

Catholic Ecclesiology and Authority
Fourth Sunday on Ordinary Time Authority
(January 29, 2006)

Scripture Readings

Deut 18:15–20; Ps 95; 1 Cor 7:32–35; Mark 1:21–28.

Summary

The thematic homilies elaborate key points seen in the solemnities and feasts. This first one examines the nature of the Church's authority and guidance by the Holy Spirit. It thus augments discussion in the preceding homily for Christ the King. Mark underscores Christ's divine authority. Fr. Roach refers his audience to some prayers and teachings "that express God's authority entrusted to the Church." Faith is a free act. So, we are called to be discerning about which teaching is authoritative, and which authority legitimately comes from God. Seeking guidance from God through the Church contrasts with the modern tendency to regard the self as the sole authority in religious matters. The latter brings to an end anything resembling faith.

Homily

THE GOSPEL FOR THIS Sunday says it all. If God exists, as the Creator manifestly does, and if God has revealed himself, as the Creator has revealed himself by God's Word becoming one of us in Jesus (the Incarnation), then the principal question for anyone who responds to God is, who speaks for God? Who speaks with God's Authority? No one has the faith Jesus the Christ asks us to have until one recognizes this Authority and submits. For this reason I can state, as I did in the opening sentence, that today's gospel says it all.

Jesus joined in a synagogue in Capernaum on the Sabbath. According to Saint Mark, this would be the first Sabbath after Jesus began to teach. Capernaum is a village on the north shore of the Sea of Galilee, which really is a lake. Jesus made this village his base from which he launched his teaching in Galilee.

The word "synagogue" comes from a Greek word for an assembly. The term for our Church—*ekklesia*, *ecclesia*, Greek and Latin—is another Greek word for an assembly. Our original term for the Church, *ecclesia*, comes from the Greek for "being called out" into an assembly, and synagogue also comes from a Greek term meaning "being led out" to assemble. Hardly a big difference! I think the differing terminology came about because of the use of terms in the Greek translation of the Hebrew Scriptures, in which *ekklesia* was used to translate the Hebrew term for the whole people whom God called out from the midst of other people to assemble as God's chosen people. Therefore, the Jewish people used another term for their smaller assemblies gathered in local areas.

Sadly, in English, we use the term "Church," which comes from a word that developed late in the Greek language and was used to designate "the Lord's house," which, of course, is the building and not the assembly. Universally, whether we Catholics use a word derived from *ecclesia*, as do those who speak Romance languages, or from the other Greek word that gave us Church, as do we who have Germanic language roots, we all consecrate the space within the building in which God's People assemble for worship (i.e., the sanctuary) because the assembly is sacred; we are the Body of Christ. We should never treat the sanctuary as a social hall.

Jesus joined his people's assembly in Capernaum one Sabbath at the beginning of his teaching career, and while participating he performed an exorcism. Saint Mark's report is quite clear. Whether we heard or read his report, Saint Mark assumed that we would understand why the "unclean spirit" would want to reveal Jesus as "the Holy One of God." The "unclean spirit" knew that before anyone could appreciate what being "the Holy One of God" really means, one had at least to be open to learning how Jesus through his teaching, his life, his passion, death, and resurrection would bring God's good news into our lives. Our Lord's understanding of what he as Messiah had to do was wholly different from what the majority expected. The people in the assembly in Galilee expected "the Holy One of God" to be a revolutionary leader who would enable them to overthrow the Roman yoke. Tagging Jesus with this task would spoil his mission. Therefore, the "unclean spirit" tried to out Jesus as Messiah prematurely, knowing that in doing so it would cause the people to misinterpret him.

Fortunately, the people at this assembly in Capernaum picked up on something else. Instead of screaming, "Our revolutionary leader is here," they remarked instead that Jesus taught with authority (Mark 1:27; the key term is authority). They knew that Jesus taught with authority because he did not kneel over the distraught man and begin an elaborate prayer begging God to deliver the poor man from the unclean spirit. No, Jesus simply commanded the spirit to depart, and the spirit was compelled to obey. Jesus had (still has) authority beyond any other man.

If this wondrous event took place today, we'd probably report what happened differently from the way Saint Mark reported the event. We are skeptical about demonic possession. We may well have taken what the unclean spirit said upon departing as the words of the deranged man himself just before our Lord healed him. Whichever report would be closer to what actually happened—what we like to call "literal"—it simply is true that Jesus healed a man who was in the clutches of evil, and the spirit of evil, which is personal, wanted to spoil our Lord's mission with a premature announcement of who he really is. Therefore, although reported as people two thousand years ago in this rural outpost of the Roman Empire would have perceived what happened, the report is true. Even if we reported such an event differently, even if we perceived it differently, if honest with ourselves we too would have observed a superhuman authority at work. Jesus did something wondrous that relieved a man from evil during a Sabbath assembly around two thousand years ago, and intelligent, perceptive people recognized that what he did and the way he did it revealed he had authority, and they recognized that this authority resided in and confirmed what he taught. They discerned the truth. We today, as much as the men and woman of Capernaum two thousand years ago, all need to discern with some precision what teaching is authoritative (i.e., true), and which authorities we recognize and then obey. If we obey authority not from God, we compromise our faith or simply lose it!

God's authority is embodied in Jesus the Christ, as today's gospel makes clear. In a constitutionally limited way, some of God's authority embodied in Jesus remains in the Church Jesus organized, in which Church God the Holy Spirit guarantees the preservation of his memory. Thus, we assemble each Sunday to fulfill our Lord's command to "Do this in Memory of me!" God the Holy Spirit then assures that our Lord really is present. Those who accurately discern this authority and obey this authority have living faith; those who don't either have defective or dead faith, or no faith at all.

In religious matters, at least here in the United States, the majority, it seems, have decided that each individual should be his/her own sole authority. To understand when this decision to be one's sole authority in all religious matters brings faith to an end, we need to distinguish between a good conscience, and other states of conscience (such as a bad conscience, an innocently but wrongly informed conscience, etcetera). We need also distinguish between legitimate authorities and illegitimate, as well as learn to accurately recognize the constitutional limits God has placed on even legitimate authority. Put abstractly, this may seem a daunting task; but no matter how daunting the task seems, we all must meet the challenge.

Perhaps, the task will become easier if we start with a couple of examples. A faith formation teacher approached me last week, and asked if I would approve him cutting back on the curriculum so that he could instead insist that the students learn the Apostles' Creed. I was not surprised; I was merely horrified, again. These are young men and women who want to receive the Sacrament of Confirmation. They should have known the Apostles' Creed by memory years ago. And, they should be able to explain in age appropriate terms what each article of the Creed means. This is true of every member of the Church from before receiving his or her first Holy Communion on!

Furthermore, each person should know by memory the prayers we use to recite the rosary. These prayers include the Apostles' Creed, the Our Father, the Hail Mary, and the lesser doxology known as the "Glory be." The other prayers some who recite the rosary use are add-ons and not necessary. All Catholics in our rite should also know how to recite the rosary, which requires knowing something about meditating on the mysteries of faith. The rosary is not required, but knowing the prayers used to say the rosary and how to meditate the mysteries is required of all who claim to be Catholic. We are meant to pray the rosary, not wear it.

Repeatedly, as recently as this past week, in communicating with me, persons have referred to First Holy Communion as if it were a distinct sacrament. It is not! All Catholics should know the seven sacraments and be able to explain each. Holy Communion is only part of a sacrament, the Sacrament of the Holy Eucharist, which we in the Roman rite refer to as the Mass (a Latinate word). A more precise term is the Eucharistic Sacrifice.

Other rites commonly refer to this sacrifice as the Divine Liturgy. Holy Communion, when properly received, is a fuller participation in the Eucharistic Sacrifice than participating only by praying with the assembly and learning from the Word. The fuller participation of receiving the Bread of Life and drinking from the Cup of Salvation requires, first, baptism into the Body of Christ and, when of the age designated in one's rite, the Sacrament of Confirmation. Then, if one has sinned, including if one has sinned by violating the third commandment, one is required to have recourse to the Sacrament of Penance (Confession) before receiving again. And, if we rightly receive the Eucharist, we prayerfully and gratefully participate in the whole liturgy. Only the sick and those otherwise impaired are permitted to receive Holy Communion apart from participation in the Mass (Divine Liturgy, Eucharistic Sacrifice). First Holy Communion is simply the occasion when a competent authority judges that a person is sufficiently prepared—physically, emotionally, and intellectually—for the fuller participation in the Eucharistic Sacrifice that occurs when he/she will receive the Body and Blood of the Lord.

I repeat that anyone who claims to be a Catholic should be able to list the seven sacraments and explain in an age-appropriate way what each one signifies and by it signification, effects.

Some time back, a person almost my age summoned up sufficient courage to ask what in the Bible I was talking about when I referred to the Sermon on the Mount. I fear there are many like this parishioner who lack her courage and humility. They're too afraid or too ashamed to ask. For those who lack this good woman's courage and humility, I'll point out that the Sermon on the Mount comprises that part of the Gospel according to Saint Matthew now marked off as chapters 5–7 inclusive. In this passage, Saint Matthew, with great artistry, compiled a summary of our Lord's teaching and presented his teaching as a single sermon. I'm at a loss how one can really be Catholic, and not know this summary of Jesus' teaching. There is another and shorter summary in the Gospel according to Saint Luke (6:20–49). And, I trust everyone knows, or will promptly learn, what part of the Sermons we refer to as the Beatitudes.

There are other basics that express God's authority entrusted to the Church. For example, there is the list of laws from the Old Testament that are correctly called the Decalogue, which means Ten Words, and often popularly referred to as the Ten Commandments. We consider these laws binding *as the Church interprets them*, which is distinctly different in a number of cases from what they originally meant. There also are six precepts of the Church. Rightly interpreted, the Decalogue and the Church's precepts set forth obligations for all Catholics that we fail to obey at our peril. All

Catholics should know and rightly understand these laws and precepts! There is no one not mentally impaired in this parish who is incapable of coming to know and understand this material. Learning these truths, including memorizing some, constitutes the absolute minimum in what we refer to as faith formation.

The second example is one I've stressed for the full Year of the Eucharist: namely, what is minimally required for one to receive Holy Communion worthily. When these requirements are defied and one still receives, the person commits a mortal sin. Not a weekend goes by during which I don't notice one or more examples of an objectively sinful violation of these requirements. I sometimes leave the altar feeling I've been an enabler of sin.

Speaking of sin, I don't see how a person can put him/herself forward for a sacrament, such as the Sacrament of Confirmation, without adequate and age-appropriate knowledge of the material I've mentioned in these examples.

If one starts with these examples, a person will not find it difficult to begin to learn, then, how to detect the limits of even legitimate authority, which requires learning how one's own conscience should work when judging between truth and falsity or between right and wrong. A person would do well to start with Just War Doctrine and the doctrine's relevance in our day. I say this a good doctrine with which to start because the great Saint Augustine of Hippo (354–430), the North African who founded what we call Western Christian civilization, provided the starting point for the theological reflection that has led to this doctrine.

In the thirteenth century, Saint Thomas Aquinas provided the summary of the doctrine that has guided reflection from then until the present. You can read this brilliant summary in Saint Thomas's *Summa Theologiae* (*A Summary of Theology*).[1] Saint Thomas's summary of the doctrine refers repeatedly to Saint Augustine, and in each reference provides the principal texts in the New Testament that Saint Augustine and all others since have had to wrestle with in order to justify the use of deadly force. The texts seem to state clearly that Jesus forbade this use. These principal texts are in the order they are presented in Saint Thomas's brief article on Just War: Matthew 26:52; Matthew 5:39; and Romans 12:19. Catholics who vote and who fail to wrestle with this doctrine are not living up to their faith.

By providing these examples of what we as Catholics should know, even some by memory, I hope I've shown what the primary meaning of authority is for our Lord. "And his teaching made a deep impression on them because, unlike the scribes, he taught them with authority" (Mark

---

1. *Summa Theologiae* IIa-IIae q.40 a.1.

1:22). The authority resides in the teaching! The wondrous acts, such as driving out the unclean spirit, merely confirm what the hearers first detected—namely, that he taught with authority. They heard the authority in his teaching! Nothing has changed. The Lord is truly present in the words of the liturgy, because he is God's Word, and if one learns, then one meets the Lord. The Church's authority is in her teaching insofar as this teaching is part of the God-protected memory of Jesus the Christ. We call this the teaching authority of the Church.

In a very secondary sense, there is a minimum of what I call bossing authority in the Church, just as among his followers Jesus created a minimum of organization—specifically, he called the original hierarchy, the Twelve, named one of them Rock (Peter), and gave them authority; but this is about all the organizing Jesus did. Even as hierarchy, their principal task was teaching and then preserving his memory with all that means. The little bit of "bossing" authority, as I like to call it (i.e., governing authority), with which Jesus endowed his Church is the minimum required in order to maintain unity and good order. As the one among us who has a minuscule amount of this authority, I can assure all how little it is and how hard it is to exercise even this minimum. I describe exercising governing authority in this parish as "herding cats." But, I will not have failed in this office thrust upon me if there is one person who has been so instructed that he/she moved from a superstitious and tribal Catholicism toward becoming one who with appropriate understanding has come to believe the truth Jesus taught with authority. On this question of whether I've failed, the jury is still out.

From our first reading we learn that Moses, who was among other things a prophet, predicted that "God will raise up a prophet like me; you will listen to him" (Deut 18:15 [NJB]). Moses gave God's People the Torah (i.e., the Law and Instruction). Now, we hear Jesus. Jesus is like Moses in that he has given us a new law, which fulfills the old, and profound instruction. In other words, Jesus embodies the new Torah. God expects us to listen to him. We do so by listening to his memory preserved in the Church Jesus founded.

We respond to this magnificent first reading with verses from Psalm 95. This psalm traditionally is used to inaugurate the Church's day of prayer. I recommend using the psalm for one's personal prayer as well.

Our second reading is a snippet taken from a passage in Saint Paul's Letter that requires extensive explanation. We do not have time for that explanation in this homily. Therefore, I suggest that we take from this passage two of its truths that do not require the more extensive explanation. Saint Paul wrote: "I should like you to have your minds free from all worry" (1

Cor 7:32). I think we can readily understand this sentence Saint Paul wrote. [A parishioner] detected I'm a bit of a worrywart, failing in Saint Paul's admonition. So, [she] had a plaque made and framed, which plaque hangs over this computer on which I am composing this homily. The plaque reads: "Good morning Fr. Roach this is God, I will be handling all your problems today. I will not need your help. So, relax and have a great day." I read it almost every day and I'm still trying!

The second point would be Saint Paul's endorsement of celibacy. With due deference to this great saint, celibacy should not be an "escape" from marriage; instead, celibacy should be, as Saint Paul took for granted it would be, a means of dedicating more time for concerning oneself with the Lord's affairs (i.e., prayer, teaching, learning, evangelizing, working for justice and charity, etcetera). If celibacy does not result in dedicating more time to the Lord's affairs, then it is of doubtful value.

With this homily, I've tried to make clear that authority resides in truth—specifically, in the truth Jesus taught and through his Church continues to teach. This past week, we had a wondrous example of our Lord teaching through the Church he founded. Pope Benedict XVI, the Bishop of Rome, issued his first encyclical (i.e., addressed to the whole Church) letter entitled, *Deus Caritas Est* (God is Love). If you download this encyclical from the Vatican web site, it prints out in about 25 pages with all its notes. This encyclical is incredibly brilliant! We haven't seen teaching this well done in a very long time. Alleluia! Please read this encyclical! In the study group or any other forum this parish would like, I'd be honored to help parishioners uncover the richness of this brilliant writing. A friend at the cathedral in London in an email described this encyclical as a Master Class in our faith. I agree wholeheartedly!

Chapter 24

Eucharist and the Lamb of God

The Second Sunday in Ordinary Time
Once is Not Enough (January 16, 2005)

Scripture Readings

Isa 49:3, 5–6; Ps 40; 1 Cor 1:1–3; John 1:29–34.

Summary

The homily reaffirms the central place of the Eucharist discussed in previous selections here, such as Holy Thursday and *Corpus Christi*. It also significantly elaborates on Christ being called Lamb of God. Knowing Christ as the Lamb of God shows us what Christ does for us. Christ as the Lamb of God recalls the Exodus and Passover, while according to Fr. Roach "we refer to our Lord's Passion and Death as the Pascal Sacrifice." The image of a sacrificial lamb also reminds us of our sins and alienation from God. One important area we need to reflect upon is our social sins. Jesus becomes the Lamb of God re-present in the Eucharistic Sacrifice, the "Chosen One" offering redemption from evil.

Homily

*I*N THE IMMORTAL WORDS of Yogi Berra, this Sunday is "déjà vu all over again!" It wasn't enough that we celebrated the Baptism of our Lord last week in a liturgy that both closed the Christmas season and served as the First Sunday in Ordinary Time; we in a certain sense celebrate the same event again this Sunday. The Church's liturgical sense (no single person or group did this) felt that the gospel reading for last Sunday taken each year from one of the synoptic gospels would focus the Liturgy of the Word, especially during the homily, on the fact of Jesus being baptized. Therefore, this liturgical sense leads the Roman rite of the Church to celebrate again using the Gospel according to Saint John (John 1:29–34) in order to assure a complementary focus.

The first thing that strikes a reader of the gospels when contrasting the four reports is the fact that the synoptic gospels recorded the event using direct discourse, whereas Saint John the Evangelist recorded the event using indirect discourse. This is to say that Saint John the Evangelist recorded what he did by quoting the other John, Saint John the Baptist. Note the opening sentence of today's gospel: "The next day, he (Saint John the Baptist) saw Jesus coming toward him and said, 'Look, there is the lamb of God that takes away the sin of the world'" (John 1:29). If the synoptic evangelists had mentioned this bit about "the lamb of God," they would have written directly: John the Baptist saw Jesus and said that he is the lamb of God. Saint John the Evangelist, instead, wants us to hear the voice of the Baptist.

Before we discuss "the lamb of God," please note the use of the singular "sin" in the words of Saint John the Baptist. He told us that our Lord takes away the "sin" of the world, yet when we use this phrase we sing that "the lamb of God" takes away the sins of the world. Our liturgy uses both the singular and the plural. There's a somewhat different meaning. "Sin," the singular, refers to the whole mess taken collectively without referring to any individual's actual sins, whereas the plural, "sins," reminds us that individuals do what is wrong, even deadly. What I referred to as "the whole mess" consists of all physical and moral evil in our world with a special focus on death. Jesus took away this sin by rising from the dead: that is, Jesus took away this sin for those who repent of their sins. In our liturgy, we sing about the singular "sin" in the Gloria, although the Latin on which our liturgy is based uses only the plural.

I think Saint John the Evangelist chose indirect discourse when reporting what happened at the Baptism of Jesus because he did not want us to think that the expression "the lamb of God" was his. He wanted us to realize that it came from someone of great authority who preceded him.

Therefore, instead even of stating that the person of great authority who preceded him had so identified Jesus, John quoted him. In this way, he made clear that the expression was not his invention.

It is very interesting that the phrase, usually written in American English as "Lamb of God," which expression we also know from our Latin liturgy as *Angus Dei*, is found in no synoptic gospel and only twice in the Gospel according to Saint John; but the last book of our New Testament, The Revelation to John, uses the concept repeatedly. This fact is one reason why I think it is correct to credit Saint John the Evangelist as the author of The Revelation. There are scholars today who dispute this attribution because of stylistic differences in the writing of Revelation and the gospel, but I think they forget how writers like Saint John had others help them re-write. The gospel manifestly was re-written a number of times, whereas The Revelation to John is a much rawer work, as would be natural for a man scribbling while in prison.

We heard the first mention of the expression "the lamb of God" in that part of the Gospel according to Saint John proclaimed today. The second, and only other use of the expression, follows almost immediately after the segment of the gospel proclaimed at this Mass. This is what the evangelist wrote immediately after today's gospel proclamation: "The next day as John (the Baptist) stood there again with two of his disciples, Jesus went past, and John looked towards him and said, 'Look, there is the lamb of God'" (John 1:35-36).

In the synoptic gospels, the evangelists made clear that immediately following the baptism of Our Lord, God his Father made known two important facts: first, Jesus is the Son, the Beloved; and second, that God the Holy Spirit with all power rests on him as human. "Son" is a term we have difficulty with, because we no longer use it with its ancient significance. In the ancient world, a son was thought to replicate his father. In the language of our system of belief, God the Son is the same God as God the Father, just as God and God's Word are the same God. In both cases, the persons are distinguished only by their relationship, not by being different beings.

Metaphors and analogies are always somewhat inadequate. In Saint Luke's remembrance of the baptism, he understood God to have made clear who Jesus is with the following words: "You are my Son; today have I fathered you." The words actually were quoted from verse 7 of Psalm 2. They capture the content of what was made known at the Baptism of our Lord, but our use of "fathered" (or beget or have begotten) misleads. We fail to understand that the "begetting" or "fathering" is eternal, which means, using temporal language as we must, that the begetting is going on always, and has always been going on, and always will be going on.

It is not certain from the manuscripts that have survived that Saint John the Baptist ever used the expression "Son of God" to refer to Jesus. He may have used a variant expression that means almost the same thing. The editors of the New Jerusalem Bible, I think rightly, assumed that the Baptist used the variant expression. Remember that these texts were hand-copied for fifteen-hundred-years before the invention of printing, and recall also that scribes like to make language uniform. Therefore, it is highly likely that when the ancient manuscript that a scribe was copying had the variant expression and the scribe had just finished copying a synoptic gospel, he made the two gospels uniform. Thus, only some of the most ancient manuscripts have the variant expression.

According to these manuscripts, Saint John the Evangelist quoted Saint John the Baptist as follows: "And John (the Baptist) declared, 'I saw the Spirit come down on him like a dove from heaven and rest on him. I did not know him myself, but he (God) who sent me to baptise with water had said to me, "The man on whom you see the Spirit come down and rest is the one who is to baptise with the Holy Spirit," I have seen and I testify that he is the Chosen One of God" (John 1:32–34). "Chosen One of God" is the variant of "Son of God."

The variant expression, "the Chosen One of God," emphasizes that God his Father had given Jesus a mission in our world. "God the Son" emphasizes Jesus's eternal reality. I think that Saint John the Baptist was primarily concerned with our Lord's mission.

In full agreement with the synoptic gospels, both Saint Johns, evangelist and baptist, believed that God the Holy Spirit descended upon Jesus the man in a special manner. This descent occurs again when God the Holy Spirit descends upon the Church Jesus organized, which is the Body of Christ, as we remember when we celebrate Pentecost. No one really knows what exactly the metaphor of a dove refers to, literally. I was pondering this question during the week and recalled a brief visit to a friend in Arizona many years ago. I remember I waited in an enclosed Arizona style garden for my friend while he was at work. I was dozing in the warm sun when I awoke to the fluttering of a flock of doves that had suddenly descended upon what I think were mesquite trees in the garden. It was as if the doves came out of nowhere, and when they arrived made all the air in the garden vibrate. Perhaps, this kind of experience prompted the ubiquitous use of the metaphor of a dove for God the Holy Spirit.

Saint John's account of this event inaugurating our Lord's public life with his quoting Saint John the Baptist identifying Jesus as "the lamb of God" remains something special about his gospel. The expression, "the lamb of God," is so rich that it is not possible to unpack all it means in one

EUCHARIST AND THE LAMB OF GOD

homily. We start with the boy Isaac asking his father Abraham, who was preparing to kill him in sacrifice, "where is the lamb for the burnt offering?" (Gen 22:7). Then came his father Abraham's pathetic answer as he was preparing to kill his son Isaac in sacrifice, "My son, God himself will provide the lamb for the burnt offering" (Gen 22:8). God wasn't ready yet to provide "the lamb of God." Instead, God provided a ram (cf. Gen 22:13). The "lamb of God" was yet to come (cf. Heb 11:17–19).

I hesitate to go into how our understanding of the meaning of a lamb grew through the chosen people's experience of the Exodus. Almost all the words and symbols of our Holy Week, Sacred Triduum, and Easter come from these experiences as recorded in sacred Writ. We read of the lamb whose blood on the lintel and doorposts drove away the angel of death from the firstborn of the chosen people while God used disastrous death to coerce the wicked pharaoh into freeing God's people from slavery.

Then came the Passover (cf. Exod 12:1–13:16). The core of the Passover celebration is a meal of roasted lamb that persons escaping from slavery ate in haste. God instructed them to mark the lintel and both doorposts of their homes with the blood of this lamb so that the angel of death would pass them by (cf. Exod 12:22–23). God had decreed the death of all the first-born in the land of Egypt. These deaths God knew would finally force pharaoh to let God's people go free. The "blood of the lamb" protected the first-born of the chosen people from death.

[Sadly, there are Protestant Evangelical/Fundamentalists who when they read that Jesus was Mary's first-born (cf. Luke 2:7) imagine that the expression "first-born" means Mary had other children of whom Jesus was but the first. This is [a notable lack of awareness]. The term "first-born" in the sacred Scriptures means the heir; it does not necessarily mean the first in a series, except that if a woman has more children it is only the first-born male who inherits his father's name and wealth. If the first male in a family actually is the tenth child, he nevertheless is the first-born, just as was Jesus who was the only child.]

The last or tenth plague that Almighty God inflicted upon the Egyptians—the death of the first-born—meant that God disrupted the line of inheritance of every family in Egypt. In the ancient world, it is hard to imagine just how ghastly this was. The lines of inheritance among the chosen people were saved by the blood of the lamb.

Our contemporary Jewish brethren celebrate the Passover (i.e., the angel of death or the Destroyer *passing over* the homes of the chosen people with the blood of the lamb on their doors) as the Seder meal. (Actually, this Hebrew word "Seder" denotes the feast that opens the eight-day observance of the Passover.) We use the term, Passover, for what Jesus did through his

Passion, Death, and Resurrection. We also use the noun "Pasch" and the adjective "paschal" to refer to the Passover. These words come from Hebrew via Aramaic into Greek and Latin, and finally to us. Thus, we refer to our Lord's Passion and Death as the Paschal Sacrifice, which means the Passover Sacrifice. It is our Lord's blood, which is the blood of the Lamb that God provides, that tells the angel of death he is not the last word in our lives. [If you do not already know them, please learn all these words for the coming Lent and Easter!]

I confess that I'm in the dark about people who do not know they need the lamb of God and his blood in order to escape the bad consequences of what they have done, or have failed to do. I'm surprised by people who also seem not to feel the need for "the lamb of God" while in this life. They seem not to need "our daily bread" or have "our daily debts" forgiven, as we pray in the Our Father: "Give us this day our daily bread, and forgive us our trespasses as we forgive those who trespass against us." "Debts" is a better word than "trespasses," but the latter will do. I don't comprehend people who do not seem to know that they need God's answer to this prayer each day. Admittedly, a particle physicist as scientist can't figure out what our debts are, or to whom we owe them, because scientific methodology does not detect these realities. He or she as a human being, not limited to being a scientist, should be able to figure out what our debts are, because we cannot limit ourselves only to what we can know using scientific methodology. Even a particle physicist, who is a master of scientific methodology, should be aware that every major thinker with a sense of what realities lie beyond the detective powers of science has been aware that we must give an account of ourselves. What this means has been imagined in many quite different ways, but we all know that somehow we are held accountable. It's a mystery to me how anyone does not feel concern for him/herself in this regard.

Almost all who will hear and/or read this homily enjoy a measure of prosperity, and the benefits of a highly developed society. We are the fortunate of this world. We, therefore, must ask ourselves, Are people paying unjustly for our good fortune? If this question is not honestly asked and courageously answered with facts rather than ideology, then one may be sure he/she is involved in something evil incurring guilt. The Our Father calls the source of this guilt our "debts." (Again, I think "trespasses" is the weaker word and clearly a poor translation.)

Let us turn to our sacred Scriptures for some understanding of what it means that we who are fortunate in this life may be incurring guilt, if our good fortune rests on the misery of others. I fear that in my repeated efforts as the priest serving this parish to correct the popular misunderstanding of guilt as collective, I've led people into the opposite, equally insidious error.

On the one hand, God punishes only the unrepentant person for his/her actual sins, never for the sins of a parent, or the sins committed by the person's family, tribe, nation, culture, etcetera. This truth means that in this life we may never say that any suffering is punishment for the sins the person suffering has committed. Suffering occurs because sin has alienated us as the human family from God, but never is specific punishment for someone's actual sins.

On the other hand, we as individuals do commit actual sins by omission (failing to do what we ought to do) and by commission (by implication in actual social sins, some of which we benefit from and about which we've done nothing). We as the Church Jesus founded retain the sacred writings composed before Jesus was born (the Old Testament) for many reasons. A principal one is the fact that from these writings, we learn about people being severely punished for the sins they were implicated in. In the Old Testament, this sometimes is confounded with a mistaken notion of collective guilt. Nonetheless, the whole library of ancient writings, which we call the Old Testament, taken as a whole does make clear that God visits disaster upon those who benefit from social injustice while doing nothing about the injustices. In my copy of the *New Jerusalem Bible*, the prophecy of Amos takes up only fourteen pages. Reading this prophecy will help one understand how one may think of God "punishing" persons who are involved in social injustice.

Essentially, what the Old Testament thought of as punishment came about because the injustices weakened the social fabric and thus brought the society down upon all citizens, guilty and innocent alike. One may discover this process of social injustice weakening a society to the point of collapse throughout history. In the strict sense, the collapse and the misery it brings upon guilty and innocent alike is not punishment, which God metes out only to unrepentant individuals in eternity, but the social consequences of unjust policies did seem to the inspired writers of the Old Testament an indication of God's justice.

What the Old Testament taught about injustice as a social phenomenon from which some benefit lies behind one of our Lord's most famous sayings: "Then Jesus said to his disciples, 'In truth I tell you, it is hard for someone rich to enter the kingdom of Heaven. Yes, I tell you again, it is easier for a camel to pass through the eye of a needle than for someone rich to enter the kingdom of Heaven'" (Matt 19:23–24). We all who live in the United States and other developed countries are rich. We should make sure that our riches do not in any measure come from injustice. And, we should pray the Our Father with conviction—" . . . forgive us our debts, / as we have forgiven those who are in debt to us" (Matt 6:12 NJB).

Sometimes, we cannot free ourselves from unjust social structure. Saint Paul addressed his letter to Philemon to just such a person. Philemon owned slaves; and, although it took us far too long to realize the truth, slavery in any form is unjust. [As we know, the old law recognized bonded servitude while insisting on just treatment of the slave or bonded servant. Nevertheless, this acceptance of bonded servitude misled many who claimed later to follow Christ. They tolerated forms of slavery that in no way could be reconciled with justice. Slavery, as practiced in the U.S., in no way could be reconciled with justice of even the most lenient sort. Therefore, works that romanticize the institution of slavery in our country, such as *Gone With the Wind*, book and movie, does us a disservice. It took many years of wrestling with this book and movie to realize what I'm now saying.]

Obviously, the possibility of being implicated in social sin so that the social sin is counted against us individually as actual or personal sin is a truth that has contemporary relevance. It means we should check our beliefs about social and economic policies, including the use of deadly force, and our role either in promoting or changing these policies. We all should be alert to this real possibility of being implicated in sin and examine our consciences.

It is because of the enlightenment we each need in order to rightly detect evil in our lives and in our behavior, and to rightly assess our role in these evils that we need "the lamb of God." If there were not assurance that when we discover ourselves implicated in evil we could obtain forgiveness and deliverance from God's "Chosen One" who functions as our lamb of sacrifice, and with his blood deflects eternal death from our doors—if there were not assurance that these blessings of mercy can be ours, then no one of us would have the courage to become truly real about sin in our world and in our lives. A great Jesuit spiritual director said that in us there are wounds so deep and painful that they can be touched only by hands that have been pierced with nails. (I'm sorry, but aging memory won't as yet bring back his name.) The hands that were pierced with nails, and thereby became hands that can touch our deepest wounds and heal them obviously are the hands of Jesus who is "the Chosen One of God" and "the lamb of God." (Jesus also is our Enlightenment.)

Our first reading was taken from the second Song of the Servant. As mentioned many times, these four songs embedded in the prophecy of Isaiah more clearly than any other part of the Old Testament predicted how Jesus would suffer and die, thereby saving us. (The prophetic songwriter did not clearly foresee the resurrection, which is the culminating saving event.) We will hear the songs again during this coming Lent.

In today's Mass, these verses are proclaimed in order to remind us that Jesus, "the chosen One of God" and "the lamb of God," also is our true source of enlightenment, which is understanding and wisdom and more. The prophet reported in this song God's intention regarding "the Chosen One of God" as light: "I (God) shall make you (my Chosen One) a light to the nations / so that my salvation may reach the remotest parts of the earth" (Isa 49:6). This phrase, "a light to the nations," refers not only to Jesus himself, but also to his Body, the Church he founded. The Second Vatican Council used the phrase to open its document defining the nature and mission of the Church: *Dogmatic constitution on the church*, promulgated on the 21st of November 1964, cited here from the English version of the documents, hence the use of lower case rather than capital letters.[1] Documents originally in Latin or Greek often are denoted by their opening words; thus, this document is commonly known as *Lumen Gentium*, which is Latin for the phrase "a light to the nations." The document is the Church's constitution, much of which had been unwritten or written in scattered documents from the beginning. The document does not include all that may be said, but does set down the lion's share. Therefore, just as we as Americans read the constitution of the United States, so we as Catholics ought to read the constitution of the Church.

The liturgists omitted one verse from within the section of the song proclaimed in today's Mass. Here is that omitted verse: "But I (the servant) said, 'My toil has been futile, / I have exhausted myself for nothing, to no purpose. / Yet all the while my cause was with Yahweh / and my reward with my God" (Isa 49:4). I find consolation in knowing from the prophet that the servant, who is Jesus, knew discouragement, yet was confident of God's reward.

The second reading (1 Cor 1:1–3) consists of the opening words of Saint Paul's first letter to the church he founded in Corinth, Greece. They also apply to you and me, and should be understood as addressed to us. If the words are true of you and me—in other words, if we are truly consecrated (baptized and confirmed) in Christ Jesus and faithful to our membership in God's holy people—then the blessing Saint Paul invoked upon the Corinthians he also invokes upon us: "Grace to you and peace from God our Father and the Lord Jesus Christ" (1 Cor 1:3).

---

1. Tanner, *Decrees*.

Chapter 25

Faith and Reason

The Second Sunday of Lent
Transfigured Before Our Eyes (March 12, 2006)

Scripture Readings

Gen 22:1–2, 9a, 12–13, 15–18; Rom 8:31b–34; Mark 9:2–10.

Summary

The homily explains faith and reason as compatible, while countering two influential philosophical assessments of Christianity. Many Catholic beliefs exceed what can be known by reason. Thus, appeal to revelation is needed. Yet, this does not make faith a leap away from rationality. Apparent conflicts between faith and reason mean that, in Fr. Roach's terms, "either the belief is not rightly understood or our reason has gone awry." Søren Kierkegaard embraced faith as a leap into absurdity, emblematic in Abraham's sacrifice of Isaac. Fr. Roach argues that the sacrifice instead shows Abraham's great faith in God's promises, and that what God asks is reasonable even when we do not fully comprehend it. Fr. Roach then turns his attention to Friedrich Nietzsche and his imitators. They see only weakness in Christianity. This is shortsighted according to a real grasp of Christian premises and the nature of the crucifixion. Christ voluntarily, and from a position of superior strength, submitted to suffering and death to share the consequences of our sinfulness. Christ, in his supreme wisdom and love, thus, restrains his superior power for the sake of demonstrating merciful love to sinners. Genuine strength and wisdom restrain power in the service of mercy overcoming evil. Imitating Christ yields in us a similar wisdom leading to our salvation and hopefully others.

Homily

*A*RGUABLY, THE MOST INFLUENTIAL philosopher of our time has been Friedrich Nietzsche (1844–1900). Nietzsche was born in Prussia in 1844, the son of a Lutheran minister who died insane four years after his son's birth. Nietzsche knew nothing of Christianity except the version he learned from the decadent Lutheranism of the *Evangelische Kirche*, i.e., the established Protestant church in nineteenth-century Germany. He despised this version of Christianity. From this hatred, he launched what remains the most sophisticated attack on Christianity, ever. This attack dominates higher education in the United States. If you have children in a college or university, you may be sure they are coming in contact with this attack, even if it is not named. [The Protestant state church of Germany differed from other Establishments in that it was a federation of regional churches. The unification of Germany took place quite late. Originally, each little German state had its own established church.]

Another nineteenth-century thinker shared in some measure Nietzsche's loathing of established Protestant Christianity, but reacted quite differently. Søren Aabye Kierkegaard (1813–1855), the great Danish Christian, regarded the Establishment as a massive failure, but unlike the German Nietzsche, he did not hate Christianity. Instead, he performed what he called a leap of faith. Sadly, what he meant by "leap" implied a kind of incompatibility between reason and faith, which in the long run may have done as much damage as Nietzsche's loathing.

Neither of these men had sufficient knowledge of Catholic faith to form a balanced judgment. Typical of the prejudice of the day, they felt that the founders of Protestantism had judged Catholicism and found it wanting; therefore, they did not need bother going over the same ground, although this may not have been true for Kierkegaard toward the end of his life. His last written work may indicate that he had finally found Luther's "justification by faith alone" inadequate, or even false.

I trust all know that "Establishment" refers to the state exercising control over religious affairs, with the resulting elite class of officials in both government and church. King Henry VIII of England created the pattern for all subsequent establishments when he made himself the "head of the church." His state bishops, then, sat in the House of Lords. They answered to no higher authority than the monarch.

Episcopalians come from the state church of England that Henry created; Presbyterians from the state church of Scotland, and Lutherans from a host of states churches–e.g., the state church of Denmark, of Norway, of Sweden, and also the federated state church of Germany, although this arrangement was modified following the Second World War.

Full-blown Establishment means that the state claims ultimate suzerainty over the church, which in turn becomes an arm of the state. We Catholics have submitted to some measure of this domination, but have never conceded in principle the claim of any state to run or oversee the Church. Our bishops always answer to an authority outside the jurisdiction of the state in which they live. The pope (Bishop of Rome) is the principal symbol of our independence, and the principal means whereby we remain independent of any state. Presently, a grave struggle for freedom from state control is going on in China. Establishments always corrupt the faith.

Our first reading provides the reason for mentioning Kierkegaard in particular. This great Danish Christian [Kierkegaard] thought it absurd that God should ask a father to kill his own son ("absurd" in the sense of not rational). I'm inclined to agree. But the nineteenth-century Dane and I part company over what conclusion to draw from the fact that this story is included in sacred Scripture. For Kierkegaard, it shows that faith requires a leap away from what is rational (from reason) into what is not rational. For this Catholic, the story may illustrate that what we believe exceeds what we may know from reason alone, but more significantly, this story illustrates how the content of faith (belief) developed very slowly with many stumbles and falls. Eventually, we come to see that, even if there are matters we cannot fully understand in this life, faith and reason are compatible, not contradictory.

This week, I was parked behind a van on the ferry crossing to Fauntleroy, which van bore bumper stickers proclaiming the socio/political views of the owner. One of the stickers moralized: "Those who would have you believe absurdities would make you commit atrocities." I had no doubt but that, if the owner knew who was parked behind, he/she would have classified me as one who would have you believe absurdities. Thus, a homily was born. I'm not Kierkegaard. I do not believe that the authentic faith Jesus the Christ offered us contains absurdities. I believe, instead, the rational may never be violated. When there appears to be a contradiction between faith and reason, either the belief is not rightly understood, or our reasoning has gone awry.

It's wonderful to see how the inspired authors even in the Old Testament strove mightily to make sense of what they were told God had asked of the patriarch Abraham. Even the initial version of the story with its ghastly preparations to kill Isaac given in detail up to the nearly completed human sacrifice concludes by letting God off the hook, somewhat. The hook, of course, would have consisted in hanging God with proof that he is cruel, capricious, and absurd. Instead, we learn that God had the charade stopped: "'Do not raise your hand against the boy,' the angel said. 'Do not harm him, for now I know you fear God. You have not refused me your own beloved son" (Gen 22:12).

This verse satisfied the inspired authors whose writings are collected in our Old Testament. Nevertheless, they did not dwell on what had happened on the mount in the land of Moriah. Their silence is telling. Regrettably, Kierkegaard probably never knew of the two inspired authors whose efforts to rationalize the history in the Old Testament were the best, since Luther and Calvin had removed them from the Old Testament. You may like to read Sirach (Ecclesiasticus) 44: 19–23 and Wisdom 10:5. Essentially, though, these authors do not substantially modify what was said in the verse explaining God's motive, as quoted in the preceding paragraph. Only the New Testament provided the rationality embedded in the story: "He was confident that God had the power even to raise the dead; and so, figuratively speaking, he was given back Isaac from the dead" (Heb 11:19 [also note verses 17–18]).

Faith, as stated many times before, is an innovation of the New Testament. It was clearly anticipated in the Old Testament, particularly in the story of Abraham (cf., Gen 15:6), as chapter 11 of the Letter to the Hebrews tries to spell out. But, its full significance and meaning comes only with the Christ.

As the verse I cited in the preceding paragraph suggests, Abraham's believing God anticipated the faith that Jesus offers us: "Abram put his faith in Yahweh and this was reckoned to him as uprightness" (Gen 15:6; God renames Abram, Abraham in Gen 17:5). "Put his faith" means Abram believed that God would keep his promise that Abram (Abraham) would have a son and heir despite his age and that of his wife. God bringing about something wondrous, like a miracle, is not irrational. Our faith in Jesus the Christ includes believing that God will keep his promises, but goes beyond this believing into a personal friendship with God–with–us–namely, Jesus, who is also human as we are.

There is a world of difference between what we read in Exodus, and what we read in the Gospel according to Saint John concerning friendship between a human being and God. In Exodus, we read: "Yahweh would talk to Moses face to face, as a man talks to his friend, . . .". (Exod 33:11a). In John's gospel, we read [that Jesus lays down his life for us as a friend] (John 15:13-15). If we see that in Jesus, God has become our human friend, then we know that as our friend when he asks something of us he has good reason, even when we don't understand. Is this not true of other friendships, if we've chosen our friends wisely? A friend may ask a favor of me, and not be able to explain why, yet I do it knowing that he/she had a good reason for asking.

With faith, we come to see that God is reasonable in all he asks of us, even when we're faced with evil. The inspired author of the Letter to the Hebrews knew that our father in faith, Abraham, whose believing made him upright although he did not yet know God as a friend in Jesus, had to have realized that God could make his order to sacrifice Isaac reasonable far beyond an arbitrary testing. The vision attributed to Abraham as faith must be our vision, too, when we look upon our Crucified Lord, although in our case we're looking on a friend who is God's Son, not our son. It is God the Father who has Abraham's role in the drama of our Lord's sacrifice. After all, God the Father asked God the Son to sacrifice himself. (Simply because this exceeds our ability to understand does not make a word of what I've said irrational.)

We responded to this first reading with words from Psalm 116. The psalm makes a wonderful prayer. If you take some time to pray this [entire] psalm, you'll appreciate how presently we see it in a new light as referring to one who is faithful to Jesus, and in some sense as referring to Jesus himself. The psalm repeats the verse: "I shall fulfill my vows to Yahweh, / witnessed by all his people" (Ps 116:14 and 18). Faithful friends fulfill their vows to their friend, Jesus. We made those vows at our baptism and confirmation, and renew them in every sacrament that we receive worthily.

The second reading seems to start with, if not an irrational claim, at least a paradoxical one: "If God is for us, who can be against us? Since he did not spare his own Son, but gave him up for the sake of all of us, then can we not expect that with him he will freely give us all his gifts?" (Rom 8:31b-32). How can we claim that God who gave his own Son up to sacrificial death be for us? If Abraham had killed Isaac, his son, I for one would never have trusted him. Did God the Father sacrifice Jesus in the direct way Abraham was ordered to sacrifice Isaac? If one has not done so already, one should sort this out before Holy Week and Easter.

The Father sacrificed the Son in that he asked the Son to share the consequences of our sinfulness. God did not wield a whip or drive a nail. God the Father did not crucify the Son. Mere human beings did that. Our faith has to do with why Jesus submitted to suffering and death. But, before we turn to why Jesus submitted, which Nietzsche comprehended not at all, we need to face yet another problem raised by the way Saint Paul expressed himself.

"Who can bring any accusation against those that God has chosen?" (Rom 8:33). Saint Paul wrote about what God has done as if God did not require our cooperation. At least since Luther and Calvin, Saint Paul's way of expressing himself has occasioned the greatest number of misunderstandings of our faith. In this instance, after referring to "those that God has chosen" as if the chosen ones did nothing, Saint Paul quoted the prophet Zechariah. Saint Paul did not quote the prophet word from word; rather he summed up the sense of what the prophet had said in these words: "When God grants saving justice, who can condemn?" (Rom 8:33). What the prophet actually had said is the following: "He (God) then showed me the high priest Joshua, standing before the angel of Yahweh, with Satan standing of his right to accuse him. The angel of Yahweh said to Satan, 'May Yahweh rebuke you, Satan! May Yahweh rebuke you, since he has made Jerusalem his choice. Is not this man a brand snatched from the fire?'" (Zech 3:1–2). By choosing Jerusalem, God had chosen the high priest Joshua. God's saving justice snatched him from the fire [see Zech 3:5–9]. Without going into the details of the prophecy, we nevertheless can see that the one chosen or elected high priest had a job to do, or else. Saint Paul tends to leave out this part, concentrating only on God's initiative.

Jesus submitted to suffering and death not out of weakness, but from his strength and free choice. Nietzsche and the many who have followed him see only weakness. Nietzsche believed that Christianity had made a virtue of weakness and denigrated strength. He therefore loathed the religion. I believe from his Lutheran background, he'd learned to apply Psalm 22 to Jesus: "But I am a worm, and no man; a reproach of men, and despised of the people" (Ps 22:6 Authorized Version [King James Bible]).

What Nietzsche learned about this psalm was not all wrong. All four gospels make clear in differing ways that this psalm helps us understand the crucifixion. Matthew and Mark say that Jesus intoned the opening verse before dying: "My God, my God, why have you forsaken me?" But, those who dwell on the cry of despair and the comparison to a worm miss the meaning: "Of you (my God) is my praise in the thronged assembly, / I will perform my vows before all who fear him. / The poor will eat and be filled, / those who seek Yahweh will praise him, 'May your heart live forever" (Ps 22:25–26). Those who think our Lord's crucifixion glorified weakness failed to finish reading the psalm.

In contrast, Jesus embodied and exemplified the greatest strength: the strength that can restrain power for the sake of mercy, and has the wisdom to know when restraint would be merciful and when it would not. If one does not see this strength in our Lord's suffering and death, one does not see Jesus the Christ! ["Power," as used here refers not only to physical force, such as military power, police power, etcetera, but also refers to whatever means can be employed to coerce others. Education, as distinct from indoctrination, as well as moral counsel, and the like are powerful; but, indoctrination excepted, they are not coercive. "Power" in this homily refers to what is coercive.]

Today's gospel reports how on one occasion Jesus gave three of the original hierarchy a glimpse of the power that would be hidden from doubting and unbelieving eyes, and would be revealed only to those who were open to faith after he rose from the dead. We call this event the Transfiguration.[1]

We are told that while he was transfigured, Elijah and Moses joined Jesus on this mountain. This overwhelmed especially Peter; they were frightened. Glorious power is frightening. But what was most awesome was the voice they heard from within an overshadowing cloud. The voice said: "This is my Son, the Beloved, listen to him" (Mark 9:7). This voice sounds in our liturgies, making the Son known to us. Do we listen to him?

Jesus told the three not to talk about what they'd seen until after he had "risen from the dead" (Mark 9:9). At the time they did not understand. Eventually, they learned. Nietzsche seems never to have learned.

Nietzsche is not irrelevant in this sadly anti-Catholic culture in which we live. The novelist Ayn Rand popularized him for those who chose not to slog their way through his philosophical writings. And, Ayn Rand became the guiding light for many who self-identify as conservative or libertarian. Alan Greenspan, for example, former head of our Federal Reserve Bank, was a devotee of Ayn Rand.

Ayn Rand has all the rejection of weakness as allegedly embodied in Jesus and all the hatred of Christianity, especially Catholicism, found in Nietzsche. But it is harder to discern in her writings because she has wrapped it in fiction. Nonetheless, her heroes are all Nietzsche's supermen (*Übermensch*), and her vision of strength excludes the strength of Jesus as if it were weakness.

I trust we all are becoming better able to appreciate that God's mercy is multi-faceted, that merciful love encompasses justice, and leads not only to personal salvation but also helps build healthy societies here and now. Mercy overcomes evil; it doesn't wink at it. And only merciful love brings the wisdom that knows when power should be restrained, and has the strength to restrain power when God's saving justice requires. The great English

---

1. See the homily on the Transfiguration earlier in this volume.

historian of the nineteenth century, an outstanding Catholic layman, said: "Power tends to corrupt, and absolute power corrupts absolutely."[2] God has given us in Jesus the perfect example of when and how to restrain power so that instead of corrupting us, our power becomes holy.

Perhaps it is foolish or naïve of me, but I believe not only does our personal salvation depend on learning how to imitate Jesus' understanding of strength and power in the service of merciful love and justice, but also our country's fate may hang on whether the citizenry in large numbers learn the same truth, and insist on applying the truth in our national affairs.

---

2. John Emerich Edward Dalberg Acton (1834–1902) historian and moralist.

Chapter 26

On Anti-Catholicism and Some Modern Ideologies

*The Seventeenth Sunday in Ordinary Time
God's Debtors (July 29, 2007)*

Scripture Readings

Gen 18:20–32; Ps 138; Col 2:12–14; Luke 11:1–13

Summary

The homily explains in what sense we owe a debt to God. We are indebted when our plight, caused by sin, can only be overcome by God's merciful love. In strict justice, God does not owe us mercy. We need to appreciate this and do penance. A long postscript sees Fr. Roach pay his "debt" on a prior promise to speak about contemporary anti-Catholicism. He thinks the root is two-fold. People reject God's ultimate moral authority and entrusting it to his Church. The Church can often give "reasonably clear distinctions between right and wrong," which many are apt to reject. Other factors muddy the waters for legitimate authority. Groups or individuals invoke God for absurd or dangerous purposes. History shows that attempts to create justice without God end in disaster, Marxism being a prime example. Many people also use the failings of individual Catholics to tar all of Catholicism and the Church. The Crusades and Inquisition are often used in this vein.

Fr. Roach notes that both movements involved morally complex situations, where Church teaching in fact judged the acts of individuals involved as unjust. Finally, anti-Catholicism is often fueled from within the Church by disgruntled Catholics.

Homily

*I*N THE GOSPEL PROCLAIMED for this Sunday, we heard Saint Luke's memory of the prayer our Lord taught us (Luke 11:2–4), the prayer we affectionately refer to by the words Jesus told us to use when addressing Almighty God—"Our Father." In our liturgies and in most personal prayer, we use Saint Matthew's memory of how our Lord taught this prayer (Matt 6:9–13). Saint Matthew remembered seven petitions; Saint Luke, five. Allowing for this distinction, the two memories are obviously of the same prayer.

The way we recite this prayer in English comes from a faulty translation of Saint Matthew's version, but the version is so well established in people's minds that our bishops have never tried to re-educate us. At least, we've never embraced the ending to the prayer that was interpolated into the *King James Version*—"For thine is the kingdom, and the power, and the glory, for ever, Amen." These words are not found in the original texts.

The faulty translation consists in using "trespasses" rather than "debts." "Forgive us our trespasses as we forgive those who trespass against us" should be "forgive us our debts as we forgive our debtors." This error leads us to forget that because of our sins we are in God's debt. We owe God!

Obviously, both "trespass" and "debt" are figures of speech chosen to help us appreciate our relationship with God, which we do not directly perceive, and in this life do not fully comprehend. "Debt," by making clear that we owe God, reminds us that God is not to blame for our plight. Instead, sin is. Overcoming sin, which requires forgiveness, pays God what we owe him. Herein lies the irony: it is God's merciful love that enables us to repay our debt to God. God essentially pays our debt to himself for us, but we're expected to appreciate fully the fact it is our debt God is paying for us. To this end, God asks us to contribute a little to the repayment. We call the little we contribute, penance. The key to penance comes in this prayer when we ask for God's forgiveness: "And forgive us our debts, / as we have forgiven those who are in debt to us" (Matt 6:12 NJB). Forgiving someone can be brutal penance; yet, if we do not forgive, we have no basis to ask God for his forgiveness.

Saint Luke's memory of the prayer probably took shape from the fact that he clearly understood that our debt to God comes from our sin. Therefore, the petition quoted in the previous paragraph from Saint Matthew becomes in Saint Luke's memory, "and forgive us our sins, / for we ourselves forgive each one who is in debt to us" (Luke 11:3 NJB). I think the moral of the "Our Father" is obvious. Do we forgive as we ought?

The rest of the gospel proclaimed today I also think is teaching that requires no special exposition. We are told to persevere in prayer (especially in Luke 11:5–8). We are to continue praying even when we feel that we're not being heard, or are prayers not answered. Persevere!

Then, the gospel alerts us to the truth that God answers our prayers in a way that is good for us (Luke 11:9–13). The section begins with the assurance that if we persevere in prayer, our prayer will be answered. Implicit in the section is the truth that the answer, which will be good for us when received from God's hands, may not be exactly what we asked for. In other words, our prayers may not be answered in the way we expect. Some years back a country singer, Garth Brooks, discovered this truth and turned it into a song—"Thank God for Unanswered Prayers!" The point, I believe, was to thank God for not answering his prayer for a specific woman to become his spouse. Instead, he married someone else and married well. Years later, he met the woman he asked God to inspire to marry him, and she was singularly unfit. He thanked God for not answering his prayer. Actually, according to today's gospel, God had answered the prayer, but not in the way Garth expected.

Our first reading presents the Lord God haggling over the price of justice much as a shopper in a Middle Eastern bazaar may haggle over the price of a rug. The reading is quite humorous. The event took place at the dawn of God's lengthy preparation of the people chosen to receive God's laws, covenants, and promises. In this sense, the story is primitive: it's at the beginning, which easily is two and half millennia ago. Nevertheless, it prepares us for our salvation, which took place in Jesus the Christ.

Strict justice should have wiped out the human race, which is the point of the story about Noah, the Ark, and the Flood. God's mercy stays the hand of justice, and an upright person is the intercessor who invokes God's mercy. In today's story, the upright Abraham appeals to the possibility that in wicked Sodom there are at least a few who are upright. Therefore, he begged for God to spare the sinful city. Ultimately, in Jesus, God's very Word, God will spare us all because there is one who is completely upright—namely, our Lord Jesus the Christ.

We responded to this first reading with verses from Psalm 138. We join the psalmist in praising and thanking God for answering our prayers.

The last stanza I find very helpful [Ps 138:7–8]. God has answered the last petition of this prayer with the gift of Jesus.

The second reading (Col 2:12–14) reminds us of what took place when we were baptized. We were incorporated into Christ by sacramentally sharing in his death and resurrection. We also assumed a share in his duties among us, which means we have obligations. Our Lord's duties are classified as three offices, as one might say that a senator has specific duties because of the office he holds. The Lord's offices, in which the baptized are obliged to share, are his priestly office, his prophetic office, and his office as king. Jesus is *the* priest, *the* prophet, and *the* king! We share the duties of these offices in a variety of ways.

Sharing in our Lord's priestly office requires that we pray, both in private and with the assembly. The minimum share of prayer with the assembly is what we call the Sunday obligation, which is an essential component in observing the third commandment—"Remember to keep holy the Lord's Day." Fidelity to truth is embedded in the prophetic office, and the kingly office imposes the obligation to exercise our citizenship in the pursuit of justice. We received strength to fulfill our obligations through the Sacrament of Confirmation (Chrismation). Failure to fulfill the obligations we've assumed is the principal source of sin in everyone's life.

Against this backdrop we must remember the [conclusion] of today's reading: "He has wiped out the record of our *debt* to the Law, which stood against us; he has destroyed it by nailing it to the cross . . . " (Col 2:14; emphasis added.)

Saint Paul distinguished between what circumcision literally means from using the term symbolically to mean that the Sacrament of Baptism cut sin out of us. Of course, very sadly, sin can re-enter if we fail to live up to our obligations. Not even this failure, though, stops God's merciful love. We may through repentance receive a renewal of baptismal innocence upon receiving the Sacrament of Penance and Reconciliation (Confession).

Saint Paul understood that the Law, by which he meant the Torah in its full integrity, convicted each of us of some sin or other. We, therefore, were in "debt to the Law." We use debt in exactly the same way when, for example, we speak of a person upon his release from jail upon the completion of his sentence as having paid his debt to society. We human beings could not possibly pay the debt to the Law we'd incurred. Even the innocent, such as babies, if they lived long enough, without God's mercy would only increase the debt. If our history proves anything, it confirms this truth. Only the Christ, the upright One, who chose to share our miserable lot without sharing our sin could by his uprightness pay humanity's debt to the Law.

This business about paying a debt to the Law is a forensic metaphor for what in exceptionally primitive terms Abraham was haggling with God about as reported in our first reading. God's judgment upon a sinful group (we're all Sodomites in this sense) is suspended by the presence in the group of one who is righteous. Jesus is the reason God suspended judgment until the end of time, thereby making his mercy available. Jesus paid for living among us sinners with a very miserable death. Then, in his overflowing merciful love, he rose from the dead, thereby conquering the worst that sin can do. And this he willingly shares with us. We should be overwhelmed with awe and joy and gratitude. And we certainly should not throw it all away by failing our obligations.

Postscript: Promised Comments on Anti-Catholicism

The homily to which this is a postscript sets up my response to the question about [why] the rise of anti-Catholicism at this time.[1] In my judgment, the key to understanding this frightening rise lies right within the Our Father—"thy kingdom come, thy will be done on earth as it is in heaven." [NJB: "your kingdom come, / your will be done, / on earth as in heaven" (Matt 6:10) "your kingdom come . . . " (Luke 11:2) Luke's briefer petition implies what is spelled out in Matthew's.] These petitions imply what is essential to Christian faith: God determines the distinction between what is good and bad, right and wrong. This is the claim that our culture rejects.

What we pray for in the "Our Father" is the answer to the sin at the origin of the human race. Please recall, perhaps even re-read, the story of the sin of our first parents as told in the third chapter of Genesis. This sin consisted essentially in believing we could know the difference between good and bad without God. Or, using other words, we could consistently discern what really is right and what is wrong without God's help. Or, yet another way of stating this truth: we human beings set the difference between good and bad rather than God setting the difference between good and bad, right and wrong. All sin stems from this sin. This sin is all around us today.

God began to remedy this sin by calling Abraham and beginning the process that led to God inspiring the Torah, which contains the Law that God inspired among the people he had chosen. God amplified this revelation by inspiring an historical record and great prophets. Finally, as the culmination of revelation, God's Word became one of us. If one understands the Incarnation, one realizes that there can be no further revelation. What

---

1. He refers to the question in the homily for the previous week, which is not included in this volume.

can God add to his own Word, whole and entire, God from God, Light from Light, etcetera? In Jesus, God has said everything.

Thus, the answer to what we ask for in the Our Father—"your kingdom come, your will be done, on earth as in heaven"—begins with our following what lies embedded in the memory of Jesus the Christ as preserved in the Church he founded. This memory includes his teachings and the example he set with his life, especially with his passion, death, and resurrection. We will never have exhausted what lies in this memory before Jesus comes again.

Some components of this memory lead to reasonably clear distinctions between right and wrong, good and bad. For example, sacred Tradition, not sacred Scripture alone, makes clear what is required for the Sacrament of Matrimony and other non-sacramental, but licit marriage. This component of the memory of Jesus the Christ entrusted to his Church takes out of merely human hands the determination of standards required for virtuous coupling, almost always of a sexual nature.

What God has wrought through the Church, God's Word founded does not meet with widespread approval in our day. Non-believers judge that their way of distinguishing between what is good and bad, right and wrong, leads to a morally superior understanding of sexual coupling. This has led to "marriages" deliberately rendered child-free; to considering the companionate component of marriage superior to the vocation of bearing and rearing children; to strongly supporting same-sex marriage for those whose sexual orientation so inclines them, etcetera. Those who embrace these views easily come to resent the Catholic Church for affirming that God has set standards for human sexual coupling, since they have come to disagree with some or all of these standards. Anti-Catholicism stems from the view that the snake presented in the third chapter of Genesis: human beings without reference to God can determine what's right and what's wrong.

Another instance of the same issue arises from what the Church Jesus founded knows about the sacredness of human life. The Catholic Church, for example, believes that God has drawn a clear line of protection around innocent human life. The Church believes that each human life belongs to God, and no other human being has the right to directly terminate another human being's life no matter at what stage of development except in cases of legitimate defense. Non-believers don't agree. They think they know better. They believe, for example, that abortion can be more compassionate, therefore morally superior, than any moral sanction upon abortion. They also think that mercy killing is just that, i.e., more merciful than a moral sanction against such killing. And, very commonly, they feel free to disregard the conditions that the Church believes come from God whereby one distinguishes a just war and the just conduct of war, on the one hand, from what is unjust and therefore immoral, on the other hand.

With regard to the sanctity of life, there is a full menu of issues in this category, including matters of social justice, such as the prohibition of slavery, and the recognition that torture is contrary to God's law; not to mention the just distribution of goods and services so that one and all may live and then live decently. [These issues, too, have been used by political forces in nefarious ways, not unlike the way an alleged "right" to abortion has been used. Nevertheless, although citizens must be wary, they also must take these issues seriously as essential to doing God's will.]

The fact that the Church speaks with the authority of God's Word in these and other matters leads very many who think they know better into becoming quite vociferously anti-Catholic. But, anti-Catholicism is not enough for some. They become anti-God in general, usually taking a position that is known as Promethean atheism. During my formative years, the prime example of Promethean atheism was Karl Marx (1818–1883). His atheism was not so much a denial of God's existence, but the stronger stance that if there were a "God," one should defy him. In effect, he thought "God" was a monster.

Believe it or not, there's a small element of sanity behind this position, if one believes the false premise from which the argument starts. The false assumption on which Promethean atheism rests is generally accepted, even by people who don't follow it through to its logical conclusion. This false assumption is, namely, that there are no objective criteria whereby one can tell what God has revealed, and therefore is required of us from what are preposterous, perhaps even demonic, claims made in God's name.

Without such criteria, claims made in God's name often are dangerous. This observation does not refer to something hidden or arcane; rather to something quite present. President Bush believes that God supported his decision to declare war preemptively upon Iraq. Pope John Paul II with full support from the other bishops, including the one who now is pope, said God did not support such a choice. Every major official Christian spokesperson outside the Catholic Church agreed, except for a handful of official spokespersons for Southern Baptists as well as other fundamentalists. It was the most ecumenical agreement among professed Christian leaders on a specific point that I've seen in my lifetime. Both positions about the justice of preemptively declaring this particular war could not possibly have been right, simultaneously. I believe there is a criterion whereby one can distinguish between the position that was right, and the one that was not. Instead of believing in such criteria, the new atheists condemn all who speak in

God's name, no matter what they say, while garden variety anti-Catholics focus simply on condemning the Church.

For Marx, the business of rejecting God and especially Catholicism was clear. If "God" sanctioned an unjust social system thereby requiring all the lower social orders to submit docilely to the injustices, as Marx mistakenly thought "God" did, then "God" should be defied. From Marx's point-of-view, the Church represented this unjust "God." Then, as is always the case with anti-God positions, what Marx proposed developed, especially in Soviet Communism and in Mao's China, into something worse than what he'd opposed. All in the name of "justice" without God!

Promethean atheism, which provides the ground for the anti-God movement, finds strength by pointing to horrors that some have claimed God sanctioned. The anti-God forces say that belief in God gave, and still gives evil people the right to propose anti-human behavior and claim that God authorized the actions. For example, if I for one moment thought that the fatwa ordering the murder of Salman Rushdie came from God, I would join anti-God forces. But, I don't believe this fatwa, and innumerable others have God behind them in any way. I reject the idea because I'm a Catholic. The Catholic Church claims that there is one and only one ultimate standard whereby one can determine what comes from God. This standard is Jesus the Christ whose memory his Church preserves. This claim infuriates some non-Catholics. [Persons of good will who've not received the gift of explicit faith recognize some or all of this standard by other means, without the direct assistance of Church teaching.]

This fury against Catholics was stirred up recently by the promulgation on the 29th of June, 2007, of a document from the Vatican Congregation for the Doctrine of the Faith concerned with the doctrine of the Church, often referred to as ecclesiology [*On Some Questions Regarding Aspects of The Doctrine of The Church*]. The reiterated affirmation that the Catholic Church retains in the full sense the memory of Jesus, and that this memory, which the Church officially proclaims, provides the only criteria whereby one can determine what God has revealed, no matter where found, infuriates those who want to see the Catholic Church as just one denomination, neither better nor worse than any other. Those who advocate this relativism often claim they're ecumenical.

Anti-Catholics use the failure of Catholics to live up to the standards they profess are embodied in Jesus their Savior to defend their anti-Catholicism. Catholics, too, find it hard to accept that God the Holy Spirit guarantees only the formal teaching of the Church, not the behavior of any of her members (except that God the Holy Spirit guarantees there will always be holy people among her members). Two apparent betrayals of her founder still plague the Church. Both have been exploited by anti-Catholics and anti-theists; and both are widely misinterpreted, therefore badly misunderstood. They are the Inquisition and the Crusades. Obviously, in a postscript, I'm not able to do justice to these topics. I will make instead a couple of observations.

As proposed, the Crusades had just cause. Here is what Pope Urban II said at Auvergne in France in 1095, from which statement the Crusades take their beginning: "Whoever for devotion alone, not to gain honour or money, goes to Jerusalem to liberate the Church of God can substitute the journey for all penance."[2] The liberation of which the pope spoke can be construed as defensive—defending those who need liberating—thereby coming within the concept of Just War. In the twentieth century, the Indian War that created Bangladesh was just such a liberation, and there is unanimity that this war was just. Much of what followed after the pope's statement in 1095 made a travesty of the beginning. Nevertheless, the solemn teaching of the Church was not violated. She held to the truth we now refer to as Just War doctrine. The Church held to the truth in teaching, if not in practice, because God the Holy Spirit holds the reins of the Church. Certainly, what happened in the conduct of a number of Crusades profoundly betrayed Jesus and his Church, proving for anyone who doubted that the Church is made up of sinners. The betrayals did not deform the Church's teaching. Instead, the teaching judged the betrayers. Some of the betrayers from the fourth Crusade were ex-communicated. One should remember that one of the greatest saints, Saint Francis of Assisi, was embroiled in the Crusades on the side of the truth. He was a man of Christ's peace and may well have brought about peace, if powerful people had paid attention to him.

The Inquisition is inseparable from the Crusades. Both are the product of a beleaguered society in the grip of fear. The fear was not without justification. Islam and other eastern heresies could easily have swamped Europe working from within and from without. Further, the hysteria regarding witches and the like, all of which were associated in the popular mind with heresy, easily turned into mob rule with attendant horrors where there was no Inquisition to rein in the fear and process it.

With respect to the Inquisition, the Church was betrayed by two powerful influences: 1) the uncritical use of Roman law, and 2) state interference. Roman law used torture, so Church officials thought torture was all right. We Catholics tended to defer to the wisdom of Roman law. The Church has since learned that, despite some good in Roman law, torture violates what our Lord requires his Church to believe and teach. Torture, therefore, is

---

2. Tyerman, *Crusades*, 12.

now quite formally condemned as always immoral. Furthermore, the state, in particular the Spanish Empire, found a useful tool in the Inquisition for consolidating power after driving Muslim rule from the Iberian Peninsula. The Spanish Empire also found in the Inquisition a valuable tool for controlling her colonies. Therefore, in large measure the Spanish Inquisition, despite the presence of clerics, was more an institution of the state than of the Church. Thus, the Spanish Inquisition yields a history, and generally a sad one that is distinct from the general history of the Roman Inquisition. Still, not even the Spanish Inquisition could corrupt Church teaching, although the Spanish did subvert some Church governance.

The two—the Crusades and the Inquisition—do not disprove the presence of God's sole standard for God's own revelation resident in the Memory of Jesus preserved in the Catholic Church. In fact, both historical phenomena are rightly judged by this very standard. Still, for anti-Catholics, the Crusades and Inquisition are advanced as proof that human judgment without reference to God produces a higher morality than any theistic morality. Some, then, go on to argue that theistic morality is inherently evil. Thus, we come to Promethean atheism, which caps the anti-Catholicism of our day. [It is difficult to see how in the light of the Reign of Terror, the Nazis, Soviet, Chinese and other Communisms, as well as other atheistic and militantly anti-Catholic movements that one can entertain the idea anti-theistic morality is inherently superior to morality claiming theistic inspiration.]

Before going further, I need to make clear what should be understood by all, and if not understood makes everything I've said thus far taken falsely! The Church affirms truth, *sensu aiente*. This Late Latin expression means that Catholics are meant to believe what is true, and not to accuse anyone else of being wrong. *Sensu negante*, the negative sense, says in effect, "we're right and you're wrong." We do not say that, ever! Sometimes, there is error in other systems of belief. Then we try to dialogue with those believers. We do not lose our grip on the truth, but for the love of God and others, we do not go out of our way to find error in what others believe. We try to find in what they believe what we can see is in harmony with Jesus the Christ and affirm with them. We don't even have to mention this, but we do use the Memory of Jesus the Christ preserved in the Church he founded to test whatever claims are made in God's name.

One of the toughest examples I know arises in dealing with the Qur'an. For example, the Qur'an denies that Jesus died on the Cross. This simply is wrong, and if asked point-blank I can say no other. But, by God's mercy, this error is not the only item in the Muslim system of belief. I can affirm other things. As much as possible, one proceeds *sensu aiente*. I know of no dialogue in which there are more pitfalls than in a dialogue with Muslims.

Anti-Catholicism presently is also fueled by disgruntled Catholics. Pope Benedict XVI rightly believes that these Catholics lost their faith, or their faith suffered severe damage, during what I call the silly season—the period following the Second Vatican Council during which the call to renewal was thought by many to have changed the Church. The document referred to above from the Congregation for the Doctrine of the Faith makes quite clear that no such change took place. Nevertheless, belief that this alleged change had taken place has gripped what may be the majority of Catholics. The false belief led to massive defections from the priesthood and religious life. A higher percentage of priests left active ministry in the silly season than during the Reformation during the sixteenth century.

Even many have stayed not only within the Church but remain as active priests and/or professed religious followed the prevailing spirit that said one's personal judgments about right and wrong were superior to the teaching of the Church even in cases that were not legitimately disputed. This led not only lay men and women but also priests and religious into sin. It became a devastating scene from which we've not as yet recovered, although there are signs of true hope. Some repented their errors and will do penance; others, sadly, have hardened in their resistance to the Church even while continuing to call themselves Catholic. Almost all blame the Church for one reason or another, usually for things not actually related to what really bothers them.

For very many who blame the Church for one thing or another, the deepest reason for blaming the Church and rejecting her or complaining against her, or whatever, remains the conviction that their judgments were at some earlier point and remain so now superior to what they thought were the Church's judgments. In what is perhaps a somewhat disguised form, their view is another version of the reason the snake used to persuade Eve to eat forbidden fruit. Since they'd made up their minds, why should they try to understand what they thought God commanded? Why should they even bother to learn exactly what God had commanded? They were not praying that God's will be done on earth as in heaven. They were "praying" for the right to determine for themselves what the real difference is between right and wrong.

Pope Benedict XVI believes that abuses of the liturgy with attendant loss of a sense of the sacred fed this breakdown. Therefore, even more strongly than his predecessor he is trying to call us to a renewed sense of reverence. For this reason, he issued the document permitting wider use of what is popularly called the Tridentine or Latin Mass. Renewed attention to this liturgical form within the Roman rite our Holy Father seems to believe will shame the great majority of us who have embraced the *Missale Romanum* of Pope Paul VI (the fully accurate way to refer to the way we celebrate Mass) into greater respect for sacred places and far greater reverence in our liturgical worship. Slovenly worship leads, so the Holy Father is convinced, to a critical loss of faith.

One reason people hate the pope for this view is not very obvious. During the silly season following the council, there were many who wanted to change the nature, even the feel, of a Catholic parish church. They wanted what would look and feel to them like a friendly space for people to gather rather than a sacred place, which may intimidate them with a sense of awe and sacredness. Ideally, a parish church would have both a friendly gathering space and the sanctuary, but that arrangement can be expensive. We come as close as parish finances would allow. We have the social hall separate from our sanctuary. But, our sanctuary was not arranged internally to full standard. Eventually, we'll overcome this liability.

I think people hate the pope for this document because he's right. When there is a truly sacred place, people must come to grips with adoration and prayer in God's presence. They must experience being overwhelmed by what is greater than all creation. They must be overawed by the Creator himself. In a recent allocution, the Holy Father quoted Saint Augustine concerning receiving Holy Communion: "No one eats of the flesh without having first adored it."[3] In other words, without the sense of awe and wonder, and sacredness and adoration, no one receives Holy Communion worthily. Do we meet this standard? The people who hate the pope do not want to observe the standard. They want to overturn it.

---

3. Augustine, *Expositions of the Psalms*, Psalm 98.

Chapter 27

Vanity, Humility, and Contemporary Gnosticism

The Eighteenth Sunday in Ordinary Time
Vanity (August 1, 2004)

Scripture Readings

Eccl 1:2, 2:21–23; Ps 89; Col 3:1–5, 9–1; Luke 12:13–21.

Summary

Fr. Roach contrasts authentic piety in Ecclesiastes with the pervasive Gnosticism in our culture. Qoheleth's "All is vanity" warns against escapism or wishful thinking. The apparent pessimism in Ecclesiastes in fact, Fr. Roach says, "tests and protects authentic faith" by preventing "a pseudo-faith that is a kind of escapism." Fr. Roach finds Gnosticism "the religion of wishful thinking" and highly influential in the national character. He then discusses key points of Gnostic thinking. The antidote to Gnosticism and similar anti-Catholic tendencies is embracing the Word as entrusted to the Church. This means cultivating humility (the focus of the next selection in this volume). Humility begins with recognizing God as the creator and us as creatures. Christianity holds that God's primary revelation is a person, not a secret body of knowledge. The escapism of Gnosticism tries to avoid the suffering

VANITY, HUMILITY, AND CONTEMPORARY GNOSTICISM

and evil one cannot do so in this life. Only Jesus, as God, can according to Fr. Roach "bestow life on those who are in Jesus."

Homily

THE FIRST READING FOR this Mass is famous from the use made of the book it was taken from in English and American literature, in pop culture, and through frequent citation. I hope that as we contemplate its contents, the reading will become famous in our eyes for providing a realistic foundation for our faith.

As presented in the lectionary, the reading consists of four verses taken from Ecclesiastes. The book also is known from the "name" of the author given in the opening verse and traditionally translated "Preacher," although the translating team for the NRSV claims the word is Hebrew for "Teacher." All agree that the word transliterated from Hebrew is *Qoheleth*. The NJB says the Hebrew word denoted the personage who speaks for the assembly. "Assembly" in Hebrew is *qahal*, and in Greek is *Ekklesia* (Latin, *Ecclesia*), the true name for the Church. For this reason, the author was denominated the "Preacher" in many translations of the first verse of the book in which he "names" himself. (This verse is not included in the proclamation, but is quoted below.) The NJB decided simply to provide the word transliterated into English.

As a consequence of the use of two names for the book, a variety of abbreviations are commonly used when citing the book. For example, our reading may be cited either as Qoh 1:2; 2:21-23 (NJB) or Eccl 1:2, 2:21-23 (NRSV-CE), or even as in our *Ordo*, Eccles. The first verse, not included in the proclaimed reading, goes as follows: The words of the Teacher, the son of David, king in Jerusalem. (NRSV-CE) Or, as found in the NJB, "Composition of Qoheleth, son of David, king in Jerusalem."

The word, *Qoheleth*, is not the translators' only problem with this book. The other key word for the book's message has been famously translated, "vanity." The NRSV-CE stays with tradition, so our verses (and a couple more) read in that translation as follows: Vanity of vanities, says the Teacher, / vanity of vanities! All is vanity" (1:2). The NJB broke with tradition and rendered this passage as follows: "Sheer futility, Qoheleth says. Sheer futility: everything is futile!" (1:2). The translator(s) of this book for the NJB recognized that what the word "vanity" first brings to a hearer's mind had changed. The word now suggests, first, the silliness of a good looking person, for example, standing before a mirror admiring him/herself. A person stuck on his or her beauty is vain. Therefore, when one says that another person is vain, the comment seems to imply only that the other person prizes too highly, or thinks too frequently about his/her good looks. But when Thackeray entitled his famous novel, *Vanity Fair*, he meant that what went on in the "fair" (i.e., the lives of those he was writing about) was all in vain. In other words, vanity used to mean futility; what was done in vain was futile.

Claiming that "All is vanity" or that "everything is futile" is a depressing and pessimistic claim. What is such pessimism doing in the Bible? Although this may surprise some, correctly answering this question is critical for our faith, because this book is in the Bible to test and protect authentic faith. Prayerfully reading this book helps a person prevent his or her faith from degenerating into a form of wishful thinking. And, we need an antidote to wishful thinking because whenever wishful thinking replaces authentic faith, the believer's appreciation of what is real becomes weakened. This weakening results in a pseudo-faith that is a kind of escapism or flight from reality. Such pseudo-faith is psychological sickness. The sickness has a wide range of degrees from the psychological equivalent of a bad cold onto the psychological equivalent to an advanced stage of terminal cancer. The cancerous form of pseudo-faith always includes falsely perceiving reality in ways that have serious consequences for self and others. Authentic faith, in contrast, is healthy.

Throughout the history of the Catholic Church, from the days Jesus put the basic organization into place, and then God the Holy Spirit descended upon her to this very day, Gnosticism has been the gravest threat to authentic faith. Gnosticism is the religion of wishful thinking.[1] Throughout history, Gnosticism has manifested at least three lethal ingredients. The first amounts to denying that we are merely creatures. [Some elaborated varieties of Gnosticism deny that the highest 'god' is the creator.] Instead of a creature who knows that the Creator is wholly other, despite having created the human as an image of the divine, the Gnostic claims to possess what usually is referred to as "a spark of the divine." In other words, the difference between you and me on the one hand and God on the other is a matter of degree or size, not a difference in kind. In one fell swoop, this lethal belief of the Gnostic wipes out all humility.

Humility begins in recognizing that God is God the Creator of all else that exists, and that I am a creature and most certainly not in any sense God.

The second lethal belief common to all Gnosticism consists in locating the principal source of our struggle with evil (wrongdoing, sickness, death,

---

1. In a homily for May 14, 2006 (not included in this volume) Fr. Roach speculates that much of the contemporary allure of Gnosticism for present-day intellectuals and academics is "they see it as a license to make up one's own religion or adapt an established religion and turn it into whatever one wants."

and so forth) as outside ourselves, even when the struggle has invaded us, or has been built into us. For the Gnostic, the struggle with evil is at root a cosmic struggle rather than a moral one. We escape personal evils by joining the right side in the cosmic struggle, rather than through repentance, grace, prayer, and personal reform.

The third lethal belief consists of distorting how and what God has revealed. The word "Gnostic" derives from a Greek word, *gnosis* (pronounced no-sis). Gnosis means knowledge, but came to be used not for understanding the human or natural world; instead it came to be used for, as the *Encyclopedia of Early Christianity* notes, "a 'revealed knowledge' available only to those who have received the secret teachings of a heavenly revealer."[2] For a perfect example of gnosis as a "revealed knowledge," defined in the preceding sentence, think of the angel Moroni and the Book of Mormon as Joseph Smith allegedly discovered it in upstate New York in the early nineteenth century. Smith read the book, allegedly written on buried golden tablets, through miraculous stones after the "angel" allegedly showed him where to find the tablets, which since have been irrevocably lost. This fantasy is a textbook example of Gnosticism!

Many Gnostic inventions are not nearly as crude as Smith's. The way was paved for him by widespread mistreatment of the Bible, as if the Bible were a cryptic writing come down from heaven and de-coded here by "heavenly revealers," usually preachers at revivals. A correct understanding of the Bible as a library of ancient writings that, when rightly interpreted, attest to the authentic faith of a people and culminate in the recognition that God's Word is a person would have made it very difficult for many to take Smith's religious fantasies seriously. Sadly, the healthy atmosphere created by a reasonable understanding of the Bible does not as yet exist. If it did exist, there would not have been seven and a half million of our fellow Americans willing to pay hard cash for Dan Brown's Gnostic fantasies in novel form—*The Da Vinci Code*.

Gnostic fantasies always are forms of wishful thinking.

Not all religions that included some Gnosticism are purely or exclusively Gnostic. Islam is an instance of a Gnostic spin-off religion, which might, I say only "might," have made the basic distinction between Creator and creature rightly. Pure Gnosticism at the least blurs this distinction, often even denies that the "creator" is the highest god. Still, Islam is profoundly Gnostic in the way the religion understands God's revelation. The prophet (i.e., Muhammad, the "heavenly revealer") sets the record straight about all preceding revelations, and corrects those who allegedly follow what

2. Ferguson, *Encyclopedia*, 371.

preceded him. Then he leaves what he alleges is God's word, a book called the Qur'an (Koran), from which God's law emanates. Our world is dealing with that "revealed knowledge" and the "heavenly revealer" even as I write. Catholic faith escapes this Gnosticism by recognizing that God's Word became a person just like you and me in all things but sin.

In one way or another, all Gnosticism falsifies our ways of thinking about death and dying. As I've said, Gnosticism is wishful thinking. In the wider world, you and I see the fruits of this falsification in every suicide/murderer wreaking terror. In this country, the overwhelming Gnosticism of our unofficial civil religion appears in our funeral rites, which we now most frequently refer to as memorials. It is assumed that when one dies, one automatically goes to a better place or on to a higher plane. No mention is made of the Creator-God judging us to determine if we are to be incorporated into God's Word for eternity (i.e., judgment before going to "a better place"). Passage to the better place, as I said, is assumed to take place automatically, because it is somehow our right. This assumption rests on the Gnostic belief that we are sparks of the divine. The spark simply returns to the originating fire of which it is a natural part. Wishful thinking! (Obviously, spark and fire are metaphors, but they convey the intended meaning clearly.) Qoheleth brings us back to look at death realistically.

Gnosticism falsely assumes that death is merely a rite of passage from one state of life to another. Authentic faith knows that creatures like us die, which if God does not intervene is the end of the creature. We know that if God did not intend to re-create those who in this life accept God's mercy on God's terms into persons who share the eternal life of God's beloved Word, then Qoheleth's views about the futilities of this life and the end that death brings would be the only truth. Before the book found its way onto the list (canon) of sacred Scriptures, an inspired editor added an epilogue. The inspired editor was unaware that in doing so he/she was preparing for the coming of Christ. The epilogue [concludes]: "To sum up the whole matter: fear God and keep his commandments, for that is the duty of everyone. For God will call all our deeds to judgement, all that is hidden, be it good or bad" (Qoh 12:13-14 NJB; the Epilogue to the Book of Ecclesiastes, [is] obviously written by an editor, probably after the death of Qoheleth).

Qoheleth himself ended the book as he had begun it: "Sheer futility, Qoheleth says, everything is futile." Or, as the NRSV-CE translates: "Vanity of vanities, says the Teacher; all is vanity." (Qoh or Eccl 12:8, the original ending.)

The inspired editor knew there would be a judgment, because he or she knew that God is just. The inspired editor knew that God is just alone, and also clearly knew that death is not simply a passage from one state of existence to another. These two truths taken together form the antidote to Gnosticism. The inspired editor did not know that judgment implied a re-creation after the finality of death, which recreation would be revealed as resurrection, and would take place when God's Word became one of us and we put him to death. The inspired editor knew only that God would reveal all our deeds, good and bad, in what in some way resembled open court, and would judge us accordingly. The chosen people did not yet know what this judgment implied. Nor did the editor know that God's judgment would be his Word, Jesus the Christ.

Gnosticism believes we overcome evil simply by choosing sides, much as one may choose to vote for the Democrats or the Republicans because of alleged insight into their plans for the future. If one has chosen the right side, one advances through death. If not, one falls backwards, whatever forwards and backwards mean in any given Gnosticism. For the Gnostic, death simply releases the divine spark, to go forward or backward. Death, therefore, is not realistically seen as the end of a life, a life that only God who created the life in the first place can re-create. A divine spark cannot really die. In contrast, in Jesus we start by knowing that we really die–thank you, Qoheleth–and we know that in Jesus, God will bestow life on those who are in Jesus.

The distinctions between the authentic faith that Jesus proclaims and its phony imitations dubbed Gnosticism are subtle, but very real and all-important. In our day, what I've described above as the second lethal belief common to all Gnosticisms wreaks the greatest havoc. This lethal belief whereby the Gnostic distinguishes between good and bad apes authentic faith, closely, while poisonously falsifying authentic faith. Protestant Evangelical/fundamentalists, for example, rail against Gnosticism, while failing to recognize that in the form of its second lethal belief Gnosticism has invaded their religion. Not realizing that they share in his Gnosticism, they've produced numerous books debunking *The Da Vinci Code*, despite loving its anti-Catholicism, because they know it drives a stake through the heart of what they have retained, albeit imperfectly, of historical Christianity. Brown went way beyond their own, unrecognized Gnosticism.

Fundamentalism derives from an Anglo-Irish Protestant, sometime Anglican cleric by the name of John Nelson Darby (1800–1882). Darby was a fantasist who thought himself a theologian. As fantasist, he read the Bible as a cryptic writing that needed his decoding (see the third lethal Gnostic belief explained above), and his decoding led to the delusions so popular among Protestant fundamentalists—Rapture, the Great Tribulation, numerous forms of Millennialism, Armageddon, and other noxious ideas. The success of the series of novels based on these fundamentalist delusions called the "End Times" series reveals just how widespread is this Gnosticism among fundamentalists who do not recognize that they are Gnostics! But, describing this element of Gnosticism that is at the heart of Protestant Evangelical fundamentalism would not lead us to see the worst ways in which Gnosticism poisons "religion" in our day. Instead, the second lethal belief leads to the gravest damage Gnosticism does in our culture.

Jesus repeatedly taught us, "Do not judge, and you will not be judged" (Matt 7:1). This teaching, which is expressed in many different ways in the New Testament, requires that in this life we judge only behavior (which may consist of some form of speech or omission, and may require evaluating intention, etc.), and we judge behavior only when prudently necessary. We are quite simply prohibited from judging persons as such! Therefore, for us distinguishing between good and bad, or good and evil never means knowing who is a bad person, or who is saved and who is not, or anything else that allows us to categorize a person as "good" or "bad." We don't even put a saint on the list (canon) until after he or she is dead! In the language of our pop culture, the world for one who believes as Jesus taught cannot be divided into good guys and bad guys! No one in this life has his or her head finally affixed to a white or black hat. [Please do not let innocent uses of the expressions "good guys" or "bad guys" block you from seeing my point.]

Gnosticism departs from what our Lord taught. Gnostics distinguish good from evil by distinguishing between which side a person is on. Sure, behavior may be used as a sign, but the behavior is not primary. Because of the inroads Gnosticism has made within Protestantism, it has become the "American religion." Harold Bloom wrote an excellent book defending this claim from the point of view of one who is quite sympathetic to Gnosticism, and its manifestation as the American religion.[3]

Long before I had a clue what Gnosticism is, American culture taught me to think like a Gnostic. For example, I'm old enough to remember the Second World War vividly. During that war, Stalin was Uncle Joe. He was a good guy because he was on our side. For a few years, he wore a white hat. He even sent judges at the end of the war to the Nuremberg trials. Then, as a young boy I was surprised by how quickly he lost his white hat. His hat became as black as soot, and I soon learned that he'd killed at least as many as Hitler, who always wore a black hat.

Then the labels on the hats changed. Black hats quickly came to mean communists and white hats, non-communists, with the whitest hats going to anti-communists.

---

3. Bloom, *American Religion*. Bloom's thesis is that much of American religiosity is covertly Gnostic. The book and thesis made an enduring impression on Fr. Roach.

When I was a small boy, liberals wore white hats and voted for Franklin D. Roosevelt and social security. Conservatives belonged to the America First Committee, and were suspected of having black hats in their closets. Then a few decades ago, something changed. Liberals became black-hatted wastrels, and conservatives rode in with bright white hats to save money and family values. Gnosticism taught this country to divide people into good guys and bad guys, rather than to discuss issues.

Gnosticism has long employed the division of people into good guys and bad guys to justify the use of deadly force. Deadly force may be used to wipe out bad guys. Persons my age can easily remember the old Westerns that Hollywood cranked out. Boy, did we cheer when the sheriff with the white hat blew away the bad guys in black hats! And sometimes white-hatted settlers wiped out whole legions of Indians who all deserved black hats, even if they weren't wearing any at the time. I never saw an Indian in a white hat. Not even Tonto ever wore one. Deadly force takes out bad guys. [If you're too young to have ever seen them in film, Tonto was the Lone Ranger's sidekick in famous Westerns.]

The morality that comes from authentic faith does not think this way. Instead, Catholic morality locates bad actions (and omissions) and seeks to correct these behaviors. Deadly force may be used to correct these behaviors only when the bad behaviors threaten innocent persons, their property and rights, and then only when no other means works. Finally, deadly force may be used only when prudence dictates that the use of such force will improve, not worsen the situation (i.e., decrease not increase bad behavior), and then only when persons ordering the use of deadly force have the competence to make the necessary determinations, and the proper authority to order the use of such force. Catholic morality is so much more complicated than classifying persons as good guys or bad guys.

The judgment that Qoheleth's editor assured us will take place, and that has begun in the Passion, Death, and Resurrection of God's Word become one of us—only this judgment can separate persons into good guys and bad guys. Only God can hand out white and black hats. Life after death is not automatic. We're not divine sparks that one way or another go on, even if we die wearing black hats. But, we don't have to worry about wearing a black hat, do we? [This is ironic!] We're all Americans, and don't all Americans wear white hats, and belong to the right side? The Gnostic religion I've been propagandized by all of my life tells me we do. I've reached the age at which I wouldn't bet on it. I've had to face the fact that at least one American, the one I know best (me), has sinned and needs God's mercy. And, I don't think my being born on the right side, and embracing this side as a patriotic citizen will win me forgiveness. Thank God, Jesus has won that forgiveness and bestowed it on me with his love. In this life, very few thought he was on the right side. I fear that very few actually believe he is on the right side now. At least, only a few tend to act as if they do.

I know there is no way to cheat death by choosing the right side. I listen to the news and learn of poor young people whose merciless leaders tell them they can cheat death by choosing the right side (always thought of as God's side), and then blowing themselves up as a bomb that kills those whom their handlers have taught them are bad guys by virtue of the side they are on. This system of belief denies the reality of death as surely as any illusion to the effect that we automatically go to a better place because we are a spark of the divine.

Death is death, and Qoheleth knew it. And the judgment that follows death determines one's hat for all eternity, the only hat that distinguishes between a good guy and a bad guy. God is not impressed by anyone insisting that he or she chose the right side during this life, if the choice did not mean living rightly in truth, justice, and merciful love. Unless one's choices are for truth, justice, and merciful love, God doesn't give a tinker's dam whose side one was on, or the color of one's hat in this world.

And, as for that divine spark. How pretentious can a mere creature get? The idea gives God a good laugh.

Today's gospel contains a parable that our Lord told about the unreality inherent in denying the reality of death. One may refer to the parable as a riff on Qoheleth from our Lord's advanced perspective.

Our Lord also commented on litigation prompted by greed. If a great deal of such litigation isn't going on in our day, I'm misinformed. Nevertheless, I can feel a reaction building against this kind of litigation—at least when medical doctors are being sued, but certainly not when Catholic priests are. I'm afraid this reaction will throw the baby out with the bath water. There are cases with real injuries that require just compensation. But, much less real injuries amplified by claims of pain and suffering designed to enrich alleged victims do not in justice require compensation that actually is a windfall for the alleged victim. These unjust compensations can and should be curtailed.

Our Lord's point was a bit different. He wanted, first, to counteract the notion that someone—he himself and those who would come after him proclaiming the gospel—who instruct the assembly and lead the assembled in prayer are authorities in legal matters. The rabbis who preceded him interpreted the Law, which they saw as the heart or essence of God's revelation. So, people came to them to have their cases adjudicated. Jesus also interpreted the Law; but he did so in broad terms, trying to change the way people thought about the Law and law in general. [Law equals Torah equals Pentateuch equals the legal codes in the Pentateuch.] Above all, he wanted people to see that God's revelation is not a Law. He, Jesus, is God's revelation.

Of course, following Jesus requires us to do what is right. But, God's revelation is not a law! We are supposed to figure out God's law for us from what God has written on our hearts (which includes what we call a conscience). We don't have a written code to follow. Contrast me as the priest serving this parish with an imam serving a mosque. The Muslim religion is a reactionary return to the idea that God's revelation is Law in imitation of how this was understood in Judaism around the time of Jesus. We are blessed to know that Jesus is God's revelation. He did not want a man quarreling with his brother over an inheritance to drag him into giving the impression that the faith he was teaching returns us to a notion that God's revelation consists of a Law.

Jesus then used the occasion to teach us about how to treat possessions in the light of the truth that we will all really die. Jesus probably thought of Qoheleth as he taught.

The liturgists selecting today's second reading omitted verses 6 through 8 inclusive for a very good reason. Although Saint Paul did not mean these omitted verses used as a "new" codified law, many, especially Protestants, have used them as codified law. Saint Paul intended them as a popular example of doing what is right, not as a code of law.

The reading does intend to direct us to the core of authentic morality, which we, who are raised with Christ, as the reading says, must live. Authentic morality is an unqualified commitment to truth: "do not lie to each other" (Col 3:9a). The rest follows. Because we are all raised in Christ, there are no distinctions among us whereby one group or ethnicity is better than another, whereby one gender is better than another, etcetera. The truth sets us free.

Chapter 28

The Humility of the Cross

*The Twenty-Second Sunday of the Year
Humility (August 29, 2004)*

Scripture Readings

Sir 3:17–18, 20, 28–29; Ps 68; Hebrews 12:18–19, 22–24; Luke 14:1, 7–14.

Summary

Christ's Passion teaches us a humility both uniquely Christian, and indispensable in responding to God. Christ emptied himself for our sake though he did not need to. Christian humility calls us to self-sacrifice if others may be persuaded to repent and receive God's loving mercy. Humility more generally involves keeping in perspective of who one is before God, and what one should do for others. Thus, Fr. Roach observes, "Bowing down before 'the power of God' prepares us for giving of ourselves even unto death in order to draw people from evil into the grace of God, just as Jesus did." Acknowledging God's power means recognizing that truth, justice, and mercy trump immediate self-interest. Humility in this way becomes the gateway to authentic Christian love, the topic of the next homily.

THE HUMILITY OF THE CROSS

Homily

MANY ARE UNAWARE THAT humility as our Lord taught the virtue by word and deed is uniquely Christian. Insofar as I can discover, all major religions recommend humility of one sort or another. No other religion recommends what makes unique the humility that Jesus taught.

For the most part, we are expected to learn about humility from our Lord's history, especially his Passion and Crucifixion. The narrative replaces explicit definition and exhortation. There are at least two documents in the New Testament that treat the subject explicitly: Saint Paul's Letter to the Philippians, and the First Letter of Peter. Both passages use a Greek word that means "lowliness," which we commonly translate to humility. Remarkably, the seventeenth century Anglican Authorized Version (AV, popularly known as the King James Version, KJV) translated the term as used in Philippians with dictionary literalness: "Let nothing be done through strife or vainglory; but in lowliness of mind let each esteem others better than themselves. Look not every man on his own things, but every man also on the things of others" (Phil 2:3–4 KJV). Here are the same two verses in a contemporary translation: "Nothing is to be done out of jealousy or vanity; instead, out of humility of mind everyone should give preference to others, everyone pursuing not selfish interests but those of others" (Phil 2:3–4 NJB). Between the seventeenth century and the twentieth, "lowliness" became "humility."

Lowliness would have been intensely repugnant to an ancient, pagan Greek. Modesty would have been a virtue, but not lowliness. Lowliness was abhorrent, and lowliness of mind would have been the most abhorrent. The Catholic Church had to explain a great deal to those shaped by the ancient cultures.

In the First Letter of Peter, we read again about this lowliness: "In the same way, younger people, be subject to the elders. Humility towards one another must be the garment you all wear constantly, because *God opposes the proud but accords his favour to the humble.* Bow down (literally, make yourself lowly), then, before the power of God now, so that he may raise you up in due time; *unload* all *your burden on to him*, since he is concerned about you (1 Pet 5:5–7 NJB; even in the seventeenth century, the translators of the KJV abandoned "lowliness" and used "humility" in these verses, so there is no point in a contrasting quotation. We see in this fact that the choice of an English term for the Greek "lowliness" was already changing even as other translators for the KJV used the literal equivalent from the dictionary).

In his Letter to the Philippians, Saint Paul explained what "lowliness of mind" meant by quoting a hymn sung in the Church at her beginning. It remains the best statement we have of what the humility Jesus taught in word and deed actually means, [see Phil 2:5–11]. The lessons we may take from this hymn are many. But, with respect to "lowliness of mind" (Remember Phil 2:3 quoted above in two translations), which is the humility God orders us to cultivate as a virtue, we may learn what it consists of from the hymn. It is the mind (or mindset) that Jesus had and still has. Jesus knew who he is. And, he knew what he could do to his enemies because he was in the "form of God." But, for their sake, for the sake of his enemies, he emptied himself and died on the Cross, the death of a despised slave. As sinners we were among the enemy.

When we acquire this humility, we sacrifice ourselves for others, but not willy-nilly. We sacrifice ourselves when and only when our sacrifice creates the conditions wherein others can repent their sins and receive God's mercy. God's Word became "as human beings are"—i.e., became Jesus—so that we could become as Jesus is since God has "raised him high."

The hymn does not spell out the steps that intervene between our Lord's death and his glory in which we are called to share. They are taken for granted. What the hymn does spell out is our need to recognize in Jesus "the form of God" of which he emptied himself for our sake. Unless we see the divine in Jesus, we will miss the humility that God requires. The author of First Peter had this in mind when he wrote First Peter 5:6–7, quoted above. In the hymn that Saint Paul quoted in Philippians, we read, " . . . *all beings / in the heavens, on earth and in the underworld, / should bend the knee* at the name of Jesus / and every tongue should acknowledge / Jesus Christ as Lord, / to the glory of God the Father" (Phil 2:10–11 [emphasis not added]). Humility begins by, and there is no humility without, bowing down "before the power of God."

Bowing down before the power of God means recognizing explicitly goods, such as truth, mercy, and justice, that are greater than what self-interest defines as good, and promoting those greater goods when possible.

Some who do not enjoy the grace of faith bow down "before the power of God" without knowing they are doing so. Members of AA do so when they call upon a higher power. Persons who dedicate themselves without prejudice to truth and justice bow down "before the power of God" without knowing they are doing so, as long as they do not allow an unworthy ideology to tell them what is true or just. Nevertheless, the grace of explicit faith is far and away the best invitation to "bow down" in humility.

[I hope that the alert reader noted where "genuflecting" before the Blessed Sacrament comes from. A good Semite like Saint Paul would easily use the word "name" to denote presence. Jesus Christ truly is present in the Blessed Sacrament. So, we genuflect, which means bend the knee, before the Blessed Sacrament; not before an altar, not before an icon, not even before the Cross except on Good Friday, but before the Blessed Sacrament.]

Bowing down "before the power of God" prepares us for giving of ourselves even unto death in order to draw people from evil into the grace of God, just as Jesus did. Drawing people from evil expresses merciful love. We are called to be instruments of our Lord's merciful love. Therefore, modesty, a virtue in itself, does not substitute for Christian humility. Modesty may complement humility; it does not take the place of humility.

In the Old Testament, lowliness/humility was understood as the proper stance before God. It was not yet seen that this "lowliness" may be needed before other human beings in order to save them from evil. This latter (lowliness before other human beings) is revealed in Jesus, as we've seen in the New Testament. Jesus preached about this lowliness/humility in his Sermon on the Mount: " . . . if anyone hits you on the right cheek, offer him the other as well; . . . " (Matt 5:39) " . . . I say this to you, love your enemies and pray for those who persecute you; . . . " (Matt 5:44). We perform such selfless acts rightly only when our selfless behavior leads others to repentance and forgiveness, which such acts will more often than many realize. Despite this higher standard our Lord introduced, the wonderful hymn to humility from the Old Testament that was our first reading (Sir 3:17–18, 20, 28–29) provides great wisdom about humility. I recommend the passage for prayerful reading. Do not be put off by the verse numbering. With a good Catholic edition of the Bible, such as the NJB, just turn to the third chapter of Ecclesiasticus (Sirach), and you'll find the tribute to humility clearly marked.

There is one verse that can easily mislead. As I write this, I don't know if it has been included in our proclamation. Whatever the case, here is the verse: "Do not try to understand things that are too difficult for you, / or try to discover what is beyond your powers." (Sir 3:21; if the lectionary follows the same verse numbering as the NJB, this verse was omitted from the proclamation.) Jesus ben (son of) Sirach (or Sira), who wrote the book, was not telling his students to become anti-intellectuals or to dumb down. (For the author's name, see the last verse of the book.) He was cautioning the boys in his care against mere curiosity. "Curiosity" used to name a vice, as in this example—a boy is curious to learn the intimate and private details of someone's life, which were none of his business. His desire to learn these details is prurient. (Sirach was the headmaster of a boys' school.) Furthermore, he is not emotionally mature enough to understand these intimate details. In doing so, he may well be trying to discover what lay beyond his powers to handle. The headmaster was telling his boys to stick to their lessons.

The entire homily thus far has been preparation for today's gospel. The punch line is quite direct: "For everyone who raises himself up will be humbled, and the one who humbles himself will be raised up" (Luke 14:11). Unfortunately, this punch line is like the verse from Sirach discussed in the preceding paragraph. Many misinterpret this verse, making it into a directive for the worst forms of false modesty. Surely, we've all run into the people who make a painful scene when asked to sit at the head table, or whatever: "Oh no, not me! I'm not worthy. Ask someone who's important." And so on. What a pain! This behavior has nothing to do with humility.

The last three verses probably tell us more about humility than the parable about places of honor at a formal dinner. (How often have you been to a formal dinner where the seating was a statement of rank? I think I can count my experiences of such dinners on one hand.) Luke 14:12–14 tells us not to cultivate only those who repay us with rich returns. It does take humility to spend time with those who cannot return favors in kind or better. It takes even greater humility to share with people without even creating the feeling that one expects something in return.

Again, even these few verses can be misunderstood. It's pride, arrogance in the worst form, when a benefactor rejects a humble token that a poor person wishes to offer something in return for a kindness received. A careful reading of these verses reveals that Jesus ruled this arrogance out by instructing us to invite those who could offer nothing in return.

The unique humility that Jesus Christ taught is seen in his crucifixion. This is why religions, such as Islam, deny that Jesus was crucified. I doubt that I can close this homily with a pithy definition summarizing what I hope we've thought about for this brief, but I'll offer a suggestion: The humility of Christ that we're expected to imitate requires sacrificing one's self-interest, including ego, if the sacrifice may persuade someone to repent and receive God's merciful love with all its demands.

Chapter 29

Loving One Another

The Fifth Sunday of Easter
"As I Have Loved You" (May 9, 2004)

Scripture Readings

Acts 14:21–27; Ps 145; Rev 21:1–5a; John 13:31–33a, 34–35.

Summary

Loving as Christ does marks the true Christian. The homily exhorts believers "how we are supposed to be marked" by Christian love and fidelity to truth, even when Fr. Roach notes "loving as Jesus loved is no easy matter." What does this involve? Authentic love calls us to seek truth, justice, and mercy for all. Christ's voluntary acceptance of a violent death flows from his commitment to truth. (This stands in contrast with Pilate's feigned disregard.) To love as Christ did is thus to share his adherence to truth. Seeking truth involves seeking the truth about ourselves, and what God asks of us. Finally, genuine love has to act on the truth. Mary's yes to God, repeated throughout her life, is our exemplar for living the truth of who we are before God.

Homily

WE OFTEN FORGET THAT by virtually universal custom, religious people mark themselves in some way. So, you and I can recognize an observant Jew by, among other things, what he or she will or will not eat. In other words, the followers of Judaism mark themselves by dietary laws. To a lesser degree, we can recognize a Muslim in the same way, but the most obvious marking is the manner of dress of Muslim women. There are marks for Hindus and Buddhists and others. The followers of the same religion can recognize each other, thanks to the markings; and those who are not followers of that specific religion, if knowledgeable about the markings, can recognize those who are.

Through history, we have done a bit of the same thing. Persons who vowed themselves to God according to a specific manner of living often wore clothing, called a habit, that marked them. For example, a nun would wear old-fashioned clothing and a veil. A Franciscan wore, and many still wear, a brown or black robe tied with a rope called a cincture. Diocesan priests wore black suits with a round, white collar replacing the tie that other men wore. And so forth! Catholics in general used to be recognized in much of the world each Friday, because we refused to eat meat. Initially, all these "Catholic" markings, as did almost all religious markings, had purposes other than signaling the religious profession of the marked individual, but these purposes were quickly forgotten and the habit or other sign became merely a mark. This is a principal reason that following the Second Vatican Council practically all were abolished. We are supposed to be marked by something different, as we will see in a moment.

Before turning to the way you and I are supposed to be marked so that we know each other and are known by others, let us look closely at the Friday "fish-eating" that once marked a Catholic, at least in this country. The discipline whereby we were obliged not to eat meat on Friday was intended as a penitential act meant to commemorate the day on which our Lord died on the Cross. It was not intended as a dietary law, which laws Jesus had observed among his own people. The Church, under the guidance of God the Holy Spirit, had abolished these laws almost the day she was founded. The Friday observance was not meant to be the backdoor, re-entrance of dietary laws. But, it was soon treated just that way. So, following the Second Vatican Council, the observance was almost universally abolished. We're no longer marked by fish on Friday, except in this country during Lent.

Today's gospel states unequivocally how we are supposed to be marked: Jesus said, "I give you a new commandment: / love one another; / you must love one another / *just as I have loved you.* / It is by your love for one another,

/ that everyone will recognise you / as my disciples" (John 13: 34–35; NJB with English spelling; emphasis added). God intends us to be marked so that others know who we are by loving exactly as God's Word, Jesus, loved us while he walked on this earth, and still loves us as our resurrected Lord.

The vast majority think they know what love is. The vast majority are deluded. The vast majority think that basically they are loving persons. They're kidding themselves. Only a few know what true love is, and they're probably here at Mass. It's probably the reason they are here at Mass, although participation in the Eucharistic Sacrifice is not a guarantee. It should be; but, tragically, it isn't. Nevertheless, those who love truly are drawn to the Eucharistic Sacrifice as the font of their loving.

Loving as Jesus loved is no easy matter. His love requires a living commitment to truth, justice, and mercy that few make. The commitment is a great bother and few want so to be bothered. So, very few actually love, as Jesus loved us. And the way Jesus loved us is the only fully authentic loving.

Jesus loved us as a consequence of his commitment to truth. It was through being true to God his Father, to himself, and to his friends that Jesus loved us. Jesus was even true to his enemies. There is no other way to authentic love! Although it is true, as Saint Paul put it in a kind of shorthand, that "Christ died for our sins" (1 Cor 15:3), this statement is meaningless, or even misleading if one does not understand that Jesus died as a martyr for the truth. The man who ordered his execution, the Roman procurator Pilate, knew this. Saint John saw the issue more clearly than the other evangelists. That is why he reported Pilate's self-justifying skepticism about truth: "'Truth?' Pilate said. 'What is that?'" (John 18:38). Jesus then assigned even greater guilt to those who put Pilate up to this charade, because God had given them the means to know truth as found in the Law, the prophecies, and the promises. Pilate did not have this advantage. The truths found in the Law, the prophecies, and the promises should have led the Judean theocrats ineluctably to the truth that Jesus taught about his Father and indirectly about himself (cf., John 19:11).

I trust that all are smart enough not to apply what I've just written to contemporary Jews. The judgment that Jesus passed on Judean theocrats (i.e., the Jewish leadership of his day) does not extend to Jews in our day. The equivalent of those who come under our Lord's harsh judgment today would first be lapsed or ex-Catholics. They were given the opportunity for authentic faith with the love that follows from it, and they rejected the opportunity.

The issue is truth. Jesus died a martyr for truth. He died for our sins because all sins are forms of lying. They are deadly when people insist on believing their lies rather than admit the truth. And any trace or attachment to untruth kills love. You and I can love only insofar as we stand in and for the truth!

An unflinching commitment to the truth cannot be reduced to observing laws, not even the moral law as we know it. A powerful experience I had while teaching helped me learn more about the unflinching commitment to the truth that God asks of us as the condition for God enabling us to love, truly.

The experience took place during an undergraduate class at Marquette University.[1] I was teaching a course entitled "Theology and Values." The subject was abortion. We were discussing the hard cases when something may be done that will have as an unintended side-effect the death of the fetus a mother is carrying. I presented the class with the case of a pregnant woman whose doctor confronted her with a diagnosis of cancer. She was well along in her pregnancy—I don't remember how long. Nevertheless, the doctor recommended operating on the cancer immediately, although he clearly foresaw that doing so would terminate her pregnancy i.e., the surgery to remove her cancer would have the unintended side-effect of killing the baby she was carrying.

The doctor made clear to the woman that the sooner he operated on the cancer, the better her chances of recovery. The woman countered with a question, "Would she be able to carry her baby to term?" The doctor replied, "Yes, but there would be increased risk of the cancer spreading and becoming inoperable." She chose to take her chances and brought her baby to term.

I explained to the class that she had not been morally obliged to do as she had chosen. I explained that Catholic moral theology judged that the death of her fetus, had she chosen immediate surgery, would have been an unintended side-effect of a licit surgery undertaken to save her life. Therefore, the death of the baby would not have met the criteria for an unequivocally prohibited abortion. Instead of regarding her choice as one she was obliged to make, Catholic moral theology regarded her choice as an heroic act of charity i.e., true love.

Before I could finish my example and explanation, I noticed a young lad sitting bolt upright, and very still with tears streaming down his face. The other students hadn't noticed him. He was seated on my left, the right side of the class, about half way toward the back of the classroom. No one had turned to look at him.

---

1. Fr. Roach is referring to Marquette University in Milwaukee, WI, where he taught in the Department of Theology for many years and often said Mass at local parishes. He moved away in the early 1990s. He is still well remembered by former students, colleagues, parishioners, and brother Jesuits in the area.

I quickly brought the class to a close a few minutes early, and the students streamed out. As I had hoped, the young lad hadn't moved. I was at his side in a second and as gently as I could asked him if I could help. He softly said, "No," and then said just as softly, "You were telling the story of my mother."

If you benefited from a mother's heroic love, this is a good day to say "Thank-you" and to pray for her. Happy Mother's Day!

What made the young lad's mother capable of heroic love was her prior commitment to truth. She may well have been surprised to learn this fact, but there it is. She knew the truth about herself, the truth about what it had meant for her to become pregnant, the truth about the life she was carrying, and the truth about how God blesses and rewards sacrifice. I have no idea how many of these truths she could explicate, but she knew them and her choice proved her commitment to them. Truth comes before love. Anything that mars truth destroys love. For this reason Jesus was a martyr for truth, and a person who commanded love.

In order to love as Jesus has loved us, we must share his commitment to truth. Even from the little we know, we are able to see that his mother's greatness resulted from her sharing in this commitment. An important part of our Lord's message consisted of overturning what was taken for granted in order to get to the truth. This happened at least twice in the life of the extraordinary woman whom we rightly call The Blessed Virgin Mary, the Mother of God.

Saint Luke tells the story about when Jesus, then a young lad of twelve, stayed behind in Jerusalem after his parents had set off for home without telling them (cf., Luke 2:41–50). We forget how little our Lady knew about her son at the time. She knew only that he had been conceived miraculously. Saint Luke wrote that the angel Gabriel had told her, her son would be called "Son of the Most High" and would inherit David's throne, that he also had said because of the miraculous conception her child would be called "the Son of God" (cf., Luke 1:26–38).

Although what Saint Luke reported about Jesus is accurate, we do not know how much of it Mary understood. From what Luke reported later on about Saint Joseph's and her concern and confusion when Jesus in his twelfth-year stayed behind in Jerusalem, I think we may reasonably conclude that when Jesus was conceived, and for a long time afterwards, Mary understood only that God had asked her to bear a child, miraculously conceived. And, she had done as God asked her.

Her greatness lay in knowing the truth about herself, and the truth of what God asked of her, and then doing the truth. Her greatness does not lie in the fact that she is the biological mother of Jesus. Her greatness lies in exactly what she said to the angel that God had dispatched to announce his intentions to her. At the end of their meeting, she gave the angel her response to God: "Mary said, 'You see before you the Lord's servant (the truth about herself), let it happen to me as you have said'" (Luke 1:38). With her last remark, our Lady acknowledged that she had understood what God was asking of her—i.e., she understood the truth about God.

Very few in the history of the human race have received special commissions from God, as our Lady did. Very few, indeed! And for even these very few, God authenticated his communicating with the individual by making clear that his message or request lay within established sacred Tradition and conformed to what may or should be universally known about him. Even when the sacred Tradition was beginning and still in its infancy, God authenticated his special revelations, as with the patriarch Abraham, within the context of what men generally could and should have known about him. Divine revelation never has been esoteric! Those who claim esoteric revelations are deluded. Our Lady was manifestly not deluded.

General truths are the foundation and starting point for verifying particular truths. General knowledge of God, available to our Lady in her day, verified the special knowledge Saint Luke said she acquired from an angel. Our Lady built her life on that truth. And her son tested her, not only as a lad in Jerusalem's temple, but later when teaching the people.

Our Lord's mother along with members of his extended family, who were referred to in Hebrew and Aramaic as "brothers," came to see him when he was teaching, and wanted a word with him. Jesus used the occasion to teach a strong lesson. He asked, "Who is my mother? Who are my brothers (which if one knows Aramaic means, who is my family)?" Then, he answered his own rhetorical questions: "Anyone who does the will of my Father in heaven is my brother and sister and mother" (cf., Matt 12:46–50; Mark 3:31–35; and Luke 8:19–21). It may have been a brutal way to teach, but it did and still does teach us that what counts is knowing the truth about God and doing it. Mary did, and for that reason we ask for her prayers on our behalf as the Mother of God. Happy Mother's Day!

The true mother is a woman who knows how to love; the true father is a man who knows how to love. Biology alone doesn't cut it! For this reason we often use the terms "mother" and "father" honorifically for those who are not biological mothers or fathers. Motherhood, as we salute it today in this secular holiday, is not just a biological fact.

Our first reading reminds us that in order to keep the faith in a sinful world, we must be prepared to suffer hardships (Acts 14:22). In most translations today, the English text uses the word "elders" to translate *presbyteroi* from the Greek. *Presbyteroi* denotes the men who came to be called priests.

For example, in Church documents, I am referred to as a member of the presbyterate. A bishop is a member of the episcopate; a deacon, of the diaconate. The shift from using the word "presbyter" for an ordained man to using the word "priest" became universal after the destruction of the Temple in Jerusalem when the Jewish priesthood ceased to function. The use of the word "priest" is a way of recognizing that the Eucharistic Sacrifice, at which the presbyter presides, replaces the sacrifices once offered in the Temple (Acts 14:23).

Finally, the reading reminds us of our catholicity: "On their arrival, they (Paul and Barnabas) assembled the church and gave an account of all that God had done with them, and how he had opened the door of faith to the gentiles" (Acts 14:27).

The responsorial is taken from the Psalm 145. This is one of the "alphabet" psalms—each verse begins with a letter of the Hebrew alphabet in proper sequence. The literary form is not unlike the conceit used in a popular song that celebrates this secular holiday—"M" is for ____; "O" is for ____: "T" is for ____; and so forth. I'm sorry that I've quite forgotten the lyrics. I hope you remember them. The point is that the song spells out the word "Mother" with a sentiment or verse for each letter. The psalm recites the Hebrew alphabet with a verse for each letter. It can't be replicated successfully in translation.

The second reading in poetic language provides a glimpse of what really will be the end times. God will make "the whole of creation new" (Rev 21:5). When God makes the creation new, " . . . there will be no more death, and no more mourning or sadness or pain" (Rev 21:4). In poetic language, this is what we know about the so-called "End Times," not the rubbish found in the best-selling novels of the "Left Behind" series. The mythology of "Rapture" and "Armageddon" is myth without truth.

Chapter 30

Perseverance

The Thirty-Third Sunday in Ordinary Time
Perseverance! (November 14, 2004)

Scripture Readings

Mal 3:19–20a; Ps 98; 2 Thess 3:7–12; Luke 21:5–19.

Summary

Humility leads to genuine love of God, while such love calls us to persevere. In this homily, Fr. Roach explains perseverance as a central Christian virtue. He notes its associated challenges. Christian perseverance means one seeks, according to Fr. Roach, to be one "who is faithful to the end." God fortunately gives the grace for faith to endure. A principal expression of this virtue in Catholicism is faithfulness to the assembly. Fr. Roach describes how "every sacrament contains a promise of faithfulness or perseverance." Key to faithfulness is doing what a sacrament requires of a person. In addition, some actions expressing the intent to be faithful to a sacrament can superficially appear otherwise. Dogged faithfulness to God should not be confused with fanaticism and its false certitude. Perseverance in the faith nowadays faces very real challenges. The reading from Malachi assures us that God's justice will triumph; our perseverance will be rewarded with the intense joy of sharing in the eternal life of God.

Homily

THE GOSPEL FOR THIS Sunday concludes with the sentence: "Your perseverance will win you your lives" (Luke 21:19). Persons who respond to Jesus the Christ with full and authentic faith receive what our Lord said with these words very seriously indeed. Some may miss the force of our Lord's words because they do not understand fully what "perseverance" means. I regard the word as a perfect synonym for faithfulness. The person who perseveres to the end is the person who is faithful to the end.

Before Luther thought up the slogan "justified by faith alone," everyone realized that faith had to work itself out through faithfulness or perseverance. Catholic theology came up with the expression, "the grace of perseverance." This named the help that God freely and mercifully would give so that a person could be faithful until death, so Catholic theologians said that in the last analysis a person was saved by the grace of perseverance. Where Protestantism became dominant, recognition of this saving grace of perseverance was blotted out of people's consciousness by "faith alone." In reality, faith without faithfulness isn't really a big deal.

Other things being equal, the principal and essential expression of perseverance or faithfulness is seen in participation in the assembly (i.e., the Church at prayer). In addition to fidelity to the Eucharistic Sacrifice (i.e., the Mass), every sacrament contains a promise of faithfulness or perseverance, if you prefer the latter term.

The Sacrament of Baptism contains a solemn promise to live the Catholic faith. For infants, proxies (parents or guardians) make the promise for the child. If old enough, the person receiving baptism makes the promise for him/herself. Either way, the promise made for an infant by proxy or by a person old enough to promise for him/herself, the Church enlists sponsors (Godparents) to support the newly baptized in keeping the promise. No one qualifies as a sponsor or Godparent except he or she is a faithful Catholic. (We allow non-Catholics a ceremonial role in baptism, but they are not registered as sponsors, whom we call "Godparents.") The grace of baptism whereby we die and rise with Christ can be lost through infidelity to our baptismal promises. We must persevere.

In the Sacrament of Confirmation (or Chrismation), we are strengthened by the gifts of God the Holy Spirit so that we may more readily fulfill our baptismal promises. There is staggering hypocrisy in receiving this sacrament as merely a rite of passage and then failing to fulfill its promise. There would be less sin in not receiving the sacrament.

[Regrettably, receiving first Holy Communion also is abused as a mere rite of passage and family celebration, as is the Sacrament of Confirmation.

This too is sinful. As we will see when discussing the Sacrament of the Eucharist, receiving Holy Communion is a public affirmation and a promise. The person who is lying when receiving Holy Communion is thereby sinning. In the case of children receiving first Holy Communion, if they fail to keep the promise of the sacrament, it usually is the case that the parents, not the children, are sinning.]

The Sacrament of Penance and Reconciliation requires renewing one's promises. If we have violated our promises in baptism and confirmation, God's merciful love, which is God's grace, calls us to repent, ask for forgiveness, and promise to try anew. Then, through the Church we receive God's forgiveness.

The Sacrament of the Eucharist is the central sacrament of Catholic faith. In celebrating this sacrament (the celebration we who once used Latin call the Mass) we remember our Lord's Passion, Death, Resurrection, and Ascension. The celebration renews our resurrected Lord's presence with us. In his renewed presence, we find the reality of his life, death, resurrection and ascension. Jesus's present reality is that of our resurrected Lord who has brought his human life to glory with God the Father and Holy Spirit. The celebration is an occasion for adoring God, which is the highest act of worship. Since the celebration re-presents our Lord's sacrificial life, death, and resurrection, it too is sacrificial, but precisely as a thanksgiving sacrifice, which our Lord enables us to offer, thereby giving thanks to God. Eucharist means thanksgiving.

For those who are prepared, the fullest entry into the celebration consists in receiving the Resurrected Lord as food—the Bread of Life and the Blood of the Lamb. Receiving Jesus in this form contains a promise to remain faithful. The reception is a public affirmation that one is an active member of the assembly (i.e., the Church) in good standing, and receiving Holy Communion also implies the promise one intends to continue as an active, faithful member of the Church. If one has failed this promise, the Sacrament of Penance always is available. Then one returns to receive Holy Communion without hypocrisy.

The Sacrament of Matrimony has the form of a promise or vow; in fact, two promises or vows that are exchanged reciprocally. If either promise is not rightly made there is no sacrament, which means there is no marriage. The heart of matrimony is faithful love related by its nature to reproduction. (There also is faithful love that is not linked by its nature to literally reproducing human life. Such faithful love is highly honorable, but not the form of a sacrament. It is the love found, for example, when Jesus called his disciples, his friends (cf., John 15:15). It would be hard to get more honorable than this, but because the love was not related by its nature to reproduction, Jesus did not make it a sacrament.)

The Sacrament of Holy Orders, which is tri-partite, imposes obligations, and thereby elicits promises from those who receive the sacrament at any of its three levels. Failure to strive to live up to the promises makes for grave sin.

Even the Sacrament of the Anointing of the Sick contains a promise requiring perseverance or faithfulness. The recipient of the sacrament, even in the midst of aging and sickness, promises to love life and live whatever time remains "in the sure and certain hope of the resurrection." The person implicitly promises to venerate God's gift of life as God intended. This does not imply a promise to prolong life here with every piece of advanced technology in the medical warehouse. Proper respect for God's gift of life includes an acceptance of natural death when God calls us home.

The recent election popularized the term "flip-flopping." Used negatively, this term implies the flip-flopper is inconsistent, merely expedient, wishy-washy, and certainly not one who is faithful and perseveres. Regrettably, a malicious and/or ignorant person can use the term, "flip-flopper," against someone who has recognized that it is necessary to change course in order to persevere in a higher sense. The term may also be used against someone who has repented a mistake and altered course in order to return to fidelity and persevere. We need to be aware of "flip-flopper's" negative meaning so that we can judge if the term is being used fairly or unfairly, because "flip-flopper" has been used unfairly with respect to keeping the promises in the sacraments God has given us.

For example, a person may enter a marriage and celebrate the Sacrament of Matrimony in good faith, only to learn that he/she has attempted marriage with an abuser. (Abuse can consist of physical violence, including sexual violence, or may be only verbal and emotional. Abuse consisting only of the verbal and emotional violence can be every bit as severe as abuse expressed in physical violence, including sexual violence.) When the spouse who attempted the marriage in good faith discovers that the other spouse is an abuser, faithfulness may well mean promptly getting a divorce, followed by a decree of nullity issued from a marriage tribunal of the Church. The spouse divorcing the abuser is not flip-flopping. He/she is following a higher faithfulness, remaining faithful to what God intended the sacrament to be.

A person who accepts the Sacrament of Holy Orders, thereby becoming a priest, may discover that he did so for the wrong reasons—pressure from the family, social standing, or one of a host of other wrong reasons. He then may realize that he can't live up to the promises the sacrament required of him. He may then, and he should, ask for a dispensation from the promises and permission to return to living as a layman. The Sacrament cannot be taken back, as it were. He remains a priest, but an inactive priest. (In the proper use of Catholic terminology, he is a laicized priest. "De-frocked" is a term our media picked up from English Protestantism.) If he sought a dispensation for the right reasons, he may not be a flip-flopper at all. He may have remained faithful to what the sacrament required of him by leaving the active ministry so that he would not fail while in office. Sadly, not all ex-priests are this honorable, but I have known some who are.

We could follow the pattern of a deeper faithfulness expressed by a change of course in this life through all the sacraments, but I think the point has been made. We need now to enlarge the point, and deal with conversion and repentance.

Conversions come in all kinds. Some are flip-flops in the worst sense. We've seen this in our parish. A person converts to the Catholic faith and makes a big deal out of his/her new faith for a while, and then suddenly is gone. Who knows where? Flip-flops of the worst kind! Some lose their faith, if they really had any, and wilt away, as it were. These are just flops. In a change that is quite different from the flops I just sketched, some repent of something seriously wrong or untrue in their lives, and from their repentance they become Catholics. They are answering our Lord's call, "Repent, and believe the gospel" (Mark 1:15, et al.). These folk turn their lives in the right direction. Others we call converts today actually were believers and going in the right direction before they became Catholics. I believe I am an example of this kind of conversion. I learned authentic faith from my mother, but it was incomplete. As I grew and learned more, I realized that I could not find the fulfillment of what I had learned from her in Protestant churches. I realized that the fulfillment lay within the Catholic Church, which I joined. I don't think I either flipped or flopped.

Saint Paul, perhaps, is an example of the kind of conversion God's grace provided me. Saint Paul was a good Pharisee who believed in God's law and served the law fanatically. Then he saw the light, and became a Catholic. Since he'd persecuted Catholics before his conversion, he also represents those who had to repent, and then believe the gospel. For him, it all came at once in a flash, although it took years to work out before he became the Apostle to the Gentiles (cf., Acts 9:1–31; Gal 1:11–24).

If one reading or hearing this homily is in university or has children in university, the person may well come across the psychological thesis that "conversion" is a sign of a psychiatric disorder. Most certainly, those whose "conversions" are flip-flopping in the negative sense are emotionally disturbed, but it is sheer prejudice to lump all conversions into a diagnosis of psychiatric disorder. Sadly, Saint Paul, because with hindsight he can be seen as a fanatic, often is lumped into this psychiatric category. Although I'd strongly dispute so categorizing Saint Paul, there are a number of alleged conversions that belong in the category. I think that I'd put just about everyone converted to fundamentalism of any variety into this category. Nevertheless, there is a fine line that distinguishes fanaticism from a new convert's healthy enthusiasm, and the line, no matter how fine, represents a real distinction. Authentic conversion does not bear the signs of fanaticism. Saint Paul was converted from fanaticism (persecuting Catholics) to something healthy, a fact that those who denigrate him overlook.

The article that provoked my preamble to the homily for Sunday, October 24th, presented an essential characteristic of fanaticism: i.e., a false sense of certainty. This false certainty may clearly be counterfactual, and based in demonstrably erroneous mythology. The false certainty may also provide a sense of mission from God (or from something else super-human). This mission always goes well beyond anything one can reasonably find in the life and work of Jesus the Christ. To qualify as fanaticism, this false certainty need not come from anything related to Christianity. Adolph Hitler, a true fanatic and most certainly not a Christian, based his false certainty on demonstrably erroneous myths about an alleged Aryan race, and bolstered the erroneous mythology with pseudo-science. Karl Marx, Lenin, and Stalin based their false certainties on a denial that God exists, having replaced God with an absurd theory of history buttressed by half-baked economics. These men show that the major fanaticisms of my lifetime have been non-religious or anti-religious, a fact commonly forgotten in our day. All four men were on a mission based on their false certainties, and they wreaked havoc.

As I just affirmed, fanaticism is not necessarily a religious phenomenon, although in recent years fanaticism has once again become primarily religious in its expressions, thanks to the rise of fundamentalism. Fanaticism also knows no religious boundaries. Even the Catholic Church has not been able to keep it in check, despite the fact that our system of belief excludes fanaticism by setting clear boundaries to what one may believe with certainty. (Note that what we call infallibility implies non-infallibility. Notice how little in our system of belief we think infallible.) The article that provoked my reflections on the problem of false certainty, key to fanaticism, was written by Ron Suskind and published in the magazine section of the *New York Times*, "Faith, Certainty and the Presidency of George W. Bush."[1] Suskind used signs of a false certainty based in Protestant evangelical faith to attack the president during the election campaign. He was right about the nature of "false certainty," but wrong in thinking it is characteristic of all

---

1. Suskind, "Faith, Certainty."

who hold strongly to Christianity. In applying the category to the president, Suskind could do no more than mount a strong circumstantial case. Because his case is circumstantial, I continue to pass over the particulars concerning the president. Furthermore, I know that "false certainty" is not true of all Evangelicals. The charge may be true by definition of all fundamentalists, but not true of all Evangelicals. If you want to consult truly Christian Evangelicals, type "Sojourners" into your search engine and read their website. These Evangelicals are good Christians. They are not committed to "false certainties." Despite the article's weaknesses, Suskind did bring to the fore this key to fanaticism—false certainty.

As I said above, I suspect that a conversion to any form of fanaticism is a sign of psychiatric illness, although I repeat that one should never confuse a convert's initial enthusiasm with fanaticism. And, I strongly maintain that the key to fanaticism is false certainty. I would also stress that fanatics are not just raving madmen; they even come in good suits with polite manners. Some, unfortunately, seem even to be impressive leaders. As rotten a fanatic as Hitler was, he was known as *Der Führer*, which is German for "The Leader." All fanatics have the one problem in common: false certainty.

There is another religious matter connected to fanaticism: the not uncommon religious idea that God (or history, or some other super-human force) has assigned a particular nation the task of bringing some kind of salvation to other peoples. God did not assign the British the task of civilizing other people, which became known as the White Man's Burden. This alleged messianic task was used to disguise the ambitions of empire. God did not assign the Russian czars or the emperors in Constantinople who preceded them the task of "protecting" Orthodoxy. They actually used this messianic task allegedly from God to bolster imperial claims. God never assigned the Boers in South Africa a messianic task. Their delusions in this regard led to apartheid. After Jesus the Christ, no "Israel" has messianic purpose in the world. God did not assign any saving purpose through Muhammad to Islamic political communities (the *Ummah*) nor did God assign any particular part of the world to Islamic control. The House of Saud has no messianic task, nor does any other Islamic party or potentate. And, need I add, not even the United States has a messianic task.

Instead, God has assigned all nations the task of serving justice through promoting the common good and establishing a just peace. Ironically, the task of establishing peace may require the use of force, but only as a last resort. A leading role in this task at one time or another may fall upon a specific nation, such as the United States. But, this does not mean that the U.S., or any other nation, has received a messianic task from God. National messianism is a form of fanaticism and very dangerous. In may well be true that some Protestant Evangelical theology is open to the abuse of assigning messianic tasks to this country in particular.

Returning to the bottom line about perseverance versus flip-flopping, we see that the grace of perseverance may well begin with a conversion. The grace may also be renewed through genuine repentance. These steps are not signs of negative flip-flopping. Neither is a divorce followed by a decree of nullity nor a laicization necessarily a sign that a person has been a flip-flopper. True perseverance or faithfulness does not consist in a false consistency in the sinful circumstances of this life. Instead, true perseverance always consists in seeking to do the will of God, as we pray in the Our Father—"Thy Kingdom come; thy will be done on earth as it is in heaven." God's kingdom never is arbitrary.

Before arriving at the conclusion stated in the last sentence of today's gospel—namely, "Your perseverance will win you your lives"—the gospel reported our Lord's warnings about persecution. In other words, perseverance never is a cakewalk. For the early members of the Catholic Church in the ancient world, as is the case for many members of the Church in other parts of the world today, perseverance meant risking one's life. Until the early years of the fourth century, the Roman Empire persecuted Catholics and often killed them. The challenges for us in the United States and other Western democracies to perseverance today may well be different, but they are nonetheless real. To reassure us that God will protect us during times of trial, Jesus said, "You will be hated universally on account of my name, but not a hair of your head will be lost" (Luke 21:17-19).

The liturgist's chose the first reading for this Mass not only so that we could hear the prophet assure us that God's justice will triumph, even over those who persecute us, but also to prepare us for the end of the liturgical year. In the arrangement of the books in our Bible, the Prophecy of Malachi is placed as the last book of the Old Testament because of the prophecy recorded in the concluding verse (Mal 3:24): "He (the prophet Elijah) will reconcile parents to their children and children to their parents, to forestall my putting (i.e., God putting) the country under the curse of destruction." Saint Luke begins his gospel by identifying Saint John the Baptist as the "Elijah" to whom Malachi referred in his prophecy. Saint Luke, then, stated that Saint John the Baptist "with the spirit and power of Elijah" would go before the Christ *"to reconcile fathers to their children* and the disobedient to the good sense of the upright, preparing for the Lord a people fit for him" (Luke 1:17; the words quoted directly from the concluding verse of the Prophecy of Malachi are italicized). Christmas is coming. The new liturgical year begins with the First Sunday of Advent, November 27th-28th this year.

In order to prevent us from using the sacred Scriptures to foster a spirit of vengeance, the liturgist ended our first reading too soon. Here are the last two verses of the section, only part of which we heard proclaimed: "But for you who fear my name, the Sun of justice will rise with healing in his rays, and you will come out leaping like calves from the stall, and trample on the wicked, who will be like ashes under the soles of your feet on the day when I act, says Yahweh Sabaoth. (Mal 3:20–21; "Yahweh Sabaoth" often is rendered "Lord God of hosts," in which phrase "hosts" means large armies.) Although I sympathize with the liturgists' concern not to encourage in us a spirit of revenge, I think two truths need reinforcing. First, the fate of the unrepentant is so dreadful that while they have time in this life, we should love them mercifully thereby paving the way for them to repent. What awaits them if they fail to repent is beyond imagining.

Secondly, we need also to remember that in ways we do not now comprehend, God's justice, when it is fully revealed, will make those who are sharing in God's life intensely happy. The prophet saw this truth in highly poetic form: young calves bucking and leaping in joy upon being released from the stall, their hooves pounding on the remains of the wicked. We find even greater joy than this in winning the wicked to uprightness through loving them mercifully and thereby leading them to repent; but for those who do not repent [it will not go well]. God's justice also brings those with God great joy, which I pray we all will feel as did the calves in Malachi's metaphor.

The Psalm 98 provides our response to the first reading. The psalm concludes with six lines that say it all: "Let the rivers clap their hands, / and the mountains shout for joy together, / at Yahweh's approach, for he is coming / to judge the earth; / he will judge the world with saving justice / and the nations with fairness" (Ps 98:8–9).

The second reading for this Sunday provides a cautionary lesson for all parish works of charity. Saint Paul wrote: "We urged you when we were with you not to let anyone eat who refused to work" (2 Thess 3:10). The problem with malingerers Saint Paul faced arose from their false expectation that the Lord was returning in a matter of days, so they thought there was no point in working. Malingerers always find an excuse. If one provides them with sustenance despite their phony excuses, one thereby becomes an enabler. Saint Paul insisted such enabling stop.

Tragically, there usually are many who are prepared to use Saint Paul's admonition, along with related passages elsewhere in the New Testament, to rationalize destroying essential social services and other forms of welfare. Saint Paul's words, obviously, can be used to foster insensitivity, and to blame victims and the needy. This sinful misuse of Saint Paul's admonition flourished among those who embraced a derivative Calvinist theology. American Protestant fundamentalism embraces such theology. Excuses for not loving mercifully are very popular and, sadly, have been intensely popular throughout Christian history. The excuses don't cut it with God. Nevertheless, our good works should not make us enablers of any sort.

Chapter 31

Christ as the Way, the Truth, and the Life
The Fifth Sunday of Easter
(April 28, 2002)

Scripture Readings

Acts 6:1–7; Ps 33; 1 Pet 2:4–9; John 14:1–12.

Summary

Fr. Roach explains Christ's three self-assertions of himself—as the way, truth, and life. He considers what each asks of people. Christ is the way when identifying with him is the path to sharing in the divine life. Christ is the truth as God's Word; Christ's Person is God's revelation. Eternal life in God means our continued individual existence. Nevertheless, as individuals, we will be united in the Body of Christ through the Holy Spirit. The love among the persons of the Trinity shows that our sacrifice for others is love of ourselves. Fr. Roach observes that the Church Scandal reveals that we are *all* called to holiness, which is a share in God's life. As a "kingdom of priests," baptized in Christ, we participate in Christ's priesthood. Doing so includes faithful participation in the Eucharistic Sacrifice. In some of his concluding advisement in this volume Fr. Roach reminds us, "We belong to God, as we belong to no one else or to anything else."

Homily

IN THE PERICOPE WE heard as today's gospel, Saint John reports in the sixth verse that Jesus used three predicates of himself. They are as follows:

Jesus is the *Way*. The Greek original means that Jesus is the path or way in the physical sense, but the same word also means the way or means or manner of doing something. So, Jesus shows us the way to live here and now; he shows us the way to die; and he both shows us and is in himself the way to his Father, God. Stating this last point in other words, it is only by identifying ourselves with Jesus, by becoming one with him, by sharing his very own life now can we come to the Father for all eternity.

Jesus is the *Truth*. The Greek word for truth gives us insight into some of what Jesus meant when he said that he is the Truth. The root meaning of the Greek word for truth is "not unseen," or "unable to escape unnoticed." Saint John used the Greek to express a deeper level in what Jesus meant when he said that he is the truth about God, which, of course, when fully unfolded includes the truth about everything. Jesus was not only identifying himself with God, but also saying about himself that one who really "saw" him could not help seeing what being God means. If we see Jesus with the eyes of true faith, God cannot escape unseen.

Jesus is the *Life*. When trying to capture in Greek what Jesus meant when he identified himself as the life, Saint John chose from among the Greek words for life not the one we used to make words like "biology," but the Greek word we used to make "zoology." The distinction is subtle, but from the way Saint John used the latter word to record his revelations, he understood ζωή (*Zoe*) to mean a specific living being, and not 'life' as something abstract or impersonal. In other words, Jesus did not mean "Life" in the way Star Wars uses the word "Force." Our Lord was not using the word "life" as if he were saying, "May the Βίος (*Bios*)–meaning, Life Force–be with you." He used the word for life to say that in him is personal and eternal life. We are not drops of water soon to return to the oblivion of the ocean, no longer drops. We are who we are forever, and "forever" means eternal joy, alive in Christ, if we begin his life here.

This last point regarding the truth that our lives are personal with personhood having fixed boundaries for each individual sets Catholic faith off from the other world religions. A recent article reviewing the role of vampires, zombies, genies, and the like in European literature written during the spread of empires (e.g., *Aladdin and the Magic Lamp*, 1878) made the point well. The author, Marina Warner, began the article with Ovid's famous line from his *Metamorphoses*: "All things are always changing / But nothing dies." This view of an always existing, infinitely malleable, force manifesting itself in human individuals and many other things, which undergo change without ever dying, is the prevalent view outside the Judeo-Christian tradition. (Islam is an effort to reinvent a kind of Judaism embraced by the false messiahs discussed in last week's homily.) Warner wrote: "This view from outside the Judeo-Christian tradition runs counter to notions of unique, individual integrity of identity in the Judaeo-Christian tradition, and sets up, through myriad narrative devises, a vision of personhood that is borderless, unstable and wandering, apt to take possession of other bodies and to live beyond its physical form."[1] The faith that Jesus Christ taught the world and entrusted to his Church to remember until he returns affirms that we are each unique. We enjoy "individual integrity of identity" not only in this life, but also in sharing the life of Jesus eternally, which life Jesus makes manifest is eternally unique and exists only as individual integrity of a person.

Jesus used a quaint metaphor in this gospel to teach us that we are each unique yet live as one—the concept of a mansion with many apartments. In eternity, we become like a family or a commune, living in one large home. To enjoy this reality in eternity, we must begin here. It has never been a greater challenge than in today's Church to live as one family.

In case we've missed the point about being unique yet joined as one, we are called in today's gospel to hear Jesus say: "You must believe me when I say / that I am in the Father and the Father is in me; / or at least believe it on the evidence of these works" (John 14:11). Jesus had already answered Philip's request that he show him God the Father by saying: "Anyone who has seen me has seen the Father, / so how can you say, 'Show us the Father'? / Do you not believe / that I am in the Father and the Father is in me?" (John 14:9). Although the word "Trinity" is never used in the sacred Scriptures, nor is the adjective "triune," as in the expression "the triune God," believing what these summary terms convey is essential to a minimum understanding of the faith that the Bible is about. Furthermore, there is no peace or true community except we learn what it means for us human beings that the Being, which is the one and only God, is multiple without becoming numerically more than the one and only God. The loving closeness of that mansion in which an apartment has been reserved for you and me will never be ours, except we begin to learn here what the union of multiplicity that is God means for us.

The gospel we've heard concludes with Jesus saying: "In all truth I tell you, / whoever believes in me / will perform the same works as I do myself, / and will perform even greater works, / because I am going to the Father"

1. Warner, "Imperial Gothic," 14.

(John 14:12). We should be quite clear about what these "greater works" are that believers are going to perform. They are works of merciful, self-sacrificial love in which those who are not blinded by sin can see the divine. Ours will be greater than the works Jesus performed, because they are no longer limited to the works of one individual. The Body of Christ, thanks to the outpouring of the Holy Spirit, now consists of many, many individuals united as one. If we are united in the Spirit that Jesus has sent us by going to the Father, then we will perform his greater works. I think of Saint Francis of Assisi, or Saint Ignatius of Loyola, or Saint Therese of Lisieux, or Mother Teresa, or Damien the Leper, or so many others. God knows we've never needed living members of the Body of Christ performing the greater works more than we do today!

I fear I know why we don't see these works at this moment when we in the Church in this country need them so badly. We don't realize what the union of multiplicity, that is the triune God, means for us. If we appreciated the Trinity, as we need to, we would all realize that justice for persons, mercy for another, compassion for another human being, self-sacrificing service for other persons is simultaneously love of self. When the Father asks sacrifice of the Son, God is making the sacrifice himself, because the Father and Son are one. When the Father and Son send the Holy Spirit, as in the sacraments of Baptism and Confirmation, "they" are sending "themselves," God is sending himself, because the Holy Spirit is one with the Father and the Son; "they" are one and only one God. It is "their" life we are called to live eternally. So, if you and I know what we are doing when we show mercy to a sinner in distress, we realize that we are forgiving and loving ourselves as well, because the sinner and we are one in Christ. This is the only realization that builds true community, one that is bound together in peace and justice and love.

Among the truths, we learn from the Trinity, and are expected also to live the truth that love equalizes as it unites. This love can unite as equals those who are arranged in a hierarchical ladder. For example, in the Trinity there is first God, the origin of the one and only divinity, then there is God's self-expression or Word who also is the one and only God, and finally there is God, the Holy Spirit, proceeding from the one and only divinity into the minds and hearts of what is not divine. As Father, Son, and Holy Spirit, the internal multiplicity in God is hierarchical. But, as persons there is perfectly equality. Each is equally God. We who are trying to live this divine life now in God's Church have got down the hierarchical part, but we're failing badly at the equality part. We realize that the bishop is over the parish priest, and the parish priest (pastor) is over the people, hierarchically. We forget that all are equally called to share God's life i.e., called to holiness.

The horrendous scandal we are suffering in the Church in the United States has reminded me that one of the falsehoods the Second Vatican Council intended to remove from our midst was the erroneous thought that only priests and religious were called to holiness; whereas, in truth, all the baptized are called to holiness. Horrifically, a very small percentage of priests, mostly sick, not only failed to seek holiness, but committed grave sins. Probably a small number of bishops committed even graver sins of omission through failing to stop the evils.[2] All will answer to God. Still, if one looks at the percentage of those who failed substantially to live up to the grace of the Sacrament of Holy Orders, and then compare that percentage to the percentage of those in this parish alone who seem to have rejected the grace of the Sacrament of Confirmation by never participating in the Sunday Mass, one would have to conclude as follows: if the percentage of those rejecting the holiness of the Sacrament of Holy Orders were as high as those who seem to have rejected the holiness of the Sacrament of Confirmation, there wouldn't be enough priests in this diocese to celebrate a single Mass in most of the churches of the Archdiocese on Sunday.

At the beginning of the Church, when ten of the Twelve whom Jesus had chosen as hierarchs initially failed, the Holy Spirit replaced only one— the one who committed suicide (cf., Acts 1:12–26). But, before the Holy Spirit came upon the Church at Pentecost enlivening the structure Our Lord had put in place, the ten who needed to repent had done so. They proved their repentance by their martyrdoms. This pattern in the Church is the same today as it was in the beginning.

Many people don't think about the power of the Holy Spirit and holiness because as a people we don't think of the Trinity enough. Holiness is catching, and it ferrets out sin. Saint Francis of Assisi, who had no power and wasn't a priest, ferreted out bad clerics and reformed them. The same is true for Saint Catherine of Siena, a laywoman, and many others like her. In our day, Mother Teresa of Calcutta made bishops quake. Holiness is the only real power in the Church, because the Holy Spirit enlivens, sustains, and in the end directs the Church. Holiness guarantees equality. Hierarchy is merely a tool; and when a part of the tool fails, the Holy Spirit has ways of punishing that part and even replacing it. If people are holy, hierarchs cannot get away without being holy.

I think that despite the failure of some of us to seek holiness as we ought, events in Boston show that the Holy Spirit decided to answer the prayers of some holy innocents and teach the hierarchy a lesson, reminding

---

2. This is a passing (if serious) comment early in the unfolding scandals then gaining national attention, and not yet Fr. Roach's studied or later developed views.

some bishops that as bishops they are supposed to serve only as the Holy Spirit's tools. From this scandal, I've learned something new about "The fear of the Lord." "The fear of the Lord is the beginning of knowledge; / fools despise wisdom and / instruction" (Prov 1:7 NRSV-CE). The gifts of the Holy Spirit, imparted in Baptism and strengthened in the Sacrament of Confirmation, if not deadened by the recipient's failure to respond, are traditionally listed as follows: "wisdom, understanding, counsel, fortitude (i.e., courage), knowledge, piety, and fear of the Lord."[3] ["Piety" and "fear of the Lord" actually are synonyms. The early Church formed the traditional list from Isa 11:1–2.]

In all this, we find confirmation of Jesus as the Way, the Truth, and the Life. We should start with him, so that we will end with him.

The first reading shows how the Church, empowered by the Holy Spirit adapted the Sacrament of Holy Orders in order to ordain men who would serve the Church with the power of the additional sacrament without becoming ministerial priests or bishops. They were ordained to serve by managing the material needs of the Church, thereby freeing up the Twelve to proclaim the Word in preaching, teaching, and through the sacraments. A Greek word for service is διακονία (*diakonia*), so we call the men, deacons. It is important for us to appreciate, as we think of this development, that it shows how the principles Our Lord implanted in his Church admit of development and expansion in general. Jesus when organizing his Church did not specify the diaconate, but he sent the Holy Spirit.

In today's second reading, the first Pope gave us a description of who we are as Church. The Second Vatican Council in its *Dogmatic Constitution on the Church*, issued on November 21, 1964, used the ninth and tenth verses of this passage from the First Letter of Peter as the primary description of what we are as Church. The entire second chapter of the document (sections #9 through #17 inclusive) develops the central concept of this passage. We need to attend to it, carefully and thoughtfully, so I will quote the two verses here in full: "But you (Saint Peter is addressing you and me) are *a chosen race, a kingdom of priests, a holy nation, a people to be a personal possession* to sing the praises of God who called you out of the darkness into his wonderful light. Once you were a *non-people* and now you are the People of God; once you were outside his pity; now you have received pity" (1 Pet 2:9–10; emphasis is original).

We are a chosen race not by common ethnicity, but because we are all adopted as sons and daughters in Jesus. We are a kingdom of priests, because we are baptized into Jesus who is the only full priest. The rest of

---

3. USCCB, *Catechism*, #1831.

us merely participate in his priesthood in various ways. All are baptized into his priesthood. We are all called to exercise his office as a priest by virtue of having been baptized. (The obligation doubles when we receive the Sacrament of Confirmation.) We do so in different ways, but we are all doing so "equally" if we are truly participating in this Eucharistic Sacrifice. Mere physical presence is not participation. Participation requires thought, prayer, attention, and so forth, but especially prayer. Participation is exercising Christ's priesthood. Through an additional sacrament, I have acquired further responsibilities in exercising Our Lord's priesthood, but these additional responsibilities are all directed to serving you.

We are a holy nation. Christ is our King, and we are his loyal subjects. Our commitment to Christ takes precedence over all other commitments!

We are called to be a people who are called to be God's personal possession. We belong to God, as we belong to no one else or to anything else. We belong to God because he has had pity on us. We show that we belong if we have pity on others.

Chapter 32

We Are All In God's Hands

The Twenty-First Sunday in Ordinary Time
The Hand of God (August 24, 2008)

Scripture Readings

Isa 22:19–23; Rom 11:33–36; Matt 16:13–20.

The reading from Isaiah introduces us to keys as a sign of authority, although the reading uses a case that failed. The Psalm teaches us to praise and thank God. The gospel establishes the authority of Saint Peter and his successors, who are the popes. There is no greater authority entrusted to human beings. It is God's authority. We ignore it at our peril.

    I prayed through these readings while lying on a hospital bed in the University of Washington Medical Center (the hospital of the UWMC). I had received very bad news. I now have a third cancer diagnosed to go with the previous two. This one is lodged in the pancreas. It is treatable, somewhat, but not curable. It has not as yet spread, which provides some hope.

    Digesting this news, I prayerfully read our second reading in the NRSV-CE translation I carry with me when traveling (the edition is smaller and more compact than my NJB). "O the depth of the riches and wisdom and knowledge of God! How unsearchable are his judgments and how inscrutable his ways! // 'For who has known the mind of the Lord? / Or who has been his counselor?' // 'Or who has given a gift to him to receive a gift in return?' // For from him and to him are all things. To him be the glory for ever. Amen" (Rom 11:33–36).

We are all in God's hands. I do not know how long I will be with you. I intend to serve as long as possible. When I can no longer serve, I will leave you in the sure and certain hope of the Resurrection! Meanwhile, it is not insincere or merely conventional to say, "I love you!" Richard R. Roach, S.J.

Bibliography

Ali, Abdullah Yusuf. (Transl.). *Holy Qur'an: Original Arabic Text with English Translation & Commentary*. Lahore, India (later Pakistan): Shaik Muhammad Ashraf, 1934.
Augustine, Saint. *Expositions of the Psalms*. Translated by J.E. Tweed. In *Nicene and Post-Nicene Fathers: First Series*. Vol. 8 of 15 Vols. Edited by Philip Schaff. Buffalo: Christian Literature, 1888.
American Heritage Dictionary of the English Language. 4th ed. Boston: Houghton Mifflin Harcourt, 2000.
Anonymous. "Account of a Visit from St. Nicholas." *The Troy Sentinel*, December 23, 1823.
Aquinas, Saint Thomas. *Summa Theologica*. Translated by the Fathers of the English Dominican Province. New York: Benzinger Bros., 1947.
Armstrong, Karen. *A Short History of Myth*. Edinburgh: Canongate, 2005.
Benedict XVI, Pope. *Deus Caritas Est (God is Love)*. Washington, DC: USCCB, 2006.
Bloom, Harold. *The American Religion: The Emergence of the Post-Christian Nation*. New York: Simon & Schuster, 1992.
Brown, Daniel. *The Da Vinci Code*. New York: Doubleday, 2003.
Enchiridion of Indulgences: Norms and Grants, Authorized English Edition. Totowa, NJ: Catholic Book, 1969. Revised as *The Handbook of Indulgences*, 1992. Revised as *The Manual of Indulgences*, Washington, DC: USCCB, 2006.
Ferguson, Everett, (ed.). *Encyclopedia of Early Christianity*. New York: Garland, 1990.
Foster, Donald. *Author Unknown: On the Trail of Anonymous*. New York: Henry Holt, 2000.
Kowalska, Sister Maria Faustina. *Divine Mercy in My Soul: The Diary of the Servant of God*. Stockbridge: Marian, 1987, and subsequent editions.
Larson, Edward J. *Summer of the Gods*. New York: Basic, 1997.
Lectionary for Mass for Use in the Dioceses of the United States. Second Typical Edition. 4 Volumes. Washington, DC: Confraternity of Christian Doctrine, 1998–2002.
New Revised Standard Version Bible: Catholic Edition. Division of Christian Education of the National Council of the Churches of Christ in the United States of America. Washington, DC: 1989 and 1993.
Pius XI, Pope. *Mit brennender Sorge (With Burning Anxiety)* [*On the Church and the German Reich*], papal encyclical read in German Catholic Churches on 21 March (Palm Sunday) 1937.

Pius XII, Pope. *Munificentissimus Deus: Apostolic Constitution Defining the Dogma of the Assumption.* Boston: St. Paul Books and Media, 1988.

Suskind, Ron. "Faith, Certainty and the Presidency of George W. Bush." *New York Times Magazine,* October 17, 2004.

Tanner, Norman. (ed.). *Decrees of the Ecumenical Councils.* 2 vols. Washington, DC: Georgetown University, 1990.

Tyerman, Christopher. *The Crusades: A Very Short Introduction.* United Kingdom: Oxford University, 2004.

United States Conference of Catholic Bishops. *Catechism of the Catholic Church.* USA Second Edition. Washington, DC and Rome: United States Catholic Conference of Bishops and Libreria Editrice Vaticana, 1997.

———. *Compendium: Catechism of the Catholic Church.* Washington, DC: USCCB, 2005.

———. *United States Catholic Catechism for Adults.* Washington, DC: USCCB, 2005.

Wansbrough, Henry (ed.). *New Jerusalem Bible.* New York: Doubleday, 1985.

Warner, Marina. "The Making of Imperial Gothic." *Times Literary Supplement,* April 12, 2002.

Wilford, John and Laurie Goldstein. "'Gospel of Judas' Surfaces After 1700 Years." *New York Times,* April 7, 2006.

www.ingramcontent.com/pod-product-compliance
Lightning Source LLC
Chambersburg PA
CBHW071942240426
43669CB00048B/2555